Coping with

Infertility

Coping with Infertility

Clinically Proven Ways of Managing the Emotional Roller Coaster

Negar Nicole Jacobs, Ph.D.
William T. O'Donohue, Ph.D.

Routledge
Taylor & Francis Group
New York   London

Routledge is an imprint of the
Taylor & Francis Group, an informa business

Routledge
Taylor & Francis Group
270 Madison Avenue
New York, NY 10016

Routledge
Taylor & Francis Group
2 Park Square
Milton Park, Abingdon
Oxon OX14 4RN

Printed in the United States of America on acid-free paper
10 9 8 7 6 5 4 3 2 1

International Standard Book Number-10: 0-415-95421-5 (Softcover)
International Standard Book Number-13: 978-0-415-95421-1 (Softcover)

Library of Congress Cataloging-in-Publication Data

Jacobs, Negar Nicole.
    Coping with infertility : clinically proven ways of managing the emotional roller coaster / Negar Nicole Jacobs and William T. O'Donohue.
        p. cm.
    ISBN 0-415-95421-5 (pb)
    1. Infertility--Psychological aspects. 2. Adjustment (Psychology) I. O'Donohue, William T. II. Title.

RC889.J32 2007
618.1'78--dc22   2006027420

Visit the Taylor & Francis Web site at
http://www.taylorandfrancis.com

and the Routledge Web site at
http://www.routledgementalhealth.com

This book is dedicated to the men and women at the Nevada Center for Reproductive Medicine who participated in our research project: Thank you for boldly sharing your infertility experiences in order to lessen the pain of others riding this emotional roller coaster. We would also like to thank the staff at the Nevada Center for Reproductive Medicine, especially Dr. Foulk, Caryn Thomason, and Gina Munda, for assistance with this project. We are also very grateful to the supportive and diligent team at Taylor & Francis, particularly Marsha Hecht, Joanne Freeman, Dana Bliss, Fred Coppersmith, and George Zimmar. This book would not have been possible without the unwavering support of our family members: Thanks to Scott and Eric, and to Jane, Katie, and Anna.

CONTENTS

PREFACE

Congratulations! You have chosen a book that not only stems from evidence-based, state-of-the-art techniques to battle the emotional aspects of infertility, but which also has been scientifically tested and shown to be effective in helping women learn to cope with the stress, depression, relationship problems, and grief associated with involuntary childlessness.

In a recent study, the authors of this book asked 108 women undergoing infertility treatment to participate in research designed to test the effectiveness of *Coping with Infertility: Clinically Proven Ways of Managing the Emotional Roller Coaster* (*CWI*). Using random assignment, half the women were given *CWI* immediately and asked to read it within four weeks. This group was called the Bibliotherapy Group. The other half were told they would be on a wait list and were given *CWI* at the end of the study. This group, the Control Group, served to ensure that any changes noted in the Bibliotherapy Group were not due just to time.

All participants filled out several sets of questionnaires designed to measure levels of anxiety, depression, relationship satisfaction, hope, confidence in their ability to handle infertility-related emotional distress, and motivation to stay in treatment for infertility. The initial pre-treatment evaluation was completed before anyone received *CWI*. Comparing the groups at pre-treatment showed no differences in scores on any of the measures. The post-treatment evaluation occurred four weeks later, after the Bibliotherapy Group had read *CWI* and before the Control Group had done so. The final followup evaluation occurred two months after the Bibliotherapy Group had read the book and before the Control Group had done so. Results showed that in comparison to the

Control Group, women who read *CWI* were able to lower their levels of depression significantly, as well as to increase their confidence in their ability to cope with infertility-related emotional distress, their motivation to stay in treatment for infertility, and their overall level of satisfaction with infertility treatment. In addition, evidence showed that *CWI* effectively decreased levels of anxiety, improved hope, and kept marital satisfaction from deteriorating over time. Overall, these results demonstrate that *CWI* is an effective tool in helping women battle the emotional roller coaster associated with the infertility experience.

Analysis of the data on satisfaction with the book revealed that women who read *CWI* were highly satisfied with it. Readers indicated that the book helped them better understand the emotional experience of infertility, lower their level of stress and depression regarding fertility problems, and cope more effectively with the pressures of infertility problems and infertility treatments. In addition, it led to lower levels of infertility-related depression, allowed a better understanding and more effective communication of infertility-related feelings with their partners, as well as greater emotional closeness and shared treatment decisions with their partners.

In open-ended comments about the book, readers indicated that the book offered them support, helped them realize that infertility was not their fault, and helped them understand that stress does not cause infertility. They also appreciated the stories, examples, and quotes of other couples involved with infertility treatment, which helped them realize that others felt the same way they did. For example, one participant wrote, "I liked that all the different emotions I have been going through were listed. After looking at the book I realize that I am normal for being on an 'emotional roller coaster,' and there are others out there going through the same thing." Readers also said they liked the contents of the book and the ease of using the skills taught in the book.

Many felt that these skills helped them cope better with specific infertility-related problems such as challenging irrational thinking, lowering levels of stress and depression, and improving various areas of relationship functioning. One reader said, "I just received the devastating news that due to my high levels of FSH, I need to seriously consider adoption or a donor. This came as a huge shock to my husband and me. I cried off and on for three days straight. *Coping with Infertility* really helped me to deal with my anger and depression. It also helped my husband and me to channel our energies toward solving this problem by seriously discussing all our options." Finally, readers indicated that they appreciated the writing style of the book. They felt it was laid out logically and written in a easy-to-understand way to which they could relate.

To our knowledge, no other book on the market has been scientifically tested and proven to be effective in helping readers battle the painful emotions associated with involuntary childlessness. We are gratified that women who participated in the study expressed high satisfaction with *CWI*. We sincerely hope that this book provides you with similar relief from your infertility-related emotional distress. We wish you the very best as you read this book and move along the path towards having a baby or ultimately making the decision to live without children.

INTRODUCTION
How to Get the Most Out of Coping with Infertility

The fact that you are reading this book probably means that you and/ or your partner are experiencing some of the emotional difficulties commonly associated with infertility and are looking for help in dealing with your feelings. You are not alone. Up to one in every six couples is affected by infertility.[1] Furthermore, infertility takes a huge physical and emotional toll on couples. Researchers[2] have observed that 80% of infertile patients they polled found their infertility experience to be either "stressful" or "extremely stressful." Another study[3] found that 49% of women and 15% of men considered infertility as *the most upsetting* experience of their lives.

The emotional experience of infertility can push the limits of your ability to deal with stress. We have seen many ordinarily strong and well-adjusted people struggle with the experience of infertility, not knowing how to cope with the intensity of their emotional reactions. We have also seen many relationships pushed to the limits as couples try to deal with the strain of infertility. On the other hand, we have talked with people who have gained strength from their infertility experience and who have found that infertility has enhanced their relationships.

This book has been written to help you and your partner cope with the emotional aspects of the infertility experience. Its goal is to help you turn infertility into something that increases your personal strength and brings you closer together as a couple.

Given that there are already hundreds of other self-help books for infertility on the market, you may wonder why we have decided to add another one to bookstore shelves. What makes this volume different? We have written this book to give couples with fertility problems access to clinically proven techniques that can help them deal with the emotional aspects of the infertility experience. Most books on infertility address the medical aspects, focusing on treatment technologies, how to find a doctor, and how to get pregnant. While these books are very important, they tend to ignore the stress, depression, grief, and relationship problems that often go along with infertility.

Even when these books do address the emotional aspects of infertility, most of the focus is on *what* the problems are instead of how to overcome them. Furthermore, the suggestions offered about coping with the emotional aspects of infertility are not based on tried-and-true therapeutic methods to overcome emotional distress.

LEARN TO USE SCIENTIFICALLY PROVEN TECHNIQUES TO COMBAT YOUR EMOTIONAL DISTRESS

Researchers in psychology have labored for many decades to develop and test the effectiveness of therapeutic techniques for battling depression, stress, and relationship problems. *Coping with Infertility* draws on this state-of-the-art research and describes those methods that have been *proven* effective in improving depressed mood, decreasing stress, and enhancing relationship satisfaction. We are confident that this book will help you cope with your infertility-related emotional distress and create a more enjoyable lifestyle.

Should everyone expect to be free of infertility-related distress after they have read *Coping with Infertility?* This would be an unreasonable

assumption for a number of reasons. First, the experience of infertility is inherently stressful, and most people with fertility problems will experience natural feelings of sadness, grief, and anxiety. This book has been written to help you cope with your feelings and keep them manageable. Second, not even the best therapies or self-help books can help *everyone*. People respond differently to different therapies. If after reading this book your symptoms have not improved or you are not better able to cope with them, we strongly recommend that you seek the help of a mental health professional who specializes in infertility counseling. A list of professionals and organizations that can help with infertility is included in Appendix B. If you are experiencing frequent and intense thoughts of suicide, we urge you to contact a mental health professional at once. Crisis Call hotlines and centers can be found in most towns, and they can get you in contact with mental health professionals who can offer immediate help. However, for most people, the prognosis for reducing infertility-related distress and strengthening relationships is excellent using the techniques described in this book.

TACKLE YOUR EMOTIONAL DISTRESS FROM THE COMFORT AND PRIVACY OF YOUR OWN HOME

If you are undergoing medical treatment for infertility, chances are that you have already exposed more of your private life than you are comfortable with. You have been examined intently, your work and personal schedules have been inconvenienced, and you have spent a significant amount of money trying to conceive. Our self-help method is private, convenient, and inexpensive. Many types of self-help books (called "bibliotherapy") are scientifically proven to be effective in helping people overcome emotional difficulties. It is important to note that while this book  is not a substitute for professional psychotherapy, it provides a viable alternative for those who seek access to sound treatment but do not want to spend the extra time, effort, and money involved in meeting with a therapist. It also allows you to avoid further public exposure while treating the emotional aspects of your infertility.

HOW COPING WITH INFERTILITY IS WRITTEN

We have made every effort to describe the scientifically proven, state-of-the-art techniques presented in this book in a language and style that are understandable and clear. In addition, we have included a number of features designed to make this book more "user friendly" and help you apply the techniques described to your own life:

> *Quizzes:* Each section starts off with a quiz. The quizzes have been constructed to help you figure out how much you know about the aspect of infertility being discussed and whether or not the

contents of the section will be relevant for you. The higher you score on each quiz, the more the contents of that section can help you. Before you launch into each section, we recommend that you take a few minutes to answer the quiz questions and score your responses. The quiz that appears at the end of the Introduction will help you focus on your trouble spots and highlight the sections of the book that will be of most help to you.

Quotes and Stories: Each section contains stories and quotes taken from real couples and individuals (with names changed to preserve confidentiality), who have been  generous enough to share personal stories about their emotional reactions to fertility problems. Their wish in sharing these stories is to help readers realize that they are not alone, that their emotional reactions are normal and valid, and that it is possible to get through the experience of infertility. We offer these vignettes in the hope that you find comfort and strength in them.

Assignments: Exercises and assignments interspersed throughout this book help you gain a better understanding of your infertility experience, identify your strengths and areas that need improvement, and help you apply available techniques to deal with your infertility problems. We urge you to read the book with pen in hand so you can do the assignments as you read the sections.

Summaries: Each section ends with a summary of the contents covered in section chapters and highlights techniques for combating your infertility-related distress. While it might be  tempting to read just the summaries, we recommend that you take the time to read *the entire text* carefully. The sections provide complete explanations, stories of real couples struggling with infertility, and full descriptions of how you can overcome your emotional distress.

SUCCESSFUL COPING LIES WITH YOU

Most infertile couples we have worked with have already read everything they could get their hands on about infertility and have tried everything possible to get pregnant. Failure to conceive leaves the couple devastated and fearful of getting their hopes up again by trying a new technique. Sometimes people handle their fear by being skeptical or cynical. Others protect their hope by merely dabbling with some new technique, so that it won't hurt as badly if they don't succeed in getting pregnant. While these reactions are perfectly understandable, they won't help you overcome your infertility-related distress.

You will get the most out of this book only if you challenge your skepticism and put forth your greatest effort. The techniques we describe in this book are not based on "pop" psychology; they are drawn from scientifically tested and proven therapies. However, these techniques won't do a thing for you unless you make the effort to practice them in your daily life. You are reading this book because infertility has caused emotional distress and you want to learn new ways to cope. You can either skim through the book with little effort and continue to suffer the emotional consequences of infertility, or you can take advantage of these clinically proven methods for improving your mood and strengthening your relationship.

Following the guidelines below will help you get the most out of *Coping with Infertility*:

> **Read each chapter carefully.** Every chapter is packed with information about the emotional aspects of infertility and how you can combat them. Set aside time in your busy schedule to read the material and apply it to your own life. Remember that conquering the emotional aspects of your infertility will require an investment of time and effort.
>
> **Read with your partner.** Infertility affects *both* partners, even if only one partner carries the medical factor for infertility or is experiencing depression or anxiety. Since infertility is a *couple* issue, it will take both partners working in tandem to combat it. Working through the emotional aspects together is just as important as attending medical appointments together. Thus, whenever possible, read the chapters of this book as a couple. This will give you and your partner an opportunity to discuss what you've read and how it relates to your relationship. It will also give you a chance to practice the skills taught in the book and do the assignments/exercises together.
>
> **Complete the assignments and exercises.** The assignments and exercises in this book have been designed to help you better understand your experience of infertility and let you practice the skills you need to improve your mood and strengthen

your relationship. Research has shown that people who do the assignments and practice the skills experience the most improvement. Learning how to apply the skills to your life will take time and practice. We urge you to schedule time to complete each assignment. Your investment can pay off with reduced stress, improved mood, and a stronger relationship with your partner.

We sincerely hope that this book helps you and your partner cope more effectively with the emotional aspects of infertility and, in doing so, improves your mood and allows your fertility problems to bring you closer together as a couple. This book has drawn from some of the best treatments that exist in order to help you do this. You can start right now by addressing yourself to the quiz below.

QUIZ: ZEROING IN ON YOUR TROUBLE SPOTS

This quiz will help you decide which sections of the book are the most important for you to read and study. Go through the questions/statements carefully and answer with either "yes" or "no."

_____ 1. I am confused about how best to time sex in order to conceive.

_____ 2. I don't understand the causes of infertility.

_____ 3. I'm not sure about the effectiveness of medical treatments for infertility.

_____ 4. I feel like my infertility experience has me on an emotional roller coaster ride.

_____ 5. I don't understand my (or my partner's) emotional reactions to the crisis of infertility.

_____ 6. I feel sad or depressed most of the time.

_____ 7. My infertility has left me feeling defective as a human being.

_____ 8. I don't really know how to cope with my sadness and depression.

_____ 9. My fertility problems make me feel very stressed out and anxious.

_____ 10. I worry that stress is causing my fertility problems or making them worse.

_____ 11. When I get anxious, I don't really know how to calm myself down.

_____ 12. I have a hard time coping with the stress of the holidays.

_____ 13. Infertility has negatively affected my relationship with my partner.

_____ 14. My partner and I don't see infertility as *our* problem.

_____ 15. I have failed my partner because of my infertility.

_____ 16. My partner reacts so differently to infertility that I can't understand him/her.

_____ 17. My partner and I have a hard time communicating about our fertility problems.

_____ 18. Infertility has taken a toll on our sex life.

_____ 19. I feel great sadness and grief over all the losses I've had to endure because of infertility.

_____ 20. I'm having a hard time coping with my infertility-related losses.

SCORING THE QUIZ: MOST IMPORTANT SECTIONS TO READ

If you answered "yes" to any of these questions, this book can help you. Read through the answers below to see which sections will be most relevant to you. Even if you answered "no," you may still want to read through certain sections to prevent future problems in those areas.

Reproduction, infertility, and medical treatments (Questions 1–3): If you answered "yes" to any of these questions, Section I, titled "Human Reproduction: When It Works, When It Doesn't, and Medical Treatment Options" can help you. It provides an overview of reproductive anatomy and offers important tips for improving your fertility. It also covers common causes of both male and female infertility and helps you sort through the maze of medical treatment options and their success rates. In addition, it discusses alternatives such as third-party reproduction, adoption, and child-free living.

Emotional reactions to infertility (Questions 4–8): If you answered "yes" to any of these questions, Section II, titled "Infertility: The Emotional Roller Coaster," is a must-read for you. It describes the common causes and cycle of depression in infertility. In addition, it illustrates the relationship between your mood and the way you think and act, and explains how to counteract irrational thinking. It also provides methods to improve mood and distract yourself from your depression.

Stress and Anxiety (Questions 9–12): If you answered "yes" to any of these questions, Section III, "Stress: Why It Is Not Enough to Just Relax," offers concrete help for reducing stress and anxiety. Unfortunately, the stress of infertility can exceed your ability to cope. In addition, stress can cause other problems (sleep disturbances, relationship problems, etc.). Section III covers the symptoms and common sources of stress in infertility and describes clinically proven coping skills to reduce your anxiety.

Relationship difficulties (Questions 13–18): The more "yes" responses you had, the more you need to read Section IV, "Couple Trouble: Infertility and Your Relationship." Infertility can take a huge toll on your relationship. This section describes common sources of infertility-related relationship difficulties. It also reviews common gender differences in reacting to and coping with various aspects of the infertility experience and provides clinically proven suggestions for dealing with these differences. In addition, it discusses common sexual problems encountered by couples with infertility, and suggests a number of resources for enhancing your sex life.

Grief and Loss (Questions 19–20): If you answered "yes" to either of these questions, we strongly recommend that you read Section V, "Infertility: The Mourning After." Infertility can involve many losses, all of which must be mourned in order to get through the crisis of infertility successfully. This section explains the series of emotional reactions typically involved in the grieving process and offers multiple strategies for coping with grief and loss. It also provides tips you can use to help your partner through the grieving process or share with friends who want to help you grieve your losses.

I

Human Reproduction

*When It Works, When It Doesn't, and
Medical Treatment Options*

QUIZ: WHAT'S YOUR REPRODUCTIVE IQ?

This quiz will help you identify what you do and do not know about reproduction, infertility, and various medical treatments for infertility. It will also help you identify when you are falling prey to infertility myths and discuss how to replace these myths with facts. Answer the questions below with "yes" or "no" answers.

_____ 1. Sperm is produced in the male penis.

_____ 2. Ovulation always occurs on day 14 of the menstrual cycle.

_____ 3. In order to get pregnant, a couple must have sexual intercourse around the time of the woman's ovulation.

_____ 4. People usually get pregnant as soon as they quit using birth control.

_____ 5. A woman's fertility decreases as she ages.

_____ 6. Most male factor infertility is caused by erectile difficulties.

_____ 7. Stress causes females to be infertile.

_____ 8. Infertility is rare.

_____ 9. Infertility is a woman's problem.

_____ 10. Infertility is caused by "sinful" thoughts and behaviors, such as promiscuity, masturbation, pre-marital sex, or abortions.

_____ 11. It always seems that couples get pregnant right after they adopt.

_____ 12. Fertility drugs can wreak havoc on your emotional state.

_____ 13. Success rates for assisted reproductive technologies (ART) have improved in the last several years.

_____ 14. Men with low sperm count must always rely on donor sperm.

_____ 15. IVF (*in vitro* fertilization) is more effective than GIFT (gamete intrafallopian transfer) and ZIFT (zygote intrafallopian transfer).

SCORING THE REPRODUCTIVE IQ QUIZ

Compare your responses to the answers below. The more incorrect answers, the more you need to read Section I to help you understand the process of human reproduction, the causes of infertility, and available medical treatments for infertility. Be sure to read through all the responses, even if you answered correctly.

Question 1—Production of sperm: The correct answer is no. Sperm are not produced in the penis, but in the testes (Chapter 1).

Question 2—Ovulation: The correct answer is no. The magic number of 14 is based on an ideal 28-day cycle, which most women do not have (Chapter 1).

Question 3—The importance of timing: The correct answer is yes. To maximize your chances of conception, you must engage in sexual intercourse around the time of ovulation (Chapter 1).

Question 4—Time it takes to get pregnant: The correct answer is no. The majority of couples do not get pregnant as soon as they stop taking birth control (Chapter 1).

Question 5—Fertility and age: The correct answer is yes. Women are most fertile in their twenties. Fertility dips after age 30. Refer to Chapter 1 and Table 3.2 for more information.

Question 6—The myth of erectile difficulties: The correct answer is no. Only a small percentage of infertility is caused by sexual dysfunction such as erectile dysfunction (Chapter 2).

Question 7—Stress and infertility: The correct answer is no. In actuality, infertility causes stress, not the other way around (Chapters 2 and 7).

Question 8—Infertility is common: The correct answer is no. Infertility has been estimated to affect one in every six couples (Chapters 1 and 2).

Question 9—Infertility is just a woman's problem: The correct answer is no. The incidence of male-factor and female-factor infertility is, in fact, equal (Chapter 2).

Question 10—"Sinful" causes of infertility: The correct answer is no. There is no scientific evidence that past or present behaviors, in and of themselves, cause infertility (Chapter 2).

Question 11—Infertility and adoption: The correct answer is no. While there are many anecdotal stories of people who adopt a baby after a long struggle with infertility and then spontaneously get pregnant, it is simply not true that adoption will lead to your own pregnancy (Chapter 2).

Question 12—Fertility drugs and emotions: The correct answer is yes. Many fertility drugs are actual hormones. The intensified moods and dramatic mood swings stemming from the drugs, coupled with the alternating hopes and letdowns of infertility treatments, can have a great effect on the emotional state of both partners (Chapter 3).

Question 13—ART success rates: The correct answer is yes. The Center for Disease Control reports that success rates have been climbing steadily (Chapter 3).

Question 14—Sperm count and donor sperm: The correct answer is no. Men with little to no sperm count can take advantage of a variety of drugs and methods to impregnate their partners (Chapter 3).

Question 15—IVF versus GIFT and ZIFT: The correct answer is yes. Success rates for IVF with and without ICSI are higher than those for GIFT and ZIFT (Chapter 3).

1

THE BIRDS AND THE BEES 101
Reproduction and Fertility

So you want to have a baby, but Mother Nature is not cooperating with your plans. You try and try without success, and finally turn to an infertility doctor for help. You are an intelligent person who is able to deal with complicated situations in your personal and professional life. But in the doctor's office, it is easy to get lost in the complexities of reproduction and in the technical jargon being thrown around. Even in your home life, you are bombarded with friends  and family members giving you what they call "tips" but what you call "old wives' tales" or "myths" about getting pregnant. You start to wonder if changing your diet or having sex during the full moon really will be the answer.

The best way to enhance your fertility is to have a basic understanding of the reproductive anatomy of both men and women and of normal reproduction. This knowledge will help you sort out the myths from the facts, understand the tests and treatments available, engage in more productive sexual intercourse, and feel more in control during the process of infertility treatment.

This chapter reviews reproductive anatomy and conception in a very basic and simplified manner and discusses ways this knowledge can help maximize your chances of getting pregnant.

REPRODUCTIVE ANATOMY

You may think that reproduction is a simple process. After all, our parents taught us about the birds and the bees when we were young, and we always whispered about sex with our friends. However, it is likely that what we learned back then was less fact than fiction. We may have taken sex ed classes, but who remembers back that far? The fact is that reproduction is a highly complex process that requires many factors to be successful—including a healthy reproductive system in both the male and female.

The Male Reproductive System

The male reproductive system has both external and internal parts. Figure 1.1 identifies the major parts of this system. The testes, or testicles, are a pair of oval bodies positioned behind the penis and enclosed in the scrotal sac. The testes are responsible for production of sperm and testosterone, a male hormone. Specifically, sperm are produced in hundreds of tiny tubules in the testes called seminiferous tubules. The testes are highly sensitive to heat, and their ability to produce sperm is dependent on their being constantly kept at a temperature approximately two to four degrees cooler than the normal body temperature. It is the responsibility of the scrotal sac to keep the sperm safe by regulating the temperature of the testes. This cooler temperature is maintained by the scrotal muscles, which contract to pull the testes closer to the body in cold weather and relax to drop the testes further away from the body in warmer temperatures. For these reasons, it is often recommended that men who are trying to conceive avoid tight-fitting clothes, hot tubs, and saunas.

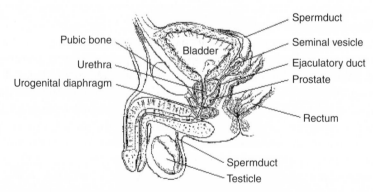

Figure 1.1 Male Reproductive Anatomy (with permission from www.pdrhealth.com)

Unlike women, whose hormone production is cyclical, men constantly produce sperm and hormones. Healthy men typically produce millions of sperm every day. Once the sperm are produced in the testes, they are pushed to the epididymis, where they stay for roughly two weeks, developing the ability to swim. The mature sperm leave the epididymis through the muscular action of this tubal duct, and enter the vas deferens. The sperm and seminal fluid are stored in the final portion of the vas deferens, called the ampullae, until ejaculation. The process of sperm production and maturation takes roughly 72 days.

When a man becomes sexually excited, the walls of the vas deferens contract and push the sperm through the seminal vesicles, the prostate, and the Cowper's glands, where the sperm are mixed with seminal fluid. The sperm and seminal fluid then enter the urethra, which runs the length of the penis. The penis contains cavernous spaces that fill with blood when sexually stimulated, resulting in an erection. During orgasm, 40–150 million sperm and are ejaculated outside the male's body.

The Female Reproductive System

The female's reproductive organs are largely contained within her body (see Figure 1.2). In ascending order from the lower portions of the female's body, the internal reproductive organs are the vagina, cervix, uterus, fallopian tubes, and ovaries. The outer genitalia include the labia majora (outer lips), labia minora (inner lips), urethral and vaginal openings, and clitoris. Except for the urethral opening, which is used for urination, the outer genitalia are involved in a woman's sexual arousal and functioning.

The vagina is a three- to five-inch inch passage lined with mucous membranes. The vagina encloses the penis during intercourse. It is capable of expanding greatly—e.g., when a baby leaves a woman's body through the vagina during birth. At the top of the vagina is the cervix, a fibrous ring of tissue that leads into the uterus. The cervix has a narrow opening called the cervical os. The cervix produces secretions that help protect the other reproductive organs from infections. It is through the cervix that the endometrial lining is shed during menstruation. The cervix also serves as the passageway for sperm to enter the uterus during intercourse. Above the cervix lies the uterus, a muscular pear-shaped organ that functions like a sack. The top, and widest part, of the uterus is called the fundus.

When an egg is fertilized, it usually implants itself in the lining of the uterus, where it is nourished and develops into a fetus. The uterus is capable of expanding to more than 40 times its size to hold a fetus

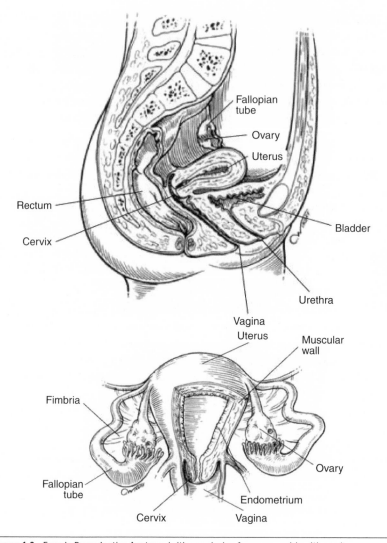

Figure 1.2 Female Reproductive Anatomy (with permission from www.pdrhealth.com)

during pregnancy. Nine months later, the uterus contracts during labor and expels the fetus down the birth canal during delivery. An unfertilized egg is shed, along with endometrial tissue, during menstruation.

The fallopian tubes arise from both sides of the fundus. These two muscular tubes, approximately four inches long, deliver the egg from the ovaries into the uterus. At the ends of the fallopian tubes are trumpet-like openings that work to "catch" the egg from the ovary during ovulation and draw it into the fallopian tube. Finally, the ovaries, roughly the size and shape of almonds, lie under the ends of the fallopian tubes at both sides of the uterus. They produce estrogen and progesterone and release at least one egg each month during ovulation. The egg may be released from either ovary during ovulation, and there is no consistent alternation of sides. If one ovary is missing or not functioning, the other ovary takes over the functions of ovulation and hormone production.

The Menstrual Cycle[1]

A woman's hormones operate in a cyclical process known as the menstrual cycle. This cycle is governed by the hypothalamus through the pituitary gland, which orchestrates a variety of hormones that result in menstruation (see Figure 1.3). Although the menstrual cycle varies in length, most women have cycles of between 26–34 days, with 28 days as the average. The first day of the cycle is marked by the first day of blood flow from the shedding of the uterine lining. Bleeding lasts for 2–3 days for some women, and 3–6 days for other women. Around the fifth day, the low levels of estrogen signal the hypothalamus to release gonadotropin-releasing hormone  (GnRH) to the pituitary gland, which reacts by releasing follicle-stimulating hormone (FSH) and some luteinizing hormone (LH). The FSH stimulates the ovary to ripen approximately 1000 ovarian follicles, or oocytes, which produce and release estrogen. Of these, one follicle will become dominant while the others eventually die. The dominant follicle will continue to absorb FSH and produce estrogen. The higher levels of estrogen signal the endometrial lining to thicken. The cervical mucous thins between days 11–13 of the cycle, resulting in clear and stringy mucous and thus a "sperm-friendly" environment.

Around day 13 of the cycle, the rise in estrogen reaches its peak, which prompts a surge in the release of LH. This surge lasts roughly 24 hours and causes the dominant follicle to ovulate, releasing the egg around day 14 of the cycle. The timing of ovulation is not precise and can vary among women. For this reason, it is important to monitor your cycle using such measures as basal body temperature, ovulation test kits, and the quality of cervical mucous. Once the egg is released, it is taken up by the ends of the fallopian tube, called the fimbria. The egg moves down the fallopian tube towards the uterus. If healthy sperm are present, fertilization will occur in the outer portion of the tube within 12–24 hours after ovulation.

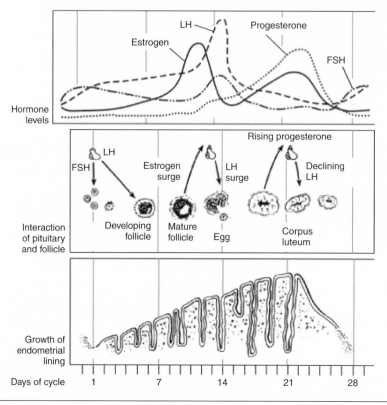

Figure 1.3 Complex Choreography of the Reproductive Hormones of Females (with permission from www.pdrhealth.com)

After the egg is released, the remaining follicle is "luteinized" by the LH surge and transforms into the corpus luteum, or "yellow body." The corpus luteum assumes responsibility for producing progesterone and estrogen for the next 10–14 days. The rise in progesterone causes a slight elevation in basal body temperature, and the cervical mucous changes back to thick and opaque. In addition, the progesterone surge causes the endometrial lining to soften and prepare for the hopeful implantation of a fertilized egg.

If pregnancy does not occur in the 14 days following ovulation, the corpus luteum stops the production of progesterone and estrogen, and eventually dies off. The unfertilized egg moves into the uterus, and the uterine lining begins to break down. In response to a decrease in progesterone, the endometrium releases chemicals called prostaglandins that cause cramps and the shedding of the endometrial lining, or menstruation. During menstruation, the low levels of estrogen signal the brain to start the next cycle.

CONCEPTION AND PREGNANCY:
THE NECESSARY ELEMENTS[2]

In order for conception to occur, a number of male and female reproductive events must take place with precise timing. The male must produce enough healthy sperm and the woman must produce a healthy egg. The number and movement quality (motility) of sperm are important because only a tiny fraction of sperm will survive the long passage ahead of them. The sperm must be deposited into the woman's vagina and travel through the cervical mucous and the fallopian tube, where it is hoped they will meet an egg. This meeting of the sperm and egg is most likely to occur within a day before or after ovulation, when the egg is released from the ovary and taken up by the fallopian tube. It is also easiest for the sperm to travel through the cervical mucous around the time of ovulation. In addition, because the woman's egg may live for as little as 12–24 hours after ovulation and the man's sperm for 24–72 hours after ejaculation, it is crucial that sexual intercourse occur as close to ovulation as possible. Ovulation typically occurs 14 days before the onset of a woman's menstrual period.

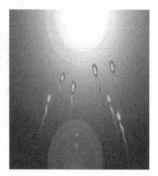

When the sperm reach the egg, they surround it and release enzymes that help them penetrate the egg. The head of one sperm will penetrate the egg, leaving its tail behind. At this point, the fertilized egg is considered an embryo and other sperm are no longer able to enter the egg. When the sperm fertilizes the egg and their chromosomes blend, conception is said to occur. Next, the embryo must be able to move through the tube and enter the uterus, which must have a lining of sufficient quality for the embryo to implant itself.

Once the embryo is successfully implanted in the uterine lining, it produces human chorionic gonadotropin hormone (HCG) for 2–3 months. HCG is often used as an early indicator of pregnancy. It is produced until the placenta of the fetus is large enough to take over the hormone production necessary to maintain pregnancy. As the fetus grows and develops, it must be held by a uterus that is sound in structure and capable of expanding greatly. In addition, the cervix must be sufficiently strong to hold the fetus inside the body without dilating too early. If all these processes occur and all these conditions are met successfully, the fetus will grow until it is fully developed and will be expelled through the vagina during labor.

Given the number of conditions and the precise timing under which they must occur in order to achieve pregnancy, it is understandable that roughly 15% of couples experience fertility difficulties.

TIPS FOR IMPROVING FERTILITY

A trip to the bookstore's infertility section will reveal shelves lined with books on tips for getting pregnant. These books discuss the best diets, vitamin or mineral supplements, and sexual positions for conception. While there is little sound scientific evidence that these types of interventions make a big difference in enhancing fertility, there are a number of other factors that, without a doubt, can maximize fertility.

Just Do It

The Nike slogan of "Just Do It" sums it up nicely. You must have sex in order to get pregnant! This sounds simplistic, but everyday stressors and other factors associated with infertility can interfere with a couple's desire and even ability to have sex. Frequently, couples find themselves too tired for sex after a long day's work or too busy at other times of the day to have sex. The emotional toll that infertility takes also can dampen the sex drive. Who wants to have sex when they're overridden with feelings of sadness, anger, guilt, or fear? In addition, medical assessment and treatment for infertility—such as being poked and prodded at the doctor's office, undergoing post-coital tests, and having to give and receive fertility drugs—can drown out the flames of romance. Despite these very understandable obstacles to making love, it is critical that you and your partner engage in sexual intercourse in order to get pregnant. Chapter 10 offers some tips for improving your sex life while trying to conceive.

Maximize Your Fertile Time

Not only do you have to have sex, but you must time intercourse just right to maximize your chances of getting pregnant. One study found that half of infertile couples did not have intercourse during the fertile time of the menstrual cycle, and 14% did not mark the

fertile time correctly.[3] The most fertile time of the cycle occurs when the female is ovulating. You can monitor this fertile time using LH kits and basal body temperature charting, checking the quality of the cervical mucous, or charting the days of the woman's monthly cycle. The first day of bleeding is considered the first day of the cycle, and ovulation occurs approximately 14 days before the first day of the cycle. If the female's cycle is regular, she can predict ovulation by subtracting 14 days from when she is due to start her period. Some doctors[4] recommend that couples have sex every other day around the time of ovulation. In a 28-day cycle, this means having sex on days 10, 12, 14, and 16. Because sperm live 24–72 hours, and because having sex every other day will give the male time to develop a good sperm supply for the next ejaculation, the above pattern will maximize the chances that sperm will be available to meet the egg when it is released at ovulation.

Watch Out for Chemicals

Some chemicals, such as those found in alcohol, illicit drugs, and even prescription or over-the-counter medications, can affect the production of sperm. Check with your doctor to see if the chemicals you are taking or have contact with can affect your fertility. Also, be sure to consult with your doctor before you discontinue use of any medications.

Chemicals found in some vaginal lubricants, especially those containing spermicides, can impede the ability of sperm to move or even kill sperm.[5] For this reason, you should read labels carefully and ask your doctor about the use of lubricants. If possible, avoid the use of lubricants, since vaginal secretions are the best and safest lubricants.

ASSIGNMENT 1.1

Talk with your partner about the ways you plan to monitor the monthly cycle and maximize your fertility. It is best for both partners to share the responsibility for marking the fertile period and for initiating sex during this time. One way of doing this is to incorporate fertility monitoring into your daily routine or even as part of sexual foreplay. You can also have a calendar that marks the fertile period in plain view. This will help both of you know when to plan for sex.

REPRODUCTION MYTHS AND FACTS[6]

Now that you've read the facts about reproduction and conception, you are less likely to fall prey to the following myths about fertility. However, just in case belief in these myths lingers, read on to distinguish between myth and fact.

Myth 1: We should get pregnant as soon as we quit using birth control.
Fact: The majority of couples do not get pregnant in the first month of trying. In fact, Dr. Menning[7] reports that only 25% of couples that have sexual intercourse without using birth control will get pregnant in the first month. Beyond this, 60% of couples conceive by six months, and 85% by the end of one year. The remaining 15% of couples are considered to have infertility problems.

Myth 2: Most couples are putting off child-bearing these days for their careers. We can afford to wait, too.
Fact: Women are most fertile in their twenties. Fertility drops after age 30 and takes a dive after age 35. While it is very difficult for professional couples to balance career and family, it is important to consider that fertility drops with age as you make your decisions about where to draw the balance. The longer you wait, the greater your risk of having infertility problems.

Myth 3: (For women) I'm sure to be fertile since I'm young.
Fact: Although your chances of infertility do increase as you age, some women in their twenties can have fertility problems. In addition to increasing age, causes for infertility in women may include hormonal problems, cysts, or structural problems of the reproductive organs.

Myth 4: (For men) I know I'm fertile because I always have a good erection and ejaculation.
Fact: Even men with no erectile or ejaculatory problems can have infertility. In addition to sexual disorders, other causes of male infertility include inadequate sperm and structural abnormalities in the reproductive organs.

Myth 5: Having a lot of sex will ensure pregnancy.
Fact: The timing of sexual intercourse is what matters in achieving pregnancy, not the frequency. To maximize your chances of conception, you must engage in sexual intercourse around the time of ovulation. This myth is problematic because it is actually recommended that men who have problems with sperm count engage in sexual inter-

course every *other* day around the time of ovulation to give their system time to produce a new supply of sperm for the next ejaculation.

Myth 6: If we chart the timing of ovulation and engage in sex during that time, we should be assured of conceiving.
Fact: Although you will definitely increase your chances of conception by engaging in sexual intercourse during ovulation, you should know that some women occassionally can menstruate without ovulating.

Myth 7: If we successfully time intercourse during ovulation, we should plan on having a healthy baby.
Fact: Unfortunately, even the sperm meeting the egg is no guarantee of a healthy baby nine months later. Natural early pregnancy loss occurs frequently in the body. In fact only roughly 31% of fertilized eggs survive to term birth, and this percentage decreases as women age.[8]

Myth 8: Ovulation occurs on day 14 each month.
Fact: This "magic" number gets thrown around because it is based on an ideal 28-day cycle. Most women do not have a perfect 28-day cycle. In general, ovulation is thought to occur approximately 14 days before a woman starts her period. However, this varies in some women. For these reasons, it is important to utilize other signs of fertility to track the timing of ovulation.

Myth 9: Since we had no problems having our other child(ren), the next conception should also be a piece of cake.
Fact: Approximately 70% of the couples experiencing infertility already have at least one child.[9] The cause of this "secondary infertility" may be related to increased maternal age or to the same types of factors that cause primary infertility.

Myth 10: Everyone else around me seems to be getting pregnant. I feel like my infertility problems are rare.
Fact: Up to one of every six couples has problems getting pregnant. However, many people are reluctant to talk openly about this painful and sensitive subject. Couples often end up suffering alone, thus missing out on potentially healing support from others.

While these myths can be scary, they are not meant to alarm you or make you lose hope of becoming pregnant. Rather, we believe that it is important for you to be educated about fact versus fiction when it comes to conception, and to use the facts to maximize your chances of having a baby.

2

WHEN REPRODUCTION DOESN'T WORK
Causes of Infertility

Infertility is a medical condition of the reproductive system in which a couple is unable to conceive after one year of engaging in sexual intercourse without the use of contraception or unable to carry a pregnancy to live birth. The time period of one year was chosen because 85% of couples achieve pregnancy within the first 12 months of trying without contraception. Of couples with infertility problems, roughly 30% have never been able to conceive (primary infertility) and approximately 70% have previously conceived but are currently unable to do so (secondary infertility). For women, rates of infertility increase with age. Researchers[1] have found that approximately 10% of females between the ages of 15 and 30 have fertility problems, while roughly 14% of those between the ages of 30 and 34 have infertility. The numbers jump dramatically to 25% among women aged 35 and older.

Since women carry and deliver a baby, there is a common misconception that infertility is the woman's problem. However, the causes of infertility can be attributed to women, men, or both. In actuality, men and women are equally affected by biological causes of infertility. Roughly 35% of cases are termed *female factor*, and approximately 35% of cases are termed *male factor*. In 20% of cases, the cause of infertility is a combination of problems in both the male and the female, and in the remaining 10% of cases the cause of infertility is unknown.

CAUSES OF INFERTILITY THAT CAN AFFECT EITHER PARTNER[2]

Before examining the typical causes of male and female factor infertility separately, let us examine some causes of infertility that can affect either partner.

Advancing Age

Increasing age is related to decreasing fertility. For women, fertility starts declining after the age of 30 and drops sharply after age 35. Because a woman is born with all her eggs, they age with her. Older eggs are more difficult to fertilize and are more likely to have chromosomal abnormalities such as Down's Syndrome. Men also experience some decrease in fertility with advancing age, due largely to dropping levels of testosterone that decrease sex drive and the ability to achieve and maintain a strong erection. Another cause of decreasing male fertility with age is medical illness. Conditions that affect some men as they age, such as diabetes or vascular disease, can affect sexual functioning and, therefore, fertility.

Miscarriages

Although miscarriage is fairly common, the chances of miscarrying increase with advancing maternal age. Additional causes of miscarriage include hormonal problems, genetic or chromosomal problems of the fetus, immunological problems, and structural problems of the reproductive organs. Other factors also have been implicated, such as infections, diseases, chemicals and environmental toxins, certain medications, and substances such as tobacco, caffeine, alcohol, and illicit drugs.

Sexually Transmitted Diseases (STDs) and Pelvic Inflammatory Disease (PID)

STDs, such as gonorrhea and chlamydia, can lead to infertility because they are often unrecognized and left untreated and can travel from the lower genitalia to affect the upper reproductive organs. Some STDs can cause women to have PID, an infection of the reproductive tract that, left untreated, can eventually lead to infertility, ectopic pregnancy (a pregnancy in the fallopian tubes instead of the uterus), and constant pelvic pain. STDs in both sexes and PID in women can cause the reproductive tracts to scar or stick together. In women, they can cause movement or blockage of the fallopian tubes, making it difficult or impossible for the egg and the sperm to make their normal journeys. In men, STDs can impair the production of sperm and their movement through the male reproductive tract. The good news is that STDs may not have these effects if they are recognized and treated properly. The bad news is that many STDs, such as chlamydia, occur silently without symptoms.

Diabetes

Diabetes, which stems from an insulin deficit, affects the body's ability to regulate sugars in the blood. Diabetes can affect fertility by damaging blood vessels and nerves. In men, diabetes can cause erectile dysfunction or retrograde ejaculation, the movement of semen backward along the reproductive tract during ejaculation. In women, uncontrolled diabetes can affect ovulation or implantation and can cause early miscarriage. Medications and treatments for diabetes, as well as careful control over blood sugar levels, can help tackle these problems.

Smoking

Smoking can affect fertility in both men and women. Studies have shown that men who smoke have sperm counts that are, on average, 15% lower than sperm counts of men who do not smoke. One small study showed that men who quit smoking increased their sperm counts dramatically. For women, smoking can affect fertility in a number of ways. Studies have shown that smoking can increase the chances of miscarriage, lengthen the time it  takes to conceive, and cause menopause to occur earlier in the woman's lifetime. In addition, smoking can interfere with the ability of the fallopian tubes to move the fertilized egg, as well as the ability of the embryo to divide, grow, and implant itself the uterus. Furthermore, it has been found that the success rates of *in vitro* fertilization are lower for women who smoke. For these and many other reasons, you may really benefit from quitting smoking.

Alcohol and Illicit Drugs

Alcohol and street drugs, especially when used excessively, can affect reproductive functioning. In men, use of these substances can  lower sperm count and quality, interfere with hormonal balance, and cause erectile dysfunction. In women, some drugs, such as marijuana, can interfere with the menstrual cycle. In addition, some substances can cause chromosomal and genetic abnormalities in the fetus if conception does occur.

Weight

Weight can affect fertility in both women and men. In underweight women, too little body fat can impede the menstrual cycle. Women who are overweight can also stop ovulating because fat can affect insulin and other hormone production. In men, being overweight can interfere with sperm production.

COMMON CAUSES OF MALE FACTOR INFERTILITY[3]

In roughly 35% of cases, the fertility problem is related to the male. Most male factor infertility stems from problems with the number or quality of sperm, blockage in the male reproductive tract, a sexual disorder, or factors such as surgeries, genital trauma, medical disorders, infections, or chemicals. Following is a brief description of some factors that can affect male fertility. For a more detailed understanding of the causes of male infertility and what is involved in a medical workup for infertility, we direct you to one of the many books specifically written on the topic.

Problems with Sperm

Problems with sperm can include the production, maturation, number, motility, and/or shape of sperm. Sperm problems are the leading cause of male infertility. Production and maturation problems can be caused by the presence of a varicocele (dilated varicose veins in the scrotum), undescended testes, surgeries, testicular trauma, hormonal problems, diseases such as mumps, orchitis, untreated STDs, extended testicular exposure to high heat levels, and infections, among other causes. Having a normal number of sperm is important to fertility because so many sperm die in the process of sexual intercourse and in the journey to meet the egg. The more sperm present in the ejaculate, the more likely it will be that a viable sperm will survive and penetrate the egg. The motility of sperm is important because sperm must be able to swim the long journey through the female reproductive tract to the egg. The shape of sperm affects their ability to penetrate the egg. Sperm heads that are too small, too big, or otherwise abnormal in shape will encounter more difficulty penetrating the shell of the egg.

Problems with Blockage

Blockages in the male reproductive tract are another cause of infertility. Such blockages can occur at various points along the tract and can be caused by congenital defects, surgeries (such as vasectomy), or infection (such as that caused by an untreated STD).

Problems with Sexual Functioning

Since conception requires successful ejaculation in the woman's vagina, some fertility problems are related to problems in achieving or maintaining an erection or to problems with premature ejaculation. However, it is important to note that most men with erectile difficulties are not infertile. Some men experience brief and transient episodes of erectile difficulties related to the "performance anxiety" of scheduled sex, postcoital tests, or having to produce a semen sample in the doctor's office. Premature ejaculation is a sexual problem, not an infertility problem. It is easily treated through a number of exercises designed to help men control their orgasms. Please refer to *The new male sexuality: The truth about men, sex, and pleasure* by Zilbergeld[4] for further reading on this topic.

Other Problems

Other factors can affect male fertility. Surgeries such as a vasectomy or surgical complications after testicular, prostate, or bladder surgeries can block the male reproductive tract. Trauma to the genitals can affect sperm production and/or its movement through the male reproductive tract. Medical disorders such as cystic fibrosis, renal disease, sickle-cell disease, diabetes, as well as infections such as those caused by STDs, can impair reproductive functioning in males. Men can also have infections of the prostate or epididymis. In addition, having a fever can affect the production of sperm, since the testes function best in an environment that is 2–4 degrees cooler than the body.

A variety of chemicals also can affect male fertility. Environmental toxins such as those used in pesticides, lead, mercury, and benzene have been implicated in male infertility. Chemicals used in chemotherapy and radiotherapy and anabolic steroids may be linked with infertility. Alcohol and illicit drugs can affect sperm quality. Even prescription medications, such as those used to treat high blood pressure, ulcers, seizures, and depression (MAO inhibitors) can cause infertility. It is important to talk with your doctor about the chemicals you are exposed to and those you ingest to investigate their potential effects on your fertility. Be sure to consult with your doctor before you discontinue use of any medications.

COMMON CAUSES OF FEMALE FACTOR INFERTILITY[5]

Infertility traditionally has been considered the woman's fault. However, only 35% of fertility is related to problems in the female, a percentage matching that of male factor infertility. Female factor infertility may be related to problems of the menstrual cycle, blockage in the reproductive tract, and/or structural problems of the uterus or cervix. Again, we direct you to one of the many books specifically written on the topic for a more detailed understanding of the causes of female infertility and what is involved in a medical workup for infertility.

Problems Related to the Menstrual Cycle

Problems with the monthly cycle can affect the process of ovulation. Irregular ovulation and hormonal problems are responsible for up to half of all female infertility. Problems with ovulation can be caused by nonfunctional ovaries, polycystic ovarian disease (PCO), hormonal imbalance, or thyroid disease.

Problems with Blockage

Blockage in the female reproductive tract accounts for approximately 40% of all female infertility. Specifically, obstruction of the fallopian tubes is responsible for 30% of female factor infertility. Blockage in the reproductive tract reduces the chances for successful union of the egg and sperm and movement of the embryo into the uterus for implantation. Blockage of the reproductive tract may also lead to ectopic pregnancy, the implantation of a fertilized egg into the fallopian tube. STDs, PID, and surgeries are common causes of infections and subsequent scarring of the reproductive tract. Endometriosis is another cause of blockage in the female reproductive tract. It occurs when the lining of the uterus grows in other places, such as the fallopian tubes or ovaries. Endometriosis can impair fertility by causing scarring and blockage. It can also interfere with sexual functioning because it is marked by severe pain around the time of menstruation.

Structural Problems of the Uterus or Cervix

While less common causes of female factor infertility, structural problems or functional abilities of the uterus or cervix can also lead to infertility. The uterus is responsible for providing for a good environment for the embryo and for nourishing the developing fetus. Fertility problems can be caused by congenital or developmental problems of the uterus, or by problems such as scarring, adhesions, polyps, or fibroids. Problems with the cervix may be related to cervical mucous or inability to support a pregnancy. Around the time of ovulation, the cervix releases a mucous that is friendly to sperm. Infections can cause problems with this cervical mucous and could lead to greater sperm death or greater difficulty for sperm to get through the mucous. If the cervix is not structurally sound, it may not be able to support a pregnancy. Specifically, if the cervical os dilates too early, loss of pregnancy may result.

INFERTILITY MYTHS AND FACTS

Now that we have covered the common causes of both male and female factor infertility, we will try to debunk some common myths about infertility.

Myth 1: Infertility is a rare problem.
Fact: Unfortunately, infertility has been estimated to affect one in every six couples. Fortunately, medical technology has advanced to the point where as many as 80% of couples with infertility can be successfully treated.

Myth 2: Since I already have a child, having another one should be no problem.
Fact: Secondary infertility, or the inability to get pregnant after at least one previous pregnancy, affects as many as 70% of infertile couples.

Myth 3: Infertility is a woman's problem.
Fact: The incidence of infertility related to male factors and female factors is equal. Thus, when a couple has problems conceiving, it is important that both the male and the female partner be evaluated for potential infertility.

Myth 4: Women who abandon traditional roles in favor of their careers are selfish and bring infertility on themselves.
Fact: While it is true that a woman's fertility decreases with advancing age, this myth completely ignores the current cultural context. In this day and age, women are not only expected to fill their traditional roles but to balance this with a career. Economic forces may demand that a woman bring in income to support a comfortable lifestyle. Not working could potentially jeopardize the financial security and well-being of the desired family. Working could jeopardize a couple's fertility. Striking a balance is not simple.

Myth 5: Infertility is caused by "sinful" thoughts and behaviors, such as promiscuity, masturbation, pre-marital sex, infidelity, incest, same-sex experiences, or abortions.

Fact: There is no religious or medical evidence that "sinful" thoughts or masturbation cause infertility, or that sexual behaviors such as promiscuity, pre-marital sex, infidelity, incest, or homosexual experiences, in and of themselves, cause infertility. The only way that sexual behaviors could be related to infertility is if an untreated STD resulted in damage to the reproductive organs. Abortions can be related to infertility only if the procedure caused scarring or damage to the reproductive tract.

Myth 6: Infertility is all in your head.
Fact: Ninety percent of infertility cases can be attributed to a physical cause. Only 10% of cases are unexplained, and some of these may remain unexplained because medical technology has not yet advanced sufficiently to find the physical cause.

Myth 7: If you just relax or take a vacation, you'll get pregnant.
Fact: Because infertility is not caused by stress, relaxing or vacationing is not likely to solve the problem. However, relaxing can improve your overall quality of life, help you cope better with the stressful experience of infertility, and allow you to make better treatment decisions and adhere to treatment regimens. In addition, couples who are relaxed or on vacation may be more likely to engage in sexual intercourse. If timed appropriately, this could improve chances of getting pregnant.

Myth 8: You'll get pregnant after you adopt a baby.
Fact: While there are many anecdotal stories of people who adopt a baby after a long struggle with infertility and then spontaneously get pregnant, it is simply not true that adoption will lead to your own pregnancy. Infertile couples who adopt have the same rates of getting pregnant afterwards as infertile couples who do not adopt.

Myth 9: Infertility indicates a sexual disorder.
Fact: In the vast majority of cases, there is no relationship between infertility and sexual dysfunction. Most people with infertility have no problems, or only temporary problems, with their sexual functioning.

Myth 10: Infertility is a sign that we would not have been good parents.
Fact: Infertility is a medical problem that has nothing to do with your parenting potential. You are very likely a loving and caring person

who has put a lot of thought into having children. The proof that this myth is untrue is evidenced by the thousands of fertile people who are terrible parents.

Myth 11: If I take a month or two off from my infertility treatments, I will ruin my chances of getting pregnant.
Fact: While continuity in your infertility treatment is important, taking a little break will not ruin your chances of conception. In fact, taking a break can help you revitalize and prepare for upcoming treatments. A break can also help bring back the sexual spark after months of scheduled sex. In addition, it can give you time to reevaluate your current treatment and consider other treatment options.

Myth 12: There's no use seeking medical help for infertility.
Fact: This is absolutely untrue. Medical technology has advanced today to the point where up to 80% of couples with infertility can be helped to produce their own biological children. These odds favor at least giving it a try!

More myths, sometimes called cognitive distortions, are discussed in Sections II, III, and IV on depression, stress, and relationship difficulties.

3

ADDRESSING THE PROBLEM
Medical Treatments for Infertility

The state of medical technology today can give infertile couples great hope about the prospect of having a baby. Better diagnostic procedures and new reproductive technologies, as well as more specialists in the field, are increasing a couple's chances of getting pregnant. In its 1999 report on assisted reproductive technology (ART) success rates, the Center for Disease Control reported an increase in success rates since 1995,[1] when monitoring began. For example, the average live birth rate per cycle using fresh non-donor eggs or embryos rose from 19.6% in 1995 to 25.2% in 1999. Recently, it has been reported that as many as 80% of infertile couples will conceive within 4–5 years of receiving their diagnosis.[2]

This chapter provides a brief overview of the various treatments available for infertility. For a more detailed and thorough description of these treatments, we refer you to the many books and websites available on the topic. In general, there are three categories of treatments for infertility. They include non-surgical treatments, surgical treatments, and assisted reproductive technologies (ARTs). Employing ARTs using sperm, eggs, embryos, and/or reproductive organs from people other than the couple trying to conceive is called third-party reproduction. Although they are not medical treatments, this chapter also touches on adoption or choosing child-free living as other options in dealing with infertility.

NON-SURGICAL TREATMENTS
Fertility Drugs

As a woman ages, a number of hormonal changes take place that decrease her fertility. Specifically, some of these changes cause her to produce fewer follicles, make her uterus less likely to accept an embryo, and decrease the chances of the embryo developing into a live birth. For women with ovulatory disorders, either because of age or medical problems, a variety of fertility drugs can stimulate the ovaries to produce eggs. Fertility medications for ovulatory disorders cost between $100 and $2,000 per cycle and have a 36–50% success rate.[3] Fertility drugs are also used to help the female regulate her ovulation so that intercourse can be timed, as is done in artificial insemination. In addition, fertility drugs are often used along with ARTs to increase the number of viable eggs in each cycle. Furthermore, they can help prepare the uterus for implantation of the embryo and are often used with ART procedures and with third-party reproduction. Male infertility can also be treated with fertility drugs in cases where men have hormonal imbalances or must stimulate the production of sperm.

Many fertility drugs are actual hormones. As such, these drugs can cause symptoms like those experienced during the monthly menstrual cycle. The intensified moods and dramatic mood swings that result from these drugs, coupled with the naturally emotional nature of dealing with infertility and medical treatments, can greatly affect your emotional state. Some of these fertility drugs must be administered through injections, putting one partner in the uncomfortable role of having to inject the other—who, in turn, is put in the position of having to take this without too much complaining. To cope with these moods and painful situations, we recommend that you and your partner make use of the tried-and-true coping skills described in Sections II, III, and IV. These coping skills can help you gain control over your raging emotions, prevent serious depression and anxiety, and help your relationship survive the infertility crisis.

Antibiotics

If the cause of male infertility is related to an infection in the organs responsible for the production or movement of sperm, antibiotic treatment is used to clear the infection.

Artificial Insemination (AI)

Artificial insemination, or AI, is a procedure in which sperm are placed near the woman's cervix and uterus so that they may go on to fertilize the egg. The sperm can come from either the male partner, in which case the procedure is called AIH (with the "H" standing for the husband) or from a donor (AID, with "D" representing the donor). To ensure that a viable egg is available for the sperm to fertilize once they are deposited into the woman's body, AI is generally used in conjunction with methods to induce ovulation in females. AI is often useful for men with a variety of ejaculatory disorders or structural problems that interfere with the ability to deliver sperm to the woman's cervix. It is also useful for women who have poor cervical mucous or women who produce sperm antibodies.

AI is generally performed in one of two ways. First, intracervical insemination, or ICI, involves placing semen in the cervix using a syringe or cannula. Second, intrauterine insemination, or IUI, involves separating the sperm from the semen and inserting the sperm into the uterine cavity. Because IUI places the sperm closer to the fallopian tubes than does ICI, it is the generally favored AI technique. IUI costs between $150 and $300 per procedure and has a 20–25% success rate.[4]

Surgical Treatments

When obstructions of the reproductive tract are the cause of infertility, surgical techniques to unblock those obstructions can help a couple permanently restore their fertility. Surgical options may be favored to ART options because surgical solutions tend to cost less, be covered by insurance, and allow for continuing attempts at pregnancy. However, compared to ART they are more invasive and have a longer recuperation time. Surgical treatments can be used to treat scarring and adhesions caused by STDs, PID, or related to endometriosis. Surgery can also reverse tubal sterilization or tubal ligation. If uterine fibroids are the cause of infertility, surgery can remove these noncancerous masses.

Surgery can also be used to correct male factor infertility. Men who have had a vasectomy and now would like to father a child can have a vasectomy reversal. Surgery can also be performed on men whose infertility is caused by other types of blockages in their reproductive tract, such as those with varicoceles or blocked ejaculatory ducts. Surgery for varicoceles costs $1,500–$4,000 and has a 50–60% success rate.[5] Men with lowered sperm count because of blockages in their reproductive tract may also find surgery to be a solution. When low sperm count is not a result of obstructions, the testes may be producing too few or even no sperm. Men with low sperm count, whether or not caused by blockages, may be helped by new microsurgical techniques involving aspiration or extraction of sperm. Collected sperm are generally injected into an egg using a procedure called intracytoplasmic sperm injection (ICSI), discussed later in this chapter.

Assisted Reproductive Technologies (ARTS)

Assisted reproductive technologies are often tried by couples that have had no success with the treatments discussed thus far. However, ARTs are being indicated earlier these days for a variety of infertility problems, including tubal problems, low or no sperm counts, unexplained infertility, and/or advanced maternal age. The cost of ARTs varies greatly among clinics in the United States. Per-cycle costs can exceed $10,000, with a general range[6] of $7,000–$12,000. This cost can be balanced by the promising success rates.

ART procedures include in-vitro fertilization (IVF) and the closely related procedures of gamete intrafallopian transfer (GIFT), zygote intrafallopian transfer (ZIFT), and tubal embryo transfer (TET). These procedures are often combined with a variety of micromanipulation techniques.

In Vitro Fertilization (IVF) *In vitro* fertilization involves removing an egg from a woman's ovary and using a man's sperm to fertilize it outside her body in a petri dish. Once the egg is fertilized and the embryo has been incubated, it is implanted in the woman's uterus at the appropriate time and hopefully develops into a normal -term pregnancy. The specific steps involved in IVF and the adjunct procedures of GIFT and ZIFT, are:

Step 1—Follicle stimulation: Fertility drugs are given to the female during the first week of the IVF cycle. These drugs are intended to stimulate the growth of ovarian follicles containing eggs. Unlike normal ovulation, when only one follicle is released, fertility drugs stimulate the ripening of many eggs. Although multiple pregnancies may result, this process maximizes the chances of having at least one viable egg. The development of the follicles is monitored until they are ready to be released from the ovary.

Step 2—Egg recovery: The eggs are retrieved from the woman's body using an ultrasound-guided needle. This needle is generally passed through the woman's vagina and the eggs are harvested from the ovary. This procedure is done while the woman is given intravenous pain medications. Occasionally, a laproscopic procedure done under general anesthesia is used to harvest the eggs. Meanwhile, the man is asked to produce a fresh semen sample that will be used in fertilization.

Step 3—Fertilization: Once the eggs have been removed, they are placed in a petri dish along with a sample of washed sperm. The dish is allowed to incubate so fertilization can take place. Once fertilized, the embryos are moved to a new growth medium and monitored for proper development. Approximately two days later, the embryos that have developed most fully will make it to the next step.

Step 4—Embryo transfer: A number of the most developed embryos are transferred to the uterus through a catheter inserted into the woman's vagina and guided via ultrasound through her cervix and into her uterus. Generally, multiple embryos are transferred to maximize the chances of successful pregnancy. This may result in the birth of twins, triplets, or even more babies.

Step 5—Implantation: In this last step, the embryo(s) implant themselves into the uterine lining. Oftentimes, the woman is given progesterone daily to maximize the chances of developing a good uterine lining for implantation. After successful implantation, the embryos develop as in a normal pregnancy.

Gamete Intrafallopian Transfer (GIFT) Gamete intrafallopian transfer involves the same steps as IVF up to the point of egg retrieval. However, GIFT allows for fertilization to occur in a woman's fallopian tubes rather than in a laboratory petri dish. In GIFT the eggs and sperm are placed into the fallopian tube through a catheter during laparoscopic surgery. GIFT is indicated only if there is at least one healthy fallopian tube. Some couples prefer GIFT to IVF because they believe it is more natural for fertilization to take place in the woman's body rather than in a laboratory. However, GIFT is being used less these days because it requires laparoscopy, does not allow for documentation of fertilization or evaluation of embryo quality, and has success rates that are fairly similar to those of IVF.

Zygote Intrafallopian Transfer (ZIFT) Zygote intrafallopian transfer is a combination of IVF and GIFT. As in the IVF procedure, eggs are retrieved and mixed with sperm in a petri dish. The newly fertilized but undivided eggs, called zygotes, are then transferred into the fallopian tubes during laparoscopy. ZIFT is sometimes preferable to GIFT because fertilization can be detected. However, as with GIFT, ZIFT is being used less frequently because it requires laparoscopy and because of the high success rates of IVF.

Tubal Embryo Transfer (TET)   Tubal embryo transfer is another combination of IVF and GIFT. As with IVF, more developed embryos are transferred. However, as in GIFT, the embryos are transferred into the fallopian tubes (instead of the woman's uterus).

Micromanipulation Techniques

Micromanipulation techniques, such as intracytoplasmic sperm injection and assisted hatching, are often used in conjunction with ARTs. Micromanipulation techniques involve tiny micro tools driven by robotic arms. These techniques allow doctors to work with individual sperm and embryos.

Intracytoplasmic sperm injection (ICSI): Intracytoplasmic sperm injection is a new micromanipulation technique involves taking one sperm from a man's semen specimen, drawing it into a microscopic needle, then injecting it directly into a single egg. Eggs that have been fertilized through this procedure are then used in IVF-type procedures. ICSI allows men with poor sperm count to become biological fathers. ICSI costs between $500 and $2,500 (not including the price of IVF), and has roughly a 25% success rate per procedure.[7]

Assisted hatching: Assisted hatching is a micromanipulation technique designed to assist the process of embryo implantation into the uterine lining. The technique involves using an acidic solution to open the embryo's outer cover, called the zona pellucida. Helping the embryo emerge from its shell allows for easier implantation. Assisted hatching is useful for older women and when the embryo shell is thick or its cell division is slow.

Success Rates for ARTs

Success rates are measured in a number of ways. The pregnancy rate indicates successful conceptions, which are common both in assisted and unassisted reproductions. The CDC's 2003 data show that 34.4% of ART cycles using fresh non-donor eggs or embryos resulted in clinical pregnancies. However, only 82.2% of these pregnancies resulted in live births,[8] which is a more accurate indicator of success.

There are two ways to measure live birth rates. The first is the rate for live birth per egg retrieval, based on the number of live births per ART cycles in which eggs were retrieved. Sometimes eggs are retrieved but never transferred because of illness, inadequate egg production, or patient cancellation for other reasons. Thus, the rate of live births per transfer tends to be a better predictor. Another distinction must be made with respect to success rates. Sometimes the success rate does not differentiate between single births and multiple-infant births. Thus, if a woman brings home twins or triplets, this may be counted as only one success, instead of two or three. CDC data show that the incidence of multiple-infant live births using ARTs is 34.2% versus 2–5% for natural conceptions (31.0% are twins and 3.2% are triplets or more).[9]

Success rates for ARTs depend on a number of factors. The 2003 CDC report lists these factors as age, infertility diagnosis, history of previous births, previous miscarriages, previous ART cycles, number of embryos transferred, type of ART procedure, use of techniques such as ICSI, and clinic size.

Age is one of the most important factors affecting the chances of a live birth for a woman who uses her own eggs. CDC figures show that success rates are relatively stable for women in their 20s, decline steadily in the 30s, and drop dramatically after the mid-30s. In addition, women are more likely to miscarry with advancing age. The CDC data show that miscarriage rates were approximately 13% for women younger than 34, but increased to 29% for women aged 40 and to 48% for women aged 43.

Table 3.1 breaks down the success rates for ARTs by infertility diagnosis:

Table 3.1 Live ART Birth Rates Using Fresh Nondonor Eggs or Embryos by Diagnosis[10]

Diagnosis	Live births per cycle
Tubal factor	30.0%
Ovulatory dysfunction	33.9%
Diminished ovarian reserve	14.3%
Endometriosis	32.1%
Uterine factor	27.3%
Male factor	33.8%
Other cause	25.7%
Unexplained cause	30.4%
Multiple factors – female only	22.7%
Multiple factors – female and male	26.9%

Table 3.2 Live Birth Rates by Woman's Age for Women with No Previous ART and for Women with One or More Unsuccessful ART Cycles[11]

Woman's Age	Live Births Per Cycle in Women with No Previous ART	Live Births Per Cycle in Women with One or More Previous Unsuccessful ART
Below 35	38.3%	32.1%
35–37	31.2%	25.0%
38–40	20.4%	17.5%
41–42	9.5%	10.8%
Over 42	4.1%	3.7%

Table 3.3 Live Births per Retrieval for Different Types of ART Procedures[12]

Type of ART Procedure	Percent of Live Births Per Retrieval
IVF with ICSI	33.4%
IVF without ICSI	31.9
GIFT	20.8%
ZIFT	25.9%
Combination (IVF and either GIFT or ZIFT)	28.3%

Success rates for ART procedures also vary depending on whether women have previously used ART but did not give birth. CDC data indicate that in all age groups up to age 42, live birth rates among women who had already undergone an unsuccessful ART cycle were lower than those for women who had not. Table 3.2 compares the live birth rates by age for ART cycles using fresh nondonor eggs or embryos for women who have had no previous ART and for women who have had one or more ART cycles with no previous births.

With respect to success rates based on type of ART procedure used, the 2003 CDC data indicate that success rates for IVF with and without ICSI were much higher than those for cycles that used GIFT and ZIFT. Results for all age groups have been combined because of similar patterns. However, it must be noted again that success rates do vary depending on a woman's age. Table 3.3 uses this data to compare the rates of live births per retrieval using fresh nondonor eggs or embryos for different types of ART procedures.

THIRD-PARTY REPRODUCTION

You may think that it only takes two to make a baby, but in some cases it takes three, four, or even five. Third-party reproduction involves the use of donors or surrogates and is used when one or both partners cannot produce gametes (eggs or sperm) or when the woman is unable to carry the baby to term. Egg donation is used when a woman cannot produce eggs or when IVF fails. The donor can be a family member, friend, or anonymous. The donor undergoes ovarian stimulation so that her eggs can be retrieved. The donor eggs are then mixed with sperm, and the resulting embryos transferred to the woman trying to conceive. The success rate for this procedure using donor eggs is 36% per embryo transfer.[13] However this procedure can add up to $7,500 to the IVF cost.[14]

If the male partner is unable to produce a sperm sample, donor sperm can be used to fertilize the egg (wife's egg or donor egg). In addition, embryos that have been fertilized using both donor egg and sperm may be used. Genetically, this situation is equivalent to adoption, except that the wife carries the embryo to term and delivers the baby. When a woman is not able to carry a pregnancy to term, the use of a donor uterus, or surrogate, may be considered. The surrogate can carry an embryo made up of any combination of the couple's or donor's gametes.

Third-party reproduction may be a viable option. However, before you consider using any form of third-party reproduction we urge you to consider a number of factors, including moral and ethical considerations, personal concerns, possible religious prohibitions, potential reaction of family and friends, partner reactions and marital concerns, issues involving confidentiality, possible legal issues, and financial costs[15]. To address these concerns we ask you to discuss the questions posed in Assignment 3.1.

ADOPTION

For couples that do not experience success with the above reproductive options, adoption may be a viable way to have a child. While not exactly a "cure" for infertility, adoption may provide a couple with a wonderful opportunity to parent a child. Adoptions may be either open, in which case the identities of all parties are known to one another, or closed, which means the identities of the genetic parents and the adoptive parents are kept confidential. You may use a public or a private adoption agency, adopt a child born within your country or one born in a foreign country.

Before adopting, it is important for some couples to go through the grieving process of not being able to have their own biological child. Not having a biological child may involve many losses, including the experience of pregnancy and birth, breastfeeding, and having a child who is genetically related to you. However, while you may not be able to pass

---

ASSIGNMENT 3.1

The following questions are designed to help you and your partner focus on some of the many issues that involve third-party reproduction.

1. What does it mean to be a father? A mother? A parent?
2. How important is it to us to be pregnant as opposed to being parents?
3. How important is it for us to pass along our genes? How important is this to our families?
4. What are our personal, cultural, spiritual, and ethical beliefs about using third-party reproduction?
5. How would we resolve differences between us on these issues?
6. What does our religion say about using donors in the process of reproduction?
7. How would my partner/spouse react if we used third-party donation?
8. How could it affect our marriage? How would we cope with any possible marital problems brought on by third-party donation?
9. How would it affect me, my partner, and my future child if the child was only partially genetically related or not genetically related at all?
10. Do we want to know who the donor is?
11. If we know the donor, to what extent would we want to interact with him or her?
12. Would we want to tell our child?
13. Would we want to tell our family and friends about the use of donors?
14. How would we arrange legal matters with donors and/or surrogates?
15. How would we afford the costs of third-party reproduction?

---

along your family genes, you can still pass along other family traits, such as values and love. You will also be able to pass along the family name.

Some couples must also grieve over their idea of having a genetically related child that is "perfect." This child is idealized as the perfect mixture of the best physical and personality traits of both the mother and the father. While grieving this ideal is important, you must also realize that the chances of actually having this perfect child are small. Even genetically related children have disabilities and defects, and they do not always inherit your best qualities.

As with third-party reproduction, adoption can involve a number of special considerations, including personal concerns, the potential reaction of family and friends, partner reactions, issues around confidentiality, legal issues, and financial costs. If you are considering adoption, we urge you to first ponder the questions posed in the following exercise.

ASSIGNMENT 3.2

The following questions are designed to help you and your partner tackle some of the many issues involved in adoption:

1. What does it mean to be a father? A mother? A parent?
2. How important is it to us to be pregnant as opposed to being parents?
3. How important is it to us to pass along our genes?
4. How would we feel to have a child who is not similar to us in appearance or personality?
5. How important is it to our families that we have a genetically related child?
6. How would our families react to the adoption? How would they treat our children?
7. How would my partner react to adoption?
8. How could we support one another through the process of adoption and raising our child?
9. How could adoption affect our relationship/marriage? How could we cope with this?
10. How do we feel about open versus closed adoption?
11. If we have an open adoption procedure, to what extent do we want the biological parents involved in the upbringing of our child?
12. Will we use a public or a private adoption agency?
13. How do we feel about adopting a domestic-born versus an international child? How about adopting a child that is culturally or racially different?
14. How do we feel about adopting an infant versus an older child? How about a special-needs child?
15. Would we want to tell our child that he/she is adopted?
16. How would we handle legal matters and potential legal problems?
17. How would we afford the costs of adoption?

CHILD-FREE LIVING

The term "childless" traditionally has been used to describe a couple with no children. Unfortunately, this term connotes the absence of something or a deficiency[16] and is associated with tragedy, misfortune, emptiness, unhappiness, and lack of fulfillment. More recently, the term "child-free" has been used to describe couples that make the decision not to become parents. However, this definition may not apply to couples struggling with infertility.

Many infertile couples who do not feel that adoption is an option or who do not want to have a child without the experiences of pregnancy and childbirth are considering child-free living. As an increasing number of people challenge traditional beliefs, it has become more socially acceptable for couples not to have children. For more information on these topics, we refer you to The National Organization for Nonparents, founded by Ellen Peck, and to a number of books on the topic (*The Baby Trap* and *Pronatalism: The Myth of Mom and Apple Pie*, also written by Ellen Peck; *Sweet Grapes: How to Stop Being Infertile and Start Living Again* by Jean Carter and Michael Carter), which consider the meaning, issues, and decision-making process involved in remaining child-free.

Couples who choose child-free living may experience feelings of grief and mourning similar to those they experienced when they first learned of their infertility diagnosis. This is because making the choice not to have children involves many losses—the loss of pregnancy, childbirth, breastfeeding, dreams about parenting, continuity of family, and a sense of connection to other parents. Couples may also experience societal stigma and be judged as "selfish" for not having children. However, there are other ways of "parenting" and making a connection with the human family. Many couples who are child-free become involved in the lives of children of relatives or friends, as well as in their communities. A sense of nurturing and generativity also can come from raising plants or pets.

CHOOSING BETWEEN OPTIONS: FIVE TIPS FOR EFFECTIVE DECISION MAKING

Choosing between reproductive options can be very confusing. Couples often get lost in the medical jargon and their emotions when trying to decide between fertility drugs, surgery, and/or ARTs. Choosing to stop medical treatments and consider adoption or child-free living also can be very difficult. These options involve weighing many factors. In our years of experience in working with individuals and couples struggling with infertility, we have witnessed the importance of the decision-making process. The tips below have been designed to help you with some of the necessary steps.

Tip 1—Consider both short-term and long-term consequences. Successful decision makers consider both the short-term and long-term consequences of each choice. A decision often will have positive short-term consequences but questionable or negative long-term consequences, or vice-versa. For example, while it might feel good to quit painful medical treatments in the short run, it may cost you the possibility of a biological child in the long run. Conversely, it may be incredibly painful in the short run to quit medical treatments and turn to adoption, but in the long run it could save you from costly failed treatments and give you a beautiful child to parent.

Tip 2—Consider both rational and emotional factors. Rational factors include the financial costs and success rates of different options, the time needed for each option, and possible legal issues. Emotional considerations include how you and your partner would cope with all the rational factors, the emotional costs of each option, the physical and emotional energy needed, your values/morals/beliefs, how each option would affect your identity and sense of well-being, and how the reaction of others could affect you.

Tip 3—Write down the pros and cons of each option. Many people find it helpful to systematically write down the pros and cons of each option (considering short-term and long-term consequences, as well as emotional and rational factors) before making a decision. This will allow you to keep track of the factors you need to take into consideration. Sometimes seeing the lists in black and white can clarify your decision.

Tip 4—Use skills in talking with your partner. Healthy couples use the communication and problem-solving skills discussed in Chapter 10 to weigh the options and come up with a mutually agreed-upon decision. When a decision of this magnitude involves another person, the *process* by which you make the decision can be as important as the decision itself. Each partner wants to feel that he or she had a chance to voice feelings and opinions that have been heard and understood by the other partner. Understanding, validation, and compromise in the decision-making process can make a very difficult situation much easier to bear, and bring couples closer together.

Tip 5 – Reevaluate your decision. Making a decision does not mean you are stuck with it for the rest of your life. People who make solid decisions reevaluate their decisions after giving them a fair chance to work. If they find that their original decision is working well and they can cope with its consequences, they continue to pursue that decision. However, if they find that their original decision is not working as they had hoped or they cannot cope with the consequences, they go back to the drawing board. This means discussing what went wrong and how they feel about it, weighing the pros and cons of new alternatives, and using communication and problem-solving skills to make and implement a new decision. Of course, the new decision also will have to be reevaluated after a time.

COPING WITH INFERTILITY AND INFERTILITY TREATMENTS

Many aspects of infertility and its medical treatments can be emotionally overwhelming. The medical workup for infertility can be difficult, and accepting the resulting diagnosis can be incredibly painful. The diagnosis of infertility often brings about a range of stressful emotional reactions, including denial, shock, anger, depression, and anxiety. In addition, making decisions about medical treatments for infertility can be stressful. These decisions may bump you and your partner up against issues of morals and values, societal and family pressures, questions of what it means to be a parent, and possible relationship difficulties. To deal with the emotional distress of infertility and its medical treatments, we strongly urge you and your partner to read Sections II, III, and IV of this book. They cover common causes of emotional distress in infertility and describe clinically proven coping skills to lower your stress, improve your mood, and increase your relationship satisfaction.

ASSIGNMENT 3.3

This assignment is designed to help you implement some of the tips described in making good decisions. Under the "Options" column, write in the various reproductive options you are considering. Headings might be IVF versus GIFT or continuing with medical treatments versus stopping and turning to adoption. The empty squares are for you to write in the pros and cons of each option. Remember to consider both short-term and long-term consequences. You will need more room than is provided, so get another sheet of paper. Once you have filled out the table, use the skills discussed in Chapter 10 to talk with your partner and negotiate a decision. Write in the decision you have chosen to pursue at this time in the space below the table. The last step is to set a date for reevaluating your decision and going back to the drawing board if necessary. You may want to make copies of this form for future use.

Considerations	Option 1 Pros	Option 1 Cons	Option 2 Pros	Option 2 Cons	Option 3 Pros	Option 3 Cons
Financial cost						
Success rate						
Time required						
Legal issues						
Ability to cope						
Emotional cost						
Energy required						
Values, beliefs, morals						
Identity and well-being						
Reactions of others						
Other						
Other						

Your decision at this time: _____
_____
_____

Date you plan to reevaluate this decision:_____
_____
_____

SECTION I SUMMARY

- Reproduction is a highly complex process that requires many factors to be in place for success—including a healthy reproductive system for both the male and female, as well as effective sexual practices.
- Infertility is a medical condition of the reproductive system in which a couple is unable to conceive after one year of engaging in sexual intercourse without the use of contraception, or unable to carry a pregnancy to live birth.
- To get pregnant you must have sexual intercourse during the fertile time of the cycle, even if you're tired, emotionally overwhelmed, or not getting along with your partner.
- The fertile time of the cycle occurs when the woman is ovulating. Ovulation occurs roughly 14 days before the first day of a woman's period. You can monitor this fertile time by using LH kits, basal body temperature charting, checking the quality of the cervical mucous, or charting the days of the woman's monthly cycle.
- Some experts recommend that couples have sex every other day around the time of ovulation to maximize the chances of conception during the fertile time of the cycle. This is especially true for couples where infertility is related to low sperm count. In a 28-day cycle, this means having sex on days 10, 12, 14, and 16.
- Only 25% of couples that have sexual intercourse without using birth control will get pregnant in the first month. Beyond this, 60% of couples conceive by six months and 85% by the end of one year. The remaining 15% of couples are considered to have fertility problems.
- Women are most fertile in their twenties. Fertility dips after age 30 and plummets after age 35.

- Men and women are equally affected by biological causes of infertility. Roughly 35% of cases are termed female factor and another 35% are termed male factor. In 20% of cases, the cause of infertility is a combination of problems in both the male and the female. In the remaining 10% of cases the cause of infertility is unknown.
- Causes of infertility may be related to advanced maternal age; miscarriages; damage to the reproductive tract caused by STDs, PID, or other infections; diseases such as diabetes; smoking, drinking, or use of illicit drugs; and weight. Male-factor infertility is generally related to problems with sperm, blockage in the reproductive tract, and/or (more rarely) problems with sexual functioning. Female-factor infertility is mostly related to problems of the menstrual cycle, blockage in the reproductive tract, or structural problems of the uterus or cervix. Medical technology has advanced to the point at which nearly 80% of couples with infertility can be helped to produce their own biological children.
- Medical options to treat infertility include the use of fertility drugs, surgeries, and ARTs with or without the use of donors or surrogates. Other options include adoption or child-free living.

II
Infertility
The Emotional Roller Coaster

QUIZ: ARE YOU RIDING THE ROLLER COASTER?

This quiz will help you identify whether you have experienced a number of common emotional reactions to infertility and determine how infertility is affecting your mood. Answer the questions below as honestly as you can, with "yes" or "no" responses.

_____ 1. I never thought that someone as healthy as I could have fertility problems.

_____ 2. I (or my partner) at first refused to get an infertility workup partly because we were in denial.

_____ 3. Seeing pregnant women or babies makes me feel very anxious.

_____ 4. I feel like I live in constant fear of another failed pregnancy attempt or miscarriage.

_____ 5. I feel angry at my body for letting me down.

_____ 6. I get angry with my partner because of the way he or she is handling infertility.

_____ 7. I worry that something I did in the past caused my infertility.

_____ 8. Lately, I feel inadequate or worthless.

_____ 9. I don't spend as much time with family or friends since our infertility problems started.

_____ 10. I don't feel as close to my partner since our infertility problems began.

_____ 11. I feel sad every time I think about a future without a biological child.

_____ 12. My depression interferes with my ability to carry out everyday tasks.

_____ 13. I feel grief every time we get a negative pregnancy test result.

_____ 14. All our plans for the future are on hold until we have a child.

_____ 15. I feel sad and/or irritable most of the time.

_____ 16. I just don't feel like doing the things I used to do before our infertility problems started.

_____ 17. I feel like my life has been a failure.

_____ 18. I feel my life will be meaningless if we can't have a (another) child.

_____ 19. I feel like infertility has made me lose control of my life.

_____ 20. Sometimes I feel hopeless about the possibility of ever having a (another) child.

_____ 21. I feel that we are being punished with infertility.

_____ 22. Sometimes I blame my partner for our infertility problems.

_____ 23. Infertility is threatening my relationship with my partner.

_____ 24. Sometimes I have thoughts of suicide.

SCORING THE ROLLER COASTER QUIZ

The more "yes" answers you gave, the more likely you are to be riding the infertility roller coaster. Read through the responses below to learn how this section can help you better understand your emotional reactions and avoid some of the common mood traps faced by people with fertility problems. Be sure to read all the responses, even if you answered "no."

> *Shock and Surprise (Question 1):* Shock and surprise are two of the most common initial reactions to an infertility diagnosis, especially for those used to having control over their lives or who identify with being healthy. Chapter 4 will guide you through your own or your partner's shocked reaction.
>
> *Denial (Question 2):* Chapter 4 describes the various forms of denial, the dangers of denial, and how to move past denial to face your infertility.
>
> *Stress and Anxiety (Questions 3–4):* Chapter 4 will help you understand appropriate stress and anxiety and briefly introduce techniques to lower them.
>
> *Anger (Questions 5–6):* Anger often stems from feelings of loss of control over your body and emotions. It can also be related to the many losses associated with infertility and a reaction to your partner's handling infertility differently than you. Chapter 4

discusses the various causes of anger and the difference between rational anger and anger that is based on illogical thinking.

Self-Image (Questions 7–8): Some people report feelings of self-blame, negative self-image, and guilt in response to infertility. Feelings of inadequacy in the realm of reproduction can extend to feelings of unworthiness in other areas of life. Chapter 4 helps you identify and counter such illogical thinking.

Social Isolation and Relationship Problems (Questions 9-10): Some people respond to infertility by withdrawing physically or emotionally from social situations and their partners. Relationship problems can include emotional distance and loss of sexual desire. Chapter 4 discusses how you can improve your relationship and maximize your chances of getting sensitive, positive social support.

Sadness and Depression (Questions 11-12): It is important to acknowledge and allow yourself to feel your sadness. However, normal sadness can turn into more serious depression if your perceptions and interpretations of your infertility are based on illogical thinking. Chapter 4 helps you distinguish between sadness and depression and between rational and illogical thinking. It also points you toward other chapters that focus on ways to improve your mood.

Grief (Question 13): Grief is a normal, necessary part of healing. Chapter 4 describes some of the losses commonly associated with infertility and directs you toward other chapters that show you how to work through your grief.

Acceptance and Resolution (Question 14): Acceptance and resolution, which come from acknowledging and confronting painful feelings, allow you to handle your infertility-related emotional reactions so you can get on with other aspects of your life. Chapter 4 helps you identify acceptance and resolution and directs you to other chapters that can help you to attain this final stage in dealing with infertility.

Mood (Question 15): It is very common for people with fertility problems to feel sad or blue. Chapter 5 will give you a better understanding of the causes of your sadness, while Chapter 6 details effective methods for handling sadness and depression.

Inactivity (Question 16): Depression is usually associated with lack of interest in activities and less enjoyment of activities in which you do engage. Chapters 5 and 6 will help you understand how inactivity is related to your mood and how you can beat the blues by being more active.

Thoughtless Thinking (Questions 17-20): People who are depressed tend see the world in a negative light and think in irrational ways. This "thoughtless thinking" can make you feel inadequate, worthless, helpless, and even hopeless. Chapters 5 and 6 discuss how thoughts affect your mood and behavior, and how you can tackle depression by changing the way you think.

Guilt (Question 21): Many people with fertility problems believe that their infertility is a punishment for some past sin or transgression. Chapter 5 helps you understand that guilt and blame are forms of thoughtless thinking, and Chapter 6 details how you can learn to think more rationally about your infertility.

Relationship Problems (Questions 22-23): Depression and its symptoms can cause problems in relationships. Chapters 5 and 6 show how depression relates to relationship difficulties and how you can improve your relationship by lifting your spirits.

Suicide (Question 24): Extreme depression can trigger thoughts of death and suicide. You may feel that your infertility has let your partner down or that life isn't worth living if you cannot have a child. If you have serious thoughts of suicide, consult a doctor or mental health professional immediately.

4

THE EMOTIONAL JOURNEY
Common Reactions to Infertility

TWO COUPLES' STORIES

Steve and Jen

Steve was born and raised in the Midwest, the middle child in a family of three brothers. He grew up playing ball with his brothers and father and played on the varsity football team in high school. He did well academically and was popular at school. He was what you could call an "all-American guy." Several colleges around the country recruited him for his football talents. He ended up at the University of Nevada in Reno (UNR), where he met Jen.

Jen was born in the Bay Area but moved to Carson City, Nevada, with her family when she was young. She was an only child and enjoyed the parental attention focused on her but longed for a brother or sister. Her family was very traditional; her mother stayed home throughout Jen's childhood, and her father was the primary breadwinner. Her mother did teach dance classes, which was where Jen got her love of dance and fitness. She went to UNR and majored in dance, hoping to follow in her mother's footsteps.

Steve and Jen met in one of their classes at the university. They dated for a couple of years and married right after college graduation. Both knew they wanted to have kids, and discussed it thoroughly before marriage. Jen wanted a large family, since she felt she had missed out on having siblings when she was a child. She always talked about her dreams and hopes for her future family. In planning her career, she made arrangements to teach dance classes from home so she could be a stay-at-home mom just like her mother.

Jen tried to talk Steve into trying to conceive a baby shortly after their marriage, but Steve didn't feel ready. He wanted to establish his career first. He assured her that they were young, that nobody was healthier than the two of them, and that they had all the time in the world to start a family. Jen was upset because she felt Steve was more interested in hanging out with his college buddies than in their future as a couple. She worried that her dreams of being a mother would be put off indefinitely.

When Steve told Jen he was ready to start trying for a baby, she was delighted. Images of her pregnant belly, her baby shower, and a beautiful baby flooded her mind. She told all her friends that they were "trying" for a baby. Nobody was happier than her mother. The two of them poured over catalogues for baby clothes and furniture for the future nursery. They even bought a book on baby names. Jen took vitamins and worked out even harder to prepare her body for pregnancy.

At first, Steve and Jen had fun trying to conceive. Lovemaking for a baby was a very meaningful and bonding experience. After sex, they would often fall asleep in one another's arms talking about how they could be parents soon. After almost a year of trying, the fun started to wear off and the fears of not being able to get pregnant set in. Efforts to time intercourse more carefully were not successful. However, Steve continued to assure Jen that they were both young and healthy and that nothing could possibly be wrong. Jen had her doubts. One of her best friends from school had personal experience with infertility and told her to get checked out by a doctor.

Consumed by fears of not being able to have a baby, Jen went to a doctor for a workup. A series of painful tests revealed that her reproductive tract was in "perfect" shape. The doctor told her to have Steve come in for a semen analysis. When Jen told Steve that her tests came out normal and that the doctor wanted to do a workup on him, Steve, to her surprise, became very angry with her. He yelled that there was "no way" that it could be his "fault," and that she should go back and have more tests herself. He added that he never wanted to talk about this again and angrily left the room. Jen felt crushed.

After several more months of unsuccessful trying, Jen gathered the courage to bring up the topic again with Steve. She begged him to make an appointment for a semen analysis, but he again refused. Jen could not understand how her husband, who was ordinarily so loving and caring, could act this way. She sought support from friends who were experiencing infertility, and their husbands suggested she "just wait," and give Steve time. With time on her side (she was still under 30), she decided to take their advice.

The advice to wait until Steve was ready paid off. Watching his college friends become fathers and seeing the longing for motherhood in Jen's eyes, Steve finally submitted to the semen analysis. The results indicated severe male-factor infertility. Steve had severe oligospermia with abnormal morphology and motility. When given the diagnosis, Steve felt his manhood was being swept from under him. He couldn't believe what he was hearing. After all, he had played college football, was involved in his college fraternities, worked out, and was very healthy. Who was more of a man than he was? Steve began to question his identity. Worse yet, he worried what his friends would say if they knew. He told Jen not to tell anyone.

The diagnosis of infertility was devastating for Jen as well. She cried from deep within her soul. She loved Steve dearly and worried that he would not be able to pass on his genes to a child. At the same time, she was very angry with him for not getting the tests done earlier. She was now two years older than when they started, and her biological clock was ticking. Jen began to fear that she might never be a mother. Seeing pregnant women or babies felt like salt poured over her wounds. Every time she saw a pregnant woman, she unconsciously put her hand over her own belly, feeling nothing but an empty pit. She felt she no longer fit in with her friends, who were now mothers. She was not allowed to talk about her infertility with anyone, not even her own mother. Jen felt isolated and alone.

It was recommended that Steve and Jen start IVF with ICSI. In preparation for these procedures, Steve had to inject Jen daily with fertility drugs. It pained Steve that his sperm problems were the source of Jen having to endure the bulk of the painful medical treatments. Worse yet, he had to give her the shots. With each shot his guilt grew. Jen tried not to let her pain show. Although she had to endure painful shots and medical procedures and was moody and irritable from the fertility drugs, she did not want to make Steve feel worse. She was happy that he was cooperating with infertility treatments and did not want to "rock the boat." However, her pain, anger, fears, and sense of isolation grew. After the IVF failed, Jen's feelings could no longer be contained. Jen told Steve that she *had* to be able to talk with other people about their infertility and that she planned to attend a RESOLVE (an infertility support group) meeting. Steve could see that her anguish was too much for her to bear on her own and agreed to go to the meeting with her.

At the RESOLVE meeting, Steve and Jen realized that there were many other couples facing the same issues. While Steve was uncomfortable at first, he felt better after attending the meetings. Steve and Jen saw that their emotional reactions were not "crazy" but were, in fact, very normal. Steve realized that fertility was not equal to manhood. He also realized that infertility was not his "fault," that it was an issue he and Jen shared. When Steve and Jen began to communicate their feelings, they felt closer to one another. They saw that infertility could make their relationship stronger. They regarded themselves as a team fighting against their fertility problems rather than as individuals fighting against each other. Steve and Jen became pregnant in their second IVF cycle.

Stacy and Paul

Stacy was born and raised in southern California. As the oldest of four children, she grew up taking care of her younger siblings. Even during playtime, she would act the role of a caretaker with her dolls. She dreamed of the day she would be a "real" mother with a family of her own. Stacy began to experience pelvic pain at age 18. The doctors suspected endometriosis. She gave little thought to how this diagnosis could affect her fertility, especially when she accidentally became pregnant at age 19 with her high school sweetheart. Unfortunately, her boyfriend told her he didn't want the baby, since he was planning to go away to college. He urged her to have an abortion. Fearing the thought of single motherhood, she eventually gave in and terminated the pregnancy. Stacy also went away to college, studying nursing and eventually getting her degree.

One of her fellow nurses introduced her to Paul, and they began dating. Paul grew up on the East Coast, the youngest in a family of three children. His family was warm and loving, and he had a very happy childhood. His parents emphasized the importance of two things: family and hard work. He grew up expecting to be a father and planning how he could be a good provider. He worked hard in school, always making the Honor Roll or Dean's List. He learned that with effort and determination, he could accomplish anything he wanted to. With this attitude, he was able to complete law school and work his way up to junior partner in his law firm.

Stacy and Paul married. Both came from strong family backgrounds and both wanted children. They began trying to conceive after two years of marriage and expected to become pregnant within "a few tries." Stacy figured that since she had been pregnant before, she should have no problem getting pregnant again. Paul believed that since his hard work had helped him accomplish all his goals so far, conceiving a baby should also be possible. Neither of them was prepared for the diagnosis of infertility.

Stacy experienced great sadness and grief every time she started her period or got a negative response from what she came to call the "Evil Pee Test" (EPT; Early Pregnancy Test). She believed that God must be punishing her for her previous abortion by not allowing her to conceive again. After a year of unsuccessfully trying to conceive on their own, Stacy and Paul suspected infertility and went to a reproductive endocrinologist (RE) for a workup. The doctor confirmed that Stacy's endometriosis was responsible for their infertility. He suggested they try IUI or IVF.

Stacy could not believe her ears. On the one hand, she was shocked to hear the diagnosis and stunned that her endometriosis could keep her from conceiving, especially since she had conceived before. It seemed to her that all her childhood fantasies of motherhood and having a family of her own were crushed in an instant. On the other hand, she was relieved to finally understand the medical reasons for her inability to get pregnant in the past year. She realized that her infertility was not a punishment from God for her abortion but the result of a disease she had even before the abortion.

Stacy and Paul decided to take the doctor's advice. They attempted to conceive with three cycles of IUI, all without success. Next, they turned to IVF. Three cycles of IVF failed to work. With each new treatment failure, Stacy grieved another loss. She felt anxious all the time, but especially during the two weeks after the embryo transfers, when she would feel both hopeful for pregnancy and fearful of another loss. She became increasingly anxious when she saw other pregnant women or babies. She worried that she might never experience the joys of pregnancy and motherhood. She cried a lot.

Stacy also worried that Paul would leave her because of her inability to give him a baby. It hurt Paul to see Stacy in such pain. Although he felt helpless at not being able to give her what she desired most, he tried to remain strong for her. He tried not to let Stacy see his sadness and grief over their fertility losses, his worry for her health during the medical treatments, or his fear that he might never be a father. He busied himself with other activities in order to get his mind off their infertility.

Stacy could not understand why Paul was "so calm" while she felt like an "emotional wreck." She accused him of not caring and resented him for being able to go on with his other activities. Paul could not understand how Stacy could think he did not care. He felt he was taking on the emotional burden by holding in his feelings so he could "be the strong one in the relationship." He thought that letting his feelings show could hurt Stacy further. He wondered why he was working so hard to afford the cost of infertility treatments that were hurting his wife both physically and emotionally. Paul also was trying to understand how all his hard work and determination was not paying off with a baby. How could it be that he was able to achieve all his other goals but could not give his wife a baby? How could it be that his law degree, intelligence, sincere intentions, determination, and hard work were now failing him? Paul started to question his belief in a fair world where perseverance pays off. He began to feel depressed, and his sense of helplessness grew.

Stacy and Paul decided to take a break from infertility treatments. They felt the need to reevaluate their plans since the IVFs were not working. During this break, they talked about their feelings. Stacy came to understand that Paul's lack of emotional displays did not mean he didn't care about having a baby. In fact, she learned that he was withholding his emotions *because* he cared so much and didn't want to hurt her. She became less resentful towards Paul. Paul came to understand that Stacy's idea of "being strong" meant sharing his feelings with her. He opened up to her about his feelings of sadness, loss, helplessness, and fear. At their doctor's suggestion, they began to "date" again, spending time together and doing things they used to do before their infertility diagnosis. Over time, they remembered what it felt like to be in a husband and wife partnership. Because they were so focused on their infertility treatments, they had forgotten that they were more than just the sum of their reproductive parts. Stacy began to remember what it felt like to not be "in cycle" and to see that there was a world outside of a house filled with fertility drugs.

Stacy and Paul reconsidered the goal of their quest for parenthood. They realized that it was more important for them to have a child than a biologically related child. They both realized that they did not want to continue living with infertility treatments. They investigated adoption and put themselves on a waiting list for a baby.

CONFRONTING OVERWHELMING EMOTIONS

The stories of Steve and Jen, and Stacy and Paul, are not uncommon. Many couples can identify with their experiences and emotional reactions. Because infertility is one of the most challenging stressors a couple can face, it has been referred to as a "life crisis." Even couples who are ordinarily very well-adjusted can find themselves feeling overwhelmed by the experience of infertility.

Infertility can take both a physical and emotional toll on a couple. Physically, infertility can be painful and draining. Medical treatments for infertility can be invasive, physically painful, embarrassing, time-consuming, and expensive. Emotional reactions to infertility have been likened to those experienced when grieving the death of a loved one or dealing with a terminal illness (see Section V). Infertility often involves grief over the loss of being able to conceive more naturally, loss of control, loss of security and faith, loss of self-confidence, loss of relationships (including sexual satisfaction), and loss through miscarriage. In addition, infertility involves losses of hopes and dreams.

Not everyone experiences the emotions detailed in this chapter, nor do they necessarily experience them in the order described. Furthermore, couples usually do not experience the same emotions at the same time, and there are common gender differences in emotional responses to infertility (see chapters 9 and 10). It is our hope that in reading about and identifying with these emotional reactions you will realize that you are not alone. Because the emotional reactions can be intense and overwhelming, many people with fertility problems feel they are "going crazy." Not only are your emotions not "crazy," they are normal and appropriate reactions to the crisis of infertility.

COMMON EMOTIONAL REACTIONS TO INFERTILITY

Surprise

The diagnosis of infertility comes as a surprise to most couples. Most of us are taught that we can control our lives. If we work hard enough, we can achieve an education, a career, a beautiful house, a fast car, and so on. Most people assume that they can extend this control to their reproductive functioning. There are many methods available to control birth: pills, condoms, spermicides, diaphragms, and even good old natural family planning. Most people assume that when they decide to stop using these methods of birth control, they can conceive easily. Realizing that they don't have the kind of control they thought they had over reproduction can come as a huge shock.

My initial reaction when hearing the word "infertility" was shock, to say the least. Neither my husband nor I have ever had any health problems that would cause us to think we would have problems conceiving.

Another aspect of surprise stems from societal expectations about parenthood. Most religious and social cultures promote reproduction. The Book of Genesis tells us to "Be fruitful and multiply." Early religions worshipped fertility gods and viewed infertility as a curse from the gods. Societal norms and governmental policies advance procreation. Young girls are primed to play the role of a mother; they are given baby dolls and taught to rock them to sleep and change diapers. Men are given the message that fatherhood is an expectation of marriage, that it is equivalent to masculinity, male potency, and power. The expectation of having children is so high that most people ask *when* you're going to have children instead of *if* you might have children.

However, not all couples react to the diagnosis of infertility with shock. Some react with relief and/or hope.

We were beating ourselves up every month trying to figure out ovulation and timing sex just right. We felt relieved to have an explanation for why it wasn't working.

Although I have low sperm count, I feel very lucky that the power of modern medicine will allow me to father a child.

Denial

Many people deny that infertility exists. "How can this be happening to me?" and "I can't believe this!" are very common reactions.

I was so afraid that if the tests showed that the infertility was due to a male problem it would affect how my wife felt about me and about our relationship. I knew how much she wanted children and how being a mother was always a dream of hers. I couldn't imagine letting her down.

Denial most likely occurs when the diagnosis of infertility is sudden or unexpected. The story of Steve and Jen illustrates this point. Steve was convinced that being young and healthy would prevent any fertility problems. While such denial can initially keep infertile couples from becoming overwhelmed by painful emotions, chronic denial can be very unhealthy. Steve's pain was understandable, but his denial went so deep that he refused to get a medical workup or treatment. This prevented Steve and Jen from accessing the possible benefits of modern reproductive technology and reduced Jen's chances of pregnancy as her maternal age advanced. Another form of Steve's denial was to blame Jen for their fertility problems and insist she get further evaluation. In addition to being unproductive, blaming your spouse is very likely to lead to relationship problems and emotional rifts. In addition, Steve did not allow Jen to tell her friends or family about their fertility problems. This severely limited their contact with potential sources of social support.

Denial can also show up in other forms. Some couples insist that the lab results were a mistake. Or they go from doctor to doctor, hoping to find one who will give them a better diagnosis. Some couples claim that they didn't really want a child anyway or otherwise discount the importance of the loss. Others busy themselves with distractions, such as becoming workaholics to take their minds off their infertility.

One of the best ways to reduce denial is to educate yourself on infertility. Read self-help books, surf the web, and talk with doctors about the topic. Many people report that they can accept their infertility much easier once they know that it is not uncommon. Talking with others about infertility also helps to reduce denial.

> *The more people I told my story to, the more I felt free. I realized I really had nothing to hide. Plus, the support helped me to cope and get through it all.*

Stress and Anxiety

Couples experience stress and anxiety during many phases of the infertility crisis, beginning with their infertility diagnosis. They fear that they may be identified as "the problem"; worry about what infertility might mean for their relationship; fear that they may never go through the experiences of pregnancy, labor, or breastfeeding; worry that they may never become parents; are upset by insensitive comments from friends and family members and at see-ing signs of fertility—pregnant women, babies in strollers, or baby commercials. The experience of infertility can also challenge a person's spiritual beliefs and ideas about how the world works. Many couples with fertility problems wonder, "Why us? Why is God not gracing us with a baby?"

> *I feel anxious every time I see young, single mothers with unwanted babies. It doesn't seem fair that God would give them babies and deny a baby to me.*

I feel anxious when I see other people who are pregnant. I feel anxious when I see people who just got married get pregnant. In the last year and a half, eight people at my work got pregnant. It's just not fair!

Infertility also challenges beliefs that hard work and determination lead to desired outcomes, as Paul learned. Having fundamental beliefs questioned can reduce your sense of security and create additional stress. Anxiety often intensifies every month as the opportunity to conceive once again comes around during ovulation. Many couples report that while they feel hopeful of having a baby each month, they also experience anxiety in anticipation of having to mourn another potential loss.

The true anxiety comes when my period starts, because for the 30 days prior I have been hoping and wishing that we would be blessed with a pregnancy.

The worst anxiety is from ovulation until I get my period. Life becomes two weeks of knowing I'm not pregnant and two weeks of wondering if maybe this time I am. And then I get anxious again when I go in for my ultrasound to find out if I can go on meds this cycle or if I have to take a month off because of the follicles still hanging around.

This anticipatory anxiety, as it is called, is often pronounced in couples with a history of miscarriages. In addition to anxiety, these couples may also experience guilt centering around the feeling that in trying for a baby they may be contributing to the death of the very thing they desire.

Anxiety is experienced by many couples in medical treatment for their infertility. The close scrutiny by the medical staff, including having to share their private lives as well as their private parts, is often quite anxiety-provoking. Most couples worry that they "must be doing something wrong" or that the slightest physical exertion could cause a miscarriage.

One way to reduce anxiety is to talk with a trusted person, such as your partner, a friend or family member, members of a support group, or a counselor. These sources of support can help you realize that your anxiety is normal and can validate your feelings. If you have questions about whether your actions might be jeopardizing your fertility or your pregnancy, medical personnel can provide you with scientific facts. One of the most important things to remember is that infertility causes stress, not the other way around. This point is discussed more fully in chapters 7 and 8, which detail other anxiety-reducing methods that include deep breathing, relaxation, and distraction.

Anger

Anger often results from feeling that you have lost control over your body, your feelings, and your life. You may feel angry at being "cheated" out of the fertility you most likely took for granted. For men, who have been social-  ized to believe that they must be in con- trol at all times, infertility can be especially maddening. Couples often are angered at having to give up control of their bodies to the medical staff at infertility treatment clinics. You may become angry at having to share personal information about your bodies, your histories, and your sexual functioning, at being probed, poked, and prodded over and over again, all the while feeling vulnerable and helpless.

Furthermore, many couples experience anger at feeling they have lost control of their emotions because of their intense reactions to the stresses of infertility. Fertility medications, which are infamous for intensifying moods and creating mood swings, can add to this feeling of losing control.

> *I am angry at my body because I feel it is failing me in a very basic and natural process. I feel angry at my family members and friends for insensitive comments, even when I realize these comments are made because they are unaware of my infertility. I feel angry at unsuspecting and innocent pregnant women just because I wish I had what they have. I feel angry at insurance companies, the government, and employers for being selfish jerks and not paying for infertility costs.*

> *I was angry at God and everyone else because I wanted a baby so badly and I felt completely helpless, powerless, and defeated.*

Couples often report being irritated or short-tempered with one another. They may feel angry toward their partner for being the cause of infertility, for not understanding, or for appearing not to care. Anger with those who live in the "fertile world" is also common. Insensitive comments by others often stir up feelings ranging from frustration to rage. Partners also tend to become angry at themselves for experiencing perfectly normal and appropriate feelings of jealousy towards others who are pregnant or have children.

In some cases, the anger is rational and appropriately focused on the many losses associated with infertility, the inconvenience and cost of medical treatments, the lack of insurance coverage for medical treatments, the insensitive comments, and the unfairness of it all. The best way to handle your anger is to recognize that it is legitimate and vent your feelings to someone you trust. Allowing yourself to experience and vent your anger is both normal and necessary. Write out your thoughts and feelings in a journal, talk with your partner or with trusted friends, "talk" with others experiencing infertility in specialized internet bulletin boards or chat rooms, or attend infertility support group meetings.

In other cases the anger is irrational and inappropriately directed at such targets as abortion rights activists, people who abuse their children, or even your own past behaviors. This type of anger is most likely masking underlying feelings of sadness, pain, and grief that you have not yet acknowledged. Thinking through these feelings and talking them over with someone you trust may help you sort your emotions and get to the root of the problem. Anger directed inward is most likely based on an inaccurate perception of self-blame.

Guilt and Negative Self-Image

People have a need to find causes for the events that happen to them. Because infertility sometimes has no cause that makes sense, they search their lives and histories for some "sin" they have committed for which they are now being punished. People often attribute their infertility to previous thoughts or actions involving masturbation, promiscuity, premarital sex, infidelity, incest, same-sex experiences, or abortions. They believe that they may be able to receive forgiveness for these perceived sins through suffering. Thus, they are likely to place themselves in emotionally or physically painful situations in hopes of atoning for their sins and receiving forgiveness. They may deprive themselves of things that give them pleasure or volunteer for painful treatments.

While feelings of guilt and self-blame are normal reactions to infertility, it is critical to remind yourself that fertility has nothing to do with worthiness. Think of all the people in the world who abuse their children but keep on having more, or the everyday "saints" you know who have no children. Try to identify when your thoughts are not based on any logical or scientific evidence. Chapter 6 will show you how to identify and challenge thoughts not based on logic. *The reality is that there is no scientific or medical connection between infertility and past "sins"* such as premarital sex or abortions. Masturbation does not cause endometriosis; lying, cheating or stealing do not cause uterine fibroids; infidelity does not cause poor quality sperm; and "impure" thoughts do not cause miscarriages.

The only way that previous sexual behaviors could be related to infertility is if the sexual contact resulted in infection that damaged the reproductive organs or if an abortion caused scarring or damage to the reproductive tract. Furthermore, there is no evidence that suffering will lead to a restoration of fertility. Remember, you are not responsible for the cause of your infertility, but you are responsible for how you handle it.

Sometimes feelings of guilt are overgeneralized to the point where the person feels inadequate and unworthy in every area of his or her life.

I feel dysfunctional physically. I feel defective, really. I feel like my body has completely failed me. Knowing that I have endometriosis and fibroids, I feel like a total mess on the inside. It's not a good feeling. For most of my life, I have felt really good about myself and have felt healthy for the most part, so this is a big shift for me.

Inability to reproduce grows into perceived inabilities at work, and in relationships with friends and partners. Sometimes people behave in ways that create self-fulfilling prophecies, such as when the partner who carries the infertility factor pushes the other away and divorce ensues. Other acts of self-destruction include getting fired from jobs, alcoholism, sexual acting out, and eating disorders. This type of behavior is based on illogical thinking that can be identified and challenged by using the techniques in Chapter 6.

Isolation

Because infertility can be a very difficult subject to discuss, many people end up suffering in silence. Couples who hope to keep their infertility private or avoid insensitive remarks from others may physically or emotionally withdraw from social situations. Those with fertility problems can feel alienated when their friends become pregnant and involved in their new family lives. Partners may feel that they can no longer relate to people who have children. Baby showers, christenings, and holidays can be painful reminders of what the couple may never have.

There are times when we try to avoid walking past playgrounds, because seeing all the parents with their young children is simply too painful.

We are Orthodox Jews, and there are two particular holy days when the family atmosphere is very strong. I usually go to the earliest morning service I can find so as to avoid being there with lots of young fathers and their kids.

It took me over a month to even look at my sister-in-law's baby and I have yet to look at, let alone hold, my sister's one-month-old baby. I have tried not to be where I know they will be. I don't talk much with my mother because she doesn't believe in IVF and usually says insensitive things.

These occasions also tend to be opportunities for nosy friends and family members to inquire or pressure you about when you plan to have children. Couples often find it easier to withdraw from the fertile world rather than endure discomfort, anger, and pain. Although the desire to withdraw is understandable, the unfortunate consequence of social isolation is that you may cut yourself off from potential sources of support. You can maximize your chances of receiving positive social support by reaching out to others and by educating insensitive people on how you would like to be treated.

Infertility can also cause a rift between partners. Gender differences (see Section IV) can account for misunderstandings and miscommunications between partners. Women tend to cope with infertility by expressing their emotions and immersing themselves in medical treatment. Men, on the other hand, tend to hide their feelings about infertility and cope by refusing to think about it. Problems may appear if the male partner believes his wife is too "emotional" and "obsessed" with having a baby or the female partner interprets her husband's calmness as not caring. These misunderstandings can cause partners to withdraw from one another.

My husband says he would be fine not having a biological child and adopting. He seems to have accepted the situation better than I have, which, of course, makes me frustrated and resentful that he can be so "at peace" while I'm so nuts! It's truly a vicious, never-ending cycle. It has consumed our marriage from the first day we started trying to conceive, and I only hope that we're able to survive it.

It is important for partners to remember that everyone reacts to and copes with painful situations in different ways. Outward expressions of emotions are not a good indicator of how much a person really cares. In addition, problems between partners can come about if they are in different phases of the grief process. One partner may feel anxiety and need support while the other is emotionally isolated and wants to be left alone. Although there may be many reasons for partners to pull away from one another, we strongly recommend that they do the opposite. Couples who share feelings about their grief have the potential of growing closer instead of further apart.

Sadness and Grief

Sadness and grief are natural responses to the losses associated with infertility, among them the loss of more natural conception, loss of control, loss of security and faith, loss of self-worth, loss of relationship satisfaction, and sometimes pregnancy loss. Infertility can also threaten hopes and fantasies about your dream child, the experience of being pregnant, your chances of being a biological mother or father, your life goals, and your future plans.

> *I felt incredible depression. There were times when I spent the whole day in bed. I wondered what God's plan was for me. I felt like He let me down. I prayed for hours for the strength to persevere. It takes such incredible strength and commitment to go through IVF— between the hormone shots 2–3 times a day, the sonograms and blood tests, the expense, the drain emotionally of each test result— it's really overwhelming.*

> *I experience grief every single time I start my period. It makes me so sad to think that we have to "try" again.*

Couples also report feeling sadness in response to reminders of their infertility, getting negative pregnancy test results, feeling out of control, experiencing relationship problems, and feeling alienated from the fertile world around them. Acknowledging these losses and allowing yourself to feel sadness and grief will reduce the intensity of your pain. Chapter 12 offers ways to help you cope with your sadness and grief.

While sadness is normal, it can sometimes turn into a more serious depression if you are reading illogical meaning into your infertility or are engaging in thoughtless thinking about your infertility. Thinking that your infertility is proof that you are not a worthy person or that you don't deserve a baby is based on distorted thinking and can turn natural sadness into an unnatural depression.

Acceptance and Resolution

Acceptance and resolution often come after acknowledging and working through painful feelings. Acceptance does not mean "getting over it." Most couples in treatment for infertility feel that they will never be "over it."

My heart will always ache for what could have been.

I don't think I will ever accept it. Even though we've adopted a baby, I think I will grieve not having a biological child at every baby shower, birthday party, graduation, and wedding.

Acceptance does not mean you will stop having feelings of denial, anxiety, anger, isolation, guilt, negative self-image, sadness, or grief. It just means that you will no longer experience them with the same intensity as you did at first and that they will no longer control you. You may have to "accept" your infertility over and over again—at the initial diagnosis, at each treatment failure, at each pregnancy loss, and possibly at having to consider options such as adoption, use of donors, or child-free living.

Acceptance and resolution are also marked by a return of energy, faith, self-esteem, and sense of humor. Instead of being consumed by infertility, you realize that infertility is only one aspect of your identity. You may notice a renewed interest in other aspects of your life, such as your relationship and your career. You may start making plans around your infertility so that you can get on with other facets of your life. You may redefine your priorities and reconsider your future.

I don't think you ever fully accept infertility. You just learn to cope with it and to move on.

5

BEATING THE (NOT-SO-BABY) BLUES
Common Causes of Depression in Infertility

"When are you going to have kids?" This question seems so simple, yet it can be tremendously painful for those with fertility problems. It can set you off on the "emotional roller coaster" that characterizes the infertility experience. Infertility can make you feel:

- Angry toward the insensitivity of the fertile world.
- Fearful that you may never have a biological child.
- Depressed about all the losses you have already endured and those that may lie ahead of you.
- Guilty or ashamed about your past and your fertility problems.
- Isolated from your partner, who doesn't seem to be on the same wavelength as you.
- Left out of the fertile world around you.
- Unsettled about your life goals.
- Insecure about your financial well-being.
- Uncertain about the assumptions you have always held to be true.

These feelings are common, normal reactions to infertility. But when not kept in check, they can lead to full-blown depression that robs you of joy in every aspect of your being.

Every time someone asks me when I'm going to have a baby, I die a little death inside.

WHAT IS DEPRESSION?

Depression is a combination of thoughts, feelings, and behaviors that interfere with everyday life. Depression is expressed by different people in different ways. Depressed individuals may have some or all of the symptoms described below in varying intensities.

Sadness

You feel down most of the time and tend to see both the present and future in a negative, gloomy light. You may feel that life has no meaning if you cannot reproduce and believe that the future holds no hope of your ever being happy again. You may express your mood as sadness and/or irritability. Some people cry a lot, others are often annoyed, and still others can put on a mask of happiness in public while feeling like a mountain of unhappiness on the inside.

Inactivity

You just don't feel like doing anything. Even things that used to make you happy seem uninteresting. You may have little interest in going on "dates" with your partner or being around friends and family, especially those whom you feel can't understand your experience of infertility.

Some days all I felt like doing was lying in bed and crying.

Everything seems to take too much effort, even simple things like household chores. You may not want to go to doctor's appointments or to RESOLVE meetings. In fact, you may not even feel like reading this book. Depression saps your level of energy, and activity goes way down. Many depressed people just want to sit around, sleep, or watch television, often in isolation from others.

Feelings of Worthlessness

You may feel worthless, inadequate or, worse, that you are a total failure. You may believe that your inability to reproduce makes you an unacceptable wife or husband or a worthless human being.

I feel like I let my wife down. I feel like a sorry excuse for a man. I can't even carry on the family line.

Despite other achievements in your life, you may feel that you are a failure if you cannot get pregnant. Feelings of worthlessness result from setting standards that are too high or even unachievable.

Feelings of Guilt

People who are depressed often feel like everything is their fault. They tend to take personal responsibility for things that go wrong, even if they are not responsible at all. You may have a tendency to attribute your infertility to some past transgression, such as premarital sex or an abortion, and that you deserve to be punished for your wrongs.

I feel guilty that I couldn't give my husband a baby. He deserves so much to be a father and I can't give this to him. I sometimes think that he should have married someone else, someone who could give him kids.

You may feel guilty for not being able to bring a child into this world and thus fulfill what you perceive your role to be as a husband/wife/human being. Some depressed individuals even feel guilty for feeling depressed.

Difficulties in Relationships

Depressed people have a hard time interacting with others. They may feel unworthy of being loved, see their relationship as inadequate or worthless, fail to put in the effort to make the relationship work, be unwilling to reach out to others, be irritated around others, have difficulties coping with disagreements that occur in all relationships, or have difficulties being assertive enough to get what they want out of relationships.

Nobody can understand me, not even my husband. I don't feel like I fit in with the world anymore. I can't stand being around people these days.

Physical Symptoms

People with depression can experience significant weight loss or weight gain, have difficulties sleeping or sleep too much, move very slowly or make agitated movements, or experience difficulties in thinking, concentrating, and making decisions ranging from what to wear to which infertility treatment option to pursue. Depression can also be related to loss of libido and/or temporary sexual dysfunction.

Thoughts of Death

Extreme depression may result in recurrent thoughts of death, dying, or suicide. While it is not uncommon for people to have these thoughts, it is quite a different story to act on them. If you find yourself having urges to act on your thoughts of suicide, it is imperative that you consult a doctor or mental health professional immediately.

COMMON CAUSES OF DEPRESSION IN INFERTILITY

A number of studies have investigated the relationship between mood and infertility. About half of them have found that individuals with infertility have moderately higher levels of depression than individuals with no fertility problems.[1] This is understandable since infertility can trigger a roster of acute problems and challenges.

Jeopardized Hopes and Dreams

Most people grow up with romantic dreams of getting married and starting a family at a time of their choosing. Many new couples fantasize about what their future will hold, confidently discussing how many

children they will have, how far apart, their sexes, and even their names. Couples may put great forethought into the type of parents they would like to be, the kind of lifestyle they hope to provide for their children, and the qualities they would like to instill in their children. It is not uncommon for partners to fantasize about what their "dream children" could accomplish when they grow up. And because these couples generally have been able to plan and experience success with every other endeavor into which they've put great effort, they naturally expect the same with getting pregnant and having children. When attempts at conception are unsuccessful, the couple is often faced, for the first time in their lives, with failure and an inability to achieve a goal they desire greatly.

I was just like most girls growing up. I've had the names for my children picked out since grade school, and all I ever wanted was to get married and have children and live a normal life. I met my husband when I was 14 and knew I would marry him. When we got married I was 21 and he was 23. It was so ideal. Soon after we married we found out that nothing is ever ideal.

The diagnosis of infertility can devastate dreams and hopes. It can force a couple to redefine their future, their sense of control, and their ideas about the meaning and purpose of life. Given the core nature of these losses and challenges, it is quite understandable for couples facing infertility to experience feelings of sadness.

Losses and Potential Losses of Infertility

Dr. Menning, who founded RESOLVE, has argued that the most common, appropriate, and necessary reaction to a diagnosis of infertility is grief. Infertility can threaten myriad aspects of a couple's life, resulting in many losses and potential losses.[2-6] For example, infertility can threaten the "dream child," as well as the hopes and fantasies that go along with that dream child. Infertility can also threaten dreams about what it would be like to be pregnant, give birth, breast feed, have your baby look like you, and carry on your genetic lineage.

I have always, always wanted to be a mommy, and to have this dream threatened is heartbreaking to me.

The experience of infertility can challenge your sense of control over yourself and the world, and therefore threaten your sense of security. It can also threaten your relationship with God and your sense of faith. Medical treatments for infertility can jeopardize your health, your privacy, your sexuality, your body image, your career, and your financial security. Relationships, especially with your partner, may also be at risk because of feelings of isolation, conflict, and fears of abandonment. These losses and potential losses can be sources of depression and grief.

By amplifying women's emotional responses, and creating mood swings, fertility medications can cause and worsen feelings of sadness and depression. Although this theory is not supported by all doctors, many women taking fertility medications have reported mood changes. Regardless of the source of your depression, the methods for improving your mood described in Chapter 6 can work for you.

I feel so pumped up on these [fertility] medications. My emotions are all over the place!

THE CYCLE OF DEPRESSION[7-8]

Psychologists who have studied and treated depression have developed a theory explaining why some people go beyond sadness into depression, and the factors that may maintain this depression.

Chances are that your depression stems from the way you've learned to react to situations. Just as people learn how to talk, walk, and dress, they also learn how to perceive and interpret the world, which in turn affects how they think, feel, and behave. It is likely that you have somehow learned to interpret the world in a way that makes you feel sad, hurt, and/or frustrated. Your negative thoughts and feelings tend to encourage behaviors that further your depression.

There is a connection between how you think, how you feel, and how you behave. Everyone has heard the metaphor of the cup being "half full" versus "half empty." If you see the cup as half full, you probably have been taught to put a positive spin on things and generally think in a more optimistic way. Positive thinkers tend to be happier people. If, on the other hand, you see the cup as half empty, you likely have been taught to put a negative spin on situations and think in a negative way. Negative thinkers tend to be depressed.

Consider the following example: Imagine that you leave a message for your friend Pat to call you back. After a week, Pat still hasn't called. This is the "Neutral Event" shown in Figure 5.1. The event is neither inherently negative nor positive. How you choose to interpret this neutral event will affect your feelings and possibly even your behavior. If you were the person in this example, what interpretation would you put on Pat's failure to return your call? If you are depressed, you would probably think something like, "Pat doesn't care about me." You may think that Pat must be angry with you and wonder what you have done to make Pat angry. You may also become upset with Pat, thinking Pat is irresponsible for not calling you back. These interpretations will result in your feeling sad, hurt, or angry with Pat. In turn, your feelings will probably make you either retreat a bit from your relationship with Pat or make you want to "get back at Pat" for what you perceive as Pat's attack on you. If you behave by withdrawing or counterattacking, you will unintentionally bolster your negative thinking, make yourself feel worse, and create a situation where you are minimally likely to call Pat again. Your thoughts, feelings, and actions feed off one another.

Now let's imagine that instead of thinking Pat doesn't care about you when Pat didn't return your call you instead think, "Maybe Pat is out

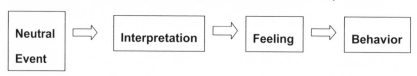

Figure 5.1

of town," or "Maybe Pat is not feeling well." This kind of thinking will be much less likely to result in reactions of sadness, hurt, or frustration with Pat. It will also make you much less likely to withdraw or counterattack. Instead, your neutral interpretation is likely to lead to neutral behavior. You will be more likely to call Pat again or send Pat a note.

Consider another example. You have just come home from a baby shower at which it seemed to you that everyone except you was pregnant. To make things worse, friends and relatives incessantly asked you why on earth you haven't gotten pregnant yet. Your aunt even inferred that you are selfish for not wanting to have a baby. You come home to your husband and start pouring out your heart about what happened and how awful it made you feel. You were hoping he would comfort and validate you, but instead he is quiet. This is the neutral event.

What interpretations would you be likely to put on your husband's silence? A negative interpretation would be to think that he isn't interested in your feelings, doesn't care about you, or is trying to be mean. Such negative interpretations will make you feel hurt, sad, depressed, or even angry with your husband. These negative thoughts and feelings will probably make you want to withdraw or get back at him, which will make the situation worse.

What are some other possible explanations for your husband's silence? Maybe he was shocked by how you were treated at the party. Maybe your sadness made him sad, too. Maybe he was tired or preoccupied with something else. Maybe he was trying to be a good listener and not interrupt you. Maybe he wanted to be validating but just didn't know what to say. The list of possible interpretations is endless. Needless to say, these explanations will result in much more neutral, or even positive, feelings and behaviors than the interpretation that he doesn't care or is being mean to you.

The connection between thoughts, feelings, and behavior is even more complicated than described above. The relationship between these factors is not just linear—i.e., thoughts influence feelings and feelings in turn influence behaviors. In reality, all these factors influence one another, as diagrammed in Figure 5.2.

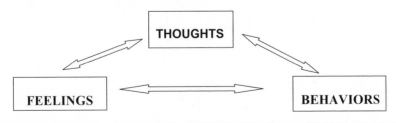

Figure 5.2

How Thoughts Influence Feelings

We've already touched on how thoughts influence feelings, but there's more. In addition to interpretations of situations influencing how you feel, it is also true that what you choose to think about will affect your mood. If your thoughts are about sadness—like when you watch sad movies, think about the lyrics of sad songs, or reflect on sad experiences in your life—you will start to feel unhappy. If, on the other hand, you choose to think about happy moments in your life, watch comedies, read joke books, or listen to upbeat music, you will start to feel happy.

How Feelings Influence Thoughts

As we've discussed, people who are depressed are inclined to see the cup as half empty and to make negative interpretations of neutral events. One of the symptoms of depression is the tendency to be plagued with *feelings of* worthlessness, inadequacy, and guilt.

How Thoughts Influence Actions

People's behaviors tend to correspond to the way they think about things. If you think about your partner's good qualities, you will likely behave in ways that enhance your relationship. On the other hand, if you dwell on the things your partner does to upset you, chances are you will not spend time with your partner or do things for him or her.

How Actions Influence Thoughts

When you're at Disneyland or at a party, you're probably thinking about how much fun you're having or about other fun times in your life. When you are studying up on infertility, reading this book, or engaged in infertility treatments, you are probably feeling productive and thinking positive thoughts about getting pregnant. On the other hand, when you are moping around the house and crying, you are most likely thinking about how bad you have it because of your fertility problems.

How Actions Influence Feelings

If you isolate yourself and sit around doing nothing, you will make yourself feel more depressed. If you force yourself to go to a party, you will probably feel better.

How Feelings Influence Actions

There is a special connection between your mood and your behavior. When you are depressed, you probably don't feel like doing anything

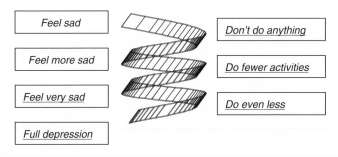

Figure 5.3

except watching TV or sleeping. When you feel happy you want to go out and celebrate. When you feel hopeful about becoming pregnant, you will try harder to comply with treatments. When you feel hopeless, you will be more likely to miss appointments or even give up.

When you are depressed you generally don't feel like engaging in activities, so you tend to sit around and do nothing. However, doing nothing will make you feel more depressed. The more depressed you feel, the less active you become. The fewer activities you engage in, the more depressed you will feel. This is a negative and vicious cycle (see Figure 5.3). Depression and inactivity feed on one another and pull you down. Luckily, the cycle can work in the opposite direction. The more pleasant activities you engage in, the better you will feel. The better you feel, the more you will want to engage in pleasant activities. The key is to force yourself to participate in activities that could improve your mood, even if you don't feel like being active.

Now that you understand the relationships between thoughts, feelings, and behaviors, let us turn our attention to how to utilize this understanding to enhance your mood. It logically follows that in order to change your mood, you must change your thoughts and/or your behaviors. Chapter 6 will show you how to improve your mood by thinking in a more positive manner and becoming more active.

6

COPING WITH DEPRESSION
You Are What You Think

Think back to the last time you felt depressed. What thoughts were going through your head just before you noticed feeling depressed? Chances are they were negative or self-deprecating. One way you can take advantage of the interaction of thoughts, feelings, and actions is to change the way you view and interpret your surroundings. If you see the world in a negative way, you will start to feel depressed and behave in a depressed manner. If, on the other hand, you can learn to view things in a more positive manner, your mood and behavior will also be more positive.

ACCURATE VERSUS INACCURATE PERCEPTIONS

We want to make a clear distinction between the natural reaction of sadness that often accompanies infertility and the unnatural depression associated with thinking about infertility in an irrational manner. Most people who have been diagnosed with fertility problems accurately perceive that they are faced with many potential losses. Thinking about and dealing with such losses will naturally result in sadness, which is very normal. It is important to allow yourself to experience this sadness and grieve the losses. However, an infertility diagnosis is just that, and nothing more. If you are reading more meaning into the diagnosis, entertaining such thoughts as "My infertility means I'm a failure," or "I deserve this because of how bad I was as an adolescent," or "My life will have no meaning if I can't conceive," then these inaccurate perceptions will turn your natural sadness into an unnatural depression.

These inaccurate perceptions are sometimes called "thoughtless thinking" or "twisted thinking." They are also called "automatic thoughts" because you have probably become so used to having them that they feel natural and automatic to you. This chapter will help you notice how you think about things, pinpoint the automatic thoughts, and suggest ways to replace your twisted thinking with more rational perceptions.

ASSIGNMENT 6.1

Before you read further about the types of thoughtless thinking, please write down your answers to the following questions about your thoughts on infertility. Leave three or four blank spaces between each answer; you will fill in these spaces for a later assignment. For now, we want you to explore your thoughts/beliefs/attitudes to determine whether they are accurate or are forms of thoughtless thinking. DON'T BE TEMPTED TO SKIP OVER THIS ASSIGNMENT! The more work you put into this, the more you will get out of it. Be honest and thorough in answering the questions, because we will work with your answers later in the chapter.

1. What does the diagnosis of infertility mean to you?
2. What does it mean to be fertile? Infertile?
3. How is your self-image affected by your or your partner's biological infertility?
4. What does having a child/children mean to you?
5. What does it mean to be a parent?
6. Why do you want to have children? Can you achieve these aims with adopted children?
7. What do you believe is the purpose of marriage? Can a marriage with no genetically related children last?
8. Do you have to have children of your own in order to gain status in your family and/or in society?
9. What does it mean to be a man? Woman? Masculine? Feminine? Good husband? Good wife? Good person?
10. How do you define your identity?
11. What are your life goals? Is having a baby the only important goal in life?
12. What gives you pleasure in life? Is parenting the only source of pleasure?

TYPES OF THOUGHTLESS THINKING[1]

Researchers[2-4] who have spent many years studying the relationship between thoughts and feelings have identified ten types of thoughtless thinking that tend to make people depressed:

All-or-Nothing Thinking

This type of thinking refers to a tendency to perceive things in extreme categories, such as all good or all bad, all right or all wrong, and so on. An example of such thinking is the statement, "If I cannot conceive a child, I will never have a meaningful life." This thinking is irrational because most things in life are never completely one way or the other. Your whole life will not lack meaning if you cannot have a child. By the same token, your life will not be completely meaningful just because you can give birth.

Overgeneralization

You take one situation or one aspect of a situation and apply it to everything. That is, you draw general conclusions based on few, and generally negative, details. An example of such generalization is thinking, "I am useless as a wife if I cannot have a baby." Another form of generalization is to conclude that one bad thing that happens to you will become a never-ending pattern—e.g., one negative pregnancy test means that you'll *never* get pregnant.

Labeling and Mislabeling

Labeling involves negatively classifying yourself or others based on mistakes or shortcomings. An example of labeling is the thought, "I'm just a loser because I blew up at my partner" or "I am a defective human being since my ovaries don't work properly." Creating labels is a distorted way of thinking because people are not defined by one quality or one mistake. When you label yourself based on an incomplete analysis, you set yourself up for self-loathing. When you label others ("Those people at the baby shower are just plain stupid because they don't understand me") you create negative feelings and resentment towards them.

Mental Filter

This type of thinking involves focusing so hard on negative aspects of an event or person that your view of the whole event or person becomes negative. An example of such thinking is the statement, "If I am infertile then I can't have a good sexual relationship," or "My infertility makes me sexually unattractive."

This mental filter is like wearing a pair of sunglasses that are so dark they don't allow you to see the bright side of things; instead, everything looks gloomy, negative, and hopeless.

Disqualifying the Positive

This type of distorted thinking goes beyond the Mental Filter. Not only do you overlook positive events, you actively twist them so they seem negative, or you disqualify them as being unimportant. You believe that you're no good/worthless/unattractive and look for confirming evidence, discounting any evidence to the contrary. For example, Linda believes she is not a good wife because she carries the infertility factor. She tells Burt she would understand if he wanted to divorce her since she is not able to perform what she believes to be her duties as a wife. Burt repeatedly compliments her on what a loving, compatible partner she is and tells her how much he wants to be with her. However, Linda disqualifies these compliments and reassurances by thinking, "He's just saying that because he's my husband; he doesn't really mean it. He'd leave if he could." By transforming neutral or positive events into negative ones, you maintain your negative beliefs, even if your everyday experience proves otherwise.

Magnification or Minimization

In this form of twisted thinking, you exaggerate the importance of negative aspects or inappropriately shrink the positive aspects of a situation. You blow up your negative qualities and minimize your positive qualities, such as believing that your whole life will be ruined because of your infertility and all the things you have going for you don't really matter if you cannot have a child.

Jumping to Conclusions

This type of irrational thinking involves making negative interpretations or predictions about the future without adequate evidence to support your conclusions. It manifests itself in such beliefs as, "If I hadn't had premarital sex, I'd still be fertile," or "If I suffer enough to atone for my previous sins then God will forgive me and give me a baby." Another form of this twisted thinking is "mind reading," in which you assume your partner or others are reacting negatively to you because of your infertility.

Personalization

This type of thought distortion involves seeing yourself as the cause of some negative event, even if you have no personal responsibility for it. For example, a husband may believe that his wife's IVF treatment failed because he had mixed feelings about its cost. Or, you may believe that your best friend's miscarriage was your fault because you felt jealous of her pregnancy. Personalizing events that are beyond your control will make you feel tremendously guilty.

Should Statements

This is the belief that things should be just the way you expect or hope for them to be. You may believe that all married couples should have children or that having children is a sign of maturity. Or, you may think that you should be able to have a baby since you've been successful at everything else in your life. Many people with infertility believe that they must not feel jealous when their friends become pregnant. Should statements can be applied to others too. You may believe that your partner should understand how you are feeling. You may get very angry at reports of child abuse because you think that people who are fortunate enough to have children should never hurt them.

The problem with should statements is that they often reflect unrealistically high standards. When you fall short of these out-of-reach standards, you set yourself up for harsh self-judgment and shame. When others fall short of your expectations, you feel angry, resentful, and self-righteous.

Emotional Reasoning

This is the belief that your thoughts and feelings reflect an absolute reality. You take your thoughts and emotions as evidence of the truth. For example, you believe that your infertility makes you a failure; therefore you are a failure. Or, you feel like your infertility is overwhelming; therefore it is impossible to conquer. The problem with this line of thinking is simply that your feelings are not facts! If your thoughts are distorted to begin with, then the feelings resulting from your thoughts will have no validity either.

You may find that you relate to some of the examples of illogical thinking and argue that the beliefs are real and accurate. Statistically, they are common. However, they are not consistent with mental health and well-being. If you have twisted thoughts, you will likely feel depressed and anxious, have relationship difficulties, seek self-isolation, or have other emotional difficulties. You must learn to recognize that these are cognitive distortions and replace them with more realistic and healthy ways of thinking!

TECHNIQUES TO COUNTER THOUGHTLESS THINKING

Understanding the various types of distorted thinking and how destructive they can be is the first step in learning to "untwist" your thinking and begin interpreting the world in a more accurate manner. Researchers[5] and therapists have found that the following ten techniques have helped millions of people improve their mood by learning to think in more rational ways.

Identify the Distortion

When you notice that your thoughts are making you feel depressed, the first thing to do is identify the type of twisted thinking in which you are engaging. You can use the definitions and examples given above to help you. For example, the thought, "I am a worthless human being because I'm infertile" involves a number of distortions: labeling, overgeneralization, disqualifying the positive, all-or-nothing thinking, and jumping to conclusions. You'll notice that many forms of twisted thinking overlap. Don't worry about precisely identifying the distortion. It is much more important for you to identify *that* the thought is a distortion rather than correctly identifying *which* distortion it is.

Examine the Evidence

Like a scientist who must analyze the data to see if the hypothesis is correct, you must examine the facts in your situation to see if your beliefs are accu-

rate. Remember that feelings are not facts. You may want to ask yourself, "What is the evidence that I am a worthless human being?" Be sure to consider evidence that disconfirms your beliefs: "What is the evidence that I am not a worthless human being?" When scientists find even one piece of disconfirming evidence, they must discard or revise their original hypotheses. Since you surely have at least some qualities that make you a worthy human being, it

follows that you must throw away or at least modify your original belief that you are unworthy.

Think Experimentally

Pursuing the scientist analogy, put your beliefs to the test. If you believe that God is punishing you with infertility, talk to your local clergy person or study scriptures to see if there is any validity to your thoughts. If you believe that parenthood is a sign of maturity, look around you to see if all parents are mature and all people without children are immature. Are 12-year-olds who get pregnant mature? Are nuns who never have children immature?

Take A Survey

Another way to put your beliefs to the test is to ask others if they agree with you. Conduct a survey of your friends and tally their responses. For example, if you believe that you are worthless and unlovable because of your infertility, you could ask people close to you if they believe that people with fertility problems are not worthy of love. If you believe that you are a bad person because you feel jealous of your pregnant friends, you should ask a group of people with fertility problems if they have ever felt jealous of others' pregnancies.

Ditch the Double Standard

When you judge yourself in a harsh manner, ask yourself if you would judge a loved one in a similar situation in the same way. If your best friend told you she carried the infertility factor, would you tell her she was a useless human being? Of course not! Unfortunately, we tend to be our own worst critics and judge ourselves much more harshly than we judge others. However, it is just as ridiculous and ineffective to judge yourself severely as it is to judge another in such a negative manner. You will only feel worse if you buy stock in your distorted belief that infertility makes you worthless.

Think in Shades of Gray

When you notice yourself thinking in distorted ways, especially if you are engaging in all-or-nothing thinking, remind yourself that things are hardly ever completely one way or the other. Consider the "shades of gray" that lie in the middle of your extreme thoughts. Nobody is completely worthy or completely worthless, not even you. Thinking in shades of gray says, "I have worth in all areas of my life even if I am disappointed that my sperm count is low. All it takes is one sperm anyway!"

Another common belief held by people with fertility problems is that infertility has taken over their lives; they have lost control. While it is true that some aspects of your life, such as fertility treatments, are mostly out of your control, you still exert *some* control over the situation. For example, you could decide to switch fertility treatments, change doctors or clinics. Or even quit treatment. Furthermore, there are many other areas over which you exert more complete control, such as where you work, what you eat, and so on.

Define Terms

When you label yourself in a negative way, it is helpful to define the label you are giving yourself. For example, if you believe you are "worthless," ask yourself what it means to be worthless. According to the dictionary, a person who is worthless is someone who has no value, dignity, or honor, and someone who is low and despicable. Does anyone truly meet this definition? Every human being has at least some value and worth, so thinking that you're worthless cannot be accurate. If you believe that you're a terrible wife because you can't give your husband a child, you can consider what it means to you to be a "terrible wife" and a "good wife."

Change your Wording

Sometimes changing the words you use to describe a situation will also change how you think and subsequently feel about that situation. This is especially true with automatic thoughts that involve should statements. Instead of thinking, "I should go to Carol's baby shower," try saying, "It would be nice to go to Carol's baby shower," or "Going to Carol's baby shower would be a nice idea." People who use should statements are often trying to motivate themselves. However, should statements will make you feel guilty and probably lower your motivation. As Dr. Burns says, it is more effective to motivate yourself with a carrot than a stick.

Reattribute the Cause

When you notice that your twisted thinking involves blame, especially blame involving personalization, challenge your thinking by making a list of all possible causes for the problem. Like a scientist, try to be as objective and thorough as possible when compiling your list of alternative causes for the problem. For example, perhaps your partner has seemed uninterested in sex for the past week, and you personalize this by assuming that he or she is not sexually attracted to you because of your fertility problems. What other possible explanations exist for your partner's lack of interest? We bet you can think of many. It is possible that your partner has been feeling sick, is stressed out at work, feels unattractive himself, is tired, and so on. For better or for worse, remember that not everything is about you!

Do a Cost–Benefit Analysis

Weigh the costs and benefits of maintaining your automatic thoughts. This technique is not about evaluating the extent to which your thoughts are true or untrue but evaluating how effective it is to continue to think in such a way. For example, consider the costs and benefits of feeling, "I am worthless because of my fertility problems." The obvious costs are that your belief will make you feel depressed and your motivation to behave as a worthwhile person will go out the window. Instead, you will tend to behave in ways that confirm your worthlessness. At least you get to be right, but this isn't a great benefit. It is just not effective to maintain automatic thoughts. You will move much closer to attaining your life goals if you challenge your irrational thoughts and replace them with more accurate perceptions.

RECORDING YOUR THOUGHTLESS THINKING: THE FOUR-COLUMN TECHNIQUE[6-7]

Now that you know how to identify and challenge your automatic thoughts, you can use the following table to record, challenge, respond to, and reevaluate your twisted thinking. Clinicians who are world famous for treating depression use this format to help their clients systematically analyze their thinking. In the first column, briefly describe the situation. In the second column, write down the automatic thoughts that go along with the feelings. In column three, identify the types of thoughtless thinking that underlie the thoughts you wrote in the previous column. The fourth and most important column involves challenging your automatic thoughts using some of the techniques you learned above and writing down more rational responses to each of your automatic thoughts. A blank copy of this form at the end of the chapter will allow you to record your own automatic thoughts.

Daily Record of Thoughtless Thinking[8]

Situation	Automatic Thought(s)	Cognitive Distortion(s)	Rational Response
I just came back from the doctor and found out that my IVF procedure failed again.	God must be punishing me for all my sins.	Jumping to conclusions and mind-reading Personalization	I cannot read God's mind.
			There is no evidence that the infertility is related to my past sins. Everyone makes mistakes, and they are not all infertile. Disconfirming evidence is that many people who sin all the time have no problems getting pregnant.
You get an invitation to go to a RESOLVE meeting	I don't deserve to get support or to be helped because of my infertility	Jumping to conclusions Emotional reasoning Should statement Disqualifying the positive	Being infertile does not mean I am unworthy of support. Just because I feel I don't deserve help does not mean it is true. My infertility doesn't mean I should be alone in my struggle. I have done many good things in my life and I'm not undeserving of anything. Everyone deserves to have help through the rough spots.

ASSIGNMENT 6.2: TEST YOUR KNOWLEDGE

The following statements are taken from individuals struggling with infertility. Now that you have read about the types of thoughtless thinking and how to challenge your distorted thinking, test your knowledge by reading the following quotes, identifying the types of thoughtless thinking in those statements, and writing down a more rational response. We have modified the four-column technique into a three-column format in order for you to do this. You will likely have to use an additional piece of paper.

Automatic Thought(s)	Cognitive Distortion(s)	Rational Response
1. God knows I'd be a terrible parent so He made me infertile.		
2. I can't have a meaningful life if I can't have a baby.		
3. I feel like I am a defective human being because of my infertility.		
4. Infertility has taken over who I am. I feel like infertility is my identity.		
5. I'm a worthless partner since I can't give my wife/husband a baby.		
6. I can't even make a baby. I feel like I can't do anything right.		
7. Infertility shouldn't make me feel so down.		
8. Maybe infertility is a sign that our union is flawed.		
9. Nothing ever comes easy for me. These kinds of things always happen to me. I always have bad luck.		
10. Infertility has taken over my life. I can't control anything anymore.		
11. Parenthood is a sign of maturity. I'll never be mature if I can't have a child.		
12. I'll never overcome infertility. It is just too big a problem.		

ANSWERS TO ASSIGNMENT 6.2:

Below you'll find our answers to this assignment. Resist the temptation to read the answers without first trying to come up with your own. Remember that you will will learn from this book in proportion to the effort you put into it. Don't worry if you don't come up with the exact answers below. We were much more thorough than you need to be. It is more important that you identify automatic thoughts as forms of twisted thinking and employ the method that works best for you than it is to match up with our answers.

1. *God knows I'd be a terrible parent so He made me infertile*: Can you really read God's mind? Seriously, this is an incredibly painful thought to entertain. You must understand that such self-loathing is a common part of depression. However, these types of thoughts are not grounded in rational thinking. This statement represents the jumping-to-conclusions form of thoughtless thinking. You are assuming that you know what God is thinking and has in store for you, and concluding that people who can't have babies are people who would have poor parenting skills. Techniques with which to challenge this distorted thought:

   a. *Examine the evidence:* What is the evidence that you would be a terrible parent? How do you know what God thinks? What is the evidence that people with fertility problems would make terrible parents? Is the converse true that people without fertility problems make great parents? If these questions stump you, it's because the original thought was not rational!

   b. *Think experimentally:* Ask your clergyman or read the scriptures regarding the possible connection between "terrible parenting" and infertility. Think about all the couples you know: Are the ones without children all bad parents? Are the ones with children all good parents?

2. *I can't have a meaningful life if I can't have a baby:* This statement represents all-or-nothing thinking. You are assuming that you either will or will not have a meaningful life depending on whether you have a baby. Another implied assumption is that having a child is the only way to have a meaningful life. While it is true that having a baby is a truly meaningful experience, it is not the only meaningful experience in life. Techniques to challenge this distorted thought:

    a. *Examine the evidence, define terms, and think in shades of gray:* Are other aspects of your life (besides fertility) meaningful? What did you find meaningful before you knew you had fertility problems? Is this no longer meaningful? Is having a baby the only life goal you have? Can't your other life goals be achieved without having genetically related children? What does "meaningful" mean, anyway? Isn't there some middle ground between "meaningful" and "not meaningful?"

    b. *Take a survey:* Ask people you know without children if they believe they have meaningless lives. Ask those with children if they believe they have completely meaningful lives.

    c. *Ditch the double standard:* Would you tell your friends with infertility problems that they should give up all hope of ever having meaningful lives? Of course not. So why are you telling yourself this?

3. *I feel like I am a defective human being because of my infertility:* This statement lights up many forms of twisted thinking. You are overgeneralizing that your difficulties with fertility amount to an overall defectiveness. It represents magnification because you project a problem in one area to your being a problem as a whole. It is a form of all-or-nothing thinking because "defective" is an extreme category. Calling yourself "defective" is also a form of labeling. In addition, it represents the mental filter because your view of yourself is negatively colored by focusing on one negative aspect. Techniques to challenge this distorted thought:

    a. *Examine the evidence:* What is the evidence that my functioning is "defective" in other areas?

    b. *Ditch the double standard:* Would you tell your friends with infertility that they are defective?

    c. *Think in shades of gray:* Consider the possibility that you are a normal human being who at the moment happens to have a problem getting your reproductive organs to function as you'd like them to.

    d. *Do a cost–benefit analysis:* What are the costs and benefits of maintaining the thought that you are defective?

4. *Infertility has taken over who I am. I feel like infertility is my identity:* When you want so badly to have a baby and spend so much time and energy thinking about it and trying to get pregnant, it is easy to feel like infertility is your whole identity,

instead of just one aspect of your identity. This idea represents a magnification of infertility and a minimization of every other aspect of your identity. Techniques to challenge the magnification and minimization form of distorted thought:

a. *Examine the evidence:* List all the ways in which you identify yourself. Consider categories such as gender, race, religion, occupation, athleticism, hobbies, and so on. An example is, "I am a Caucasian Christian male lawyer who has problems with fertility. I'm also a runner and a fisherman." Another way to make other aspects of your identity more prominent is to devote more time and energy to them. For example, the person in the example could plan a fishing trip or focus on running again.

b. *Do a cost–benefit analysis:* What are the costs and benefits of regarding yourself only as an "infertile" person? The possible costs are that it could become a self-fulfilling prophecy: You could give up on fertility treatments or other alternatives by thinking and acting as if you'll never have a child.

5. *I'm a worthless partner since I can't give my wife/husband a baby:* While being able to create a baby with your partner is a wonderful experience, it is not the only way in which you can give to your partner or have worth. This thought is representative of just about every form of twisted thinking! It represents all-or-nothing thinking, since it is based on extremes of worth depending solely on one factor. It also represents overgeneralization because you are taking one aspect of being a worthy partner and applying it to everything. Calling yourself "worthless" is a form of mislabeling. Mental filter is represented, too, because you are focusing on only one aspect of partnership. This overlaps with magnification and minimization; such thinking magnifies one negative aspect and minimizes all the positive aspects of being a worthy partner. But wait, there's one more! It's a form of emotional reasoning. Just because you feel worthless does not mean that you are worthless. Since this statement is irrational in so many ways, there are also many techniques with which to challenge it:

a. *Examine the evidence:* List all the qualities that make a partner "worthy," and notice how many of these qualities you have. Since it is certain that you have at least some "worthy" qualities, you have disconfirmed your hypothesis.

Thus, you must throw away the irrational thought that you are worthless.

b. *Take a survey:* The best way to find out if your partner thinks you are worthless is simply to ask him or her. This will enhance the communication in your relationship, too.

c. *Ditch the double standard:* Would you judge your friends with infertility as "worthless" partners? If not, it does not make sense for you to do this to yourself.

d. *Think in shades of gray:* Nobody is completely worthy or worthless. Remind yourself of all the areas of your life in which you have worth, even if you are disappointed in your fertility.

e. *Define terms and change your wording:* What does "worthless" mean? Look it up. Surely you have at least some worth and value, so this word is not accurate.

f. *Do a cost–benefit analysis:* What are the costs and benefits of thinking that you are worthless? Is keeping this thought really helping you to have a better relationship? The potential costs are that you could start believing it and feel and act as if you are worthless. It could become a self-fulfilling prophecy, and you could damage your relationship.

6. *I can't even make a baby. I feel like I can't do anything right:* Because you are focusing so hard on your ability to make a baby, it is easy to understand how feeling inadequate in this area could spread to other areas. However, this automatic thought is irrational because it is simply not true that you can't do anything right. It represents overgeneralization, since you are projecting your difficulties with conception to every other domain of your life. It also represents disqualifying the positive and magnification and minimization because you are magnifying your problems with fertility and disqualifying and minimizing all your other abilities to do things well. It is also a form of mental filter in that you have focused so hard on a negative aspect of your abilities that your entire view of yourself has become negative. Finally, believing that you can't do anything right just because you feel this is true is a form of emotional reasoning. Techniques to challenge this distorted thought:

a. *Examine the evidence:* What is the evidence that you can't do anything right? What is the evidence regarding the things you do well?

      b. Think in shades of gray and change your wording: Consider the statement, "I do many things well, even though infertility is giving me a huge challenge right now."

      c. Do a cost–benefit analysis: What are the pros and cons of entertaining the thought that you can't do anything right? Again, the potential costs are that you could come to believe that the statement is true and act in a manner consistent with your belief.

7. *Infertility shouldn't make me feel so down:* This thought is a form of a should statement. Don't "should" on yourself; you probably have enough insensitive friends and family members doing that for you! Just because you see others reacting in one way to infertility doesn't mean that you should react the same way. We are all individuals, with distinct histories and circumstances that influence our reaction. Techniques to challenge this distorted thought:

      a. Examine the evidence: Infertility can be an extremely painful experience. Feeling down about it is a normal and natural response.

      b. Ditch the double standard: Would you tell your friends with infertility that they shouldn't feel so sad? Don't you hate it when your insensitive friends or family members tell you "just don't worry about it" or "just relax."

      c. Change your wording: Instead of thinking that you shouldn't feel sad, try thinking, "It would be nice if I didn't feel so sad."

8. *Maybe infertility is a sign that our union is flawed:* Are you a fortune teller? Infertility can be a challenge to many relationships, but it is no sure sign of a flawed union. Trying to read meaning into things is a form of jumping to conclusions. Techniques to challenge this distorted thought:

      a. Examine the evidence: What is the evidence that your union is flawed? Talk with your partner and objectively discuss the strengths and weaknesses of your relationship. Working on the aspects of your relationship you feel need strengthening will help lift your spirits.

      b. Ditch the double standard: Are relationships of all infertile couples flawed? On the flip side, is fertility a sign of a perfect union? Do all couples with children have perfect relationships?

      c. Reattribution: It may be that your relationship does have flaws, but it is highly unlikely that your relationship problems *caused* your infertility.

9. *Nothing ever comes easily for me. These kinds of things always happen to me. I always have bad luck:* Thinking that one event is part of a never-ending pattern of defeat or bad luck is a form of overgeneralization. It also represents all-or-nothing thinking because you believe that things are always easy or difficult, that luck is either always good or always bad. It is also a form of personalization, since you are taking responsibility for having bad luck. Techniques to challenge this distorted thought:

   a. *Examine the evidence:* Does anything ever come easily for you? Do positive things ever happen for you? Do you ever have good luck?

   b. *Think in shades of gray and change your wording:* Everyone has some abilities that come easily to them and other skills that are more of a challenge. Everyone has both good and bad things happen to them. Everyone has some good luck and some bad luck. Consider saying, "Having a baby has not come easily for me," instead of "Nothing ever comes easily for me."

10. *Infertility has taken over my life. I can't control anything anymore:* Infertility can certainly feel like it has taken over your life, but believing this is a form of emotional reasoning. Feeling that you can't control anything is also a form of all-or-nothing thinking. It also represents overgeneralization, since you are applying a lack of control in one area to all areas of your life. In addition, You are magnifying your lack of control over fertility issues and minimizing your control in other areas of your life. Techniques to challenge this distorted thought:

   a. *Examine the evidence:* List the areas in your life over which you do have control. Work on exercising this control to make yourself feel more powerful over your own life.

   b. *Think in shades of gray and change your wording:* Try saying, "I have control in many areas of my life, and I don't like not feeling in control of my fertility."

   c. *Do a cost–benefit analysis:* What are the costs and benefits of believing that you have no control over your life? The cost is feeling and even acting helpless.

11. *Parenthood is a sign of maturity. I'll never be mature if I can't have a child:* This thought is a form of all-or-nothing thinking. It is also a form of emotional reasoning since you believe that your thoughts about what constitutes maturity are factual. Techniques to challenge this distorted thought:

    a. Examine the evidence: Are all parents mature? What about 14-year-olds who have babies? What about priests and nuns who never have kids?

    b. Take a survey: Consider people you know. Are all the ones with kids mature and all the ones without kids immature?

    c. Define terms: What does it mean to be mature? What are the ways in which a person can achieve maturity?

    d. Change your wording: Try saying, "Parenthood helps some people gain maturity, and I'll have to find other ways to develop my maturity."

12. *I'll never overcome infertility. It is just too big a problem:* This thought is a form of emotional reasoning, since you are equating your thoughts with facts. Techniques to challenge this distorted thought:

    a. Examine the evidence: Consider your strengths and how you have previously coped with difficult situations. Hone your existing strengths and coping skills, and work on developing new ones.

    b. Change your wording: Try saying, "Infertility is a huge challenge, and I will have to find ways to overcome it."

    c. Do a cost–benefit analysis: What are the costs and benefits of believing that you cannot overcome infertility? Possible costs are that you will not try as hard or will give up trying.

ASSIGNMENT 6.3

Remember those questions you answered from Assignment 6.1? We asked you to leave a few blank spaces between each answer, which we'd like you to fill in for this assignment. Now that you know how to identify and counter twisted thinking we'd like you to:

1. Read over the answers you gave to the 12 questions in Assignment 6.1.
2. Decide whether the responses you gave were based on rational thinking or were forms of twisted thinking. If they were forms of thoughtless thinking, identify the type of distortion they represent.
3. Use the techniques you've learned to counter the thoughtless thinking you've identified and create a more rational response.

CHANGE YOUR BEHAVIORS: YOU ARE WHAT YOU DO

We have discussed the relationship between activities and mood. The way to capitalize on this to improve your mood is to engage in as many pleasant activities as possible. Your mood is like a bank account. Dealing with negative events and engaging in activities that aren't pleasant—such as enduring painful infertility treatments or baby showers—are withdrawals. Too many withdrawals from your bank account will put you in the "hole" financially, just as too many negative events in your life will put your mood "in the hole," so to speak. The way to balance your bank account is to make sure there are at least as many deposits as withdrawals. The same principle applies to your activities.  You must balance activities that are likely to make you feel bad with at least as many activities that are likely to make you feel good. Remember, the more you engage in pleasant activities the better your mood, and the better your mood the more likely you will continue to engage in pleasant activities.

In addition, it is important to balance activities that make you feel inadequate or incompetent with activities you've mastered that make you feel adequate and competent. For many people, infertility is their first experience of failure. To balance your emotional checkbook, it is important for you to do things that give you a sense of self-worth and make you feel like a success. Engaging in pleasant activities, including those that make you feel competent is rewarding and will distract your attention, mood, and behavior from what makes you upset.

Pleasant Activities

Researchers[9] have developed a list of activities that tend to alleviate depression and lift spirits. Table 6.1 includes highlights from this Pleasant Events Schedule, as well as a number of other enjoyable activities for you to choose from. Read over the list carefully, then circle the items you believe would be pleasurable for you. The blank spots are for you to write in your own pleasant activities.

Table 6.1 Pleasant Events Schedule

Spend time in the country	Contribute to others	Talk about sports
Meet new people	Go to a concert	Play sports
Go to the beach	Do artwork	Read holy/sacred writings
Pray	Read	Go dancing
Go to a lecture	Take a class	Go boating
Visit with family	Woodwork	Have sex
Laugh	Work crossword puzzles	Complete a challenging task
Have lunch with a friend	Take a shower	Go on a nice drive
Write stories or poetry	Play with animals	Explore
Sing	Go to a party	Go to religious functions
Join a club	Play a musical instrument	Bake or cook
Take a nap	Volunteer to help others	Do yard work or gardening
Plan or organize a party	Go on a date with your partner	Invite friends to visit
Give gifts	Get a massage/backrub	Write letters to people
Clean your house or car	Tell or listen to jokes	Talk about your health
Learn about infertility	Counsel someone else	Compliment/praise someone
Call someone	Daydream	Go to the movies
Attend RESOLVE meetings	Kiss your partner	Have a good cry
Reminisce about good times	Write in a diary	Get counseling
Meditate or do yoga	Do someone a favor	Read the newspaper
Surf the internet	Talk with your doctor	Talk about sex
Go to the library	Do people watching	Repair something
Be with happy people	Smile at people	Take a walk
List your blessings	Call old friends	Do relaxation exercises
_____	_____	_____
_____	_____	_____
_____	_____	_____

ASSIGNMENT 6.4

The only way that pleasant activities can improve your mood is if you actually engage in them. So here's your assignment:

1. Circle all the items from Table 6.1 that you find enjoyable or that you think would be good for you.
2. Fill in the blanks in Table 6.1 with additional activities. If you need extra space, write in the margins or on another piece of paper.
3. Guesstimate the number of pleasant events you already engage in on a daily basis, and multiply by THREE. This is the number of pleasant activities we want you to engage in daily.
4. On the Weekly Activities Schedule below, plan when you will engage in these daily activities. You can copy this form and use it each week to plan your activities.
5. Carry through, NO MATTER WHAT! Force yourself if you have to. If you wait until you're in the mood to do these things, you might be waiting a long time. The fact is the good mood comes after, not before, you engage in the activity.
6. Notice the connection between your level of activity and your mood. On the calendar you'll note two spaces at the bottom of each day. One space is for you to rate your level of activity on a scale from 1 to 10, with 1 representing little activity and 10 representing lots of activity. The other space is for you to rate your overall mood during that day on a scale from 1 to 10, with 1 representing the worst you've ever felt and 10 representing the best you've ever felt.
7. Reward yourself with even more pleasurable activities—such as material items, special dinners out, or vacations—for completing this assignment and engaging in all the pleasant events you planned.

Weekly Activity Schedule

Time	Sun	Mon	Tue	Wed	Thur	Fri	Sat
Morning							
Afternoon							
Evening							
Level of Activity (1–10)							
Mood Rating (1–10)							

DISTRACT FROM DEPRESSION

People who are depressed tend to spend their time dwelling on the things that make them depressed. Given the relationship between thoughts, feelings, and behaviors, the more depressed infertile couples feel, the fewer activities they'll want to engage in, and the more depressed they become. While it is important to spend some time thinking about your problems (so you can solve them), dwelling on them excessively is unhealthy.

One way to break the vicious cycle of depression is to distract your mind from thinking about the things that depress you. Instead, focus your mind on thoughts that make you happy. It almost doesn't matter what you think about, as long as it is not your problems.

Sometimes it just helped to get busy with things in my life other than my infertility. It made me feel "normal" and gave me a break from it all.

Remember that you are what you think, so think happy thoughts if you want to feel happy. Researchers from the University of Washington[10] have put together a list of distractions, discussed below, that have been used to help people deal with distress in their lives.

Distract From Your Depression by Focusing on Other Thoughts

The human mind cannot give full attention to more than one thought at a time. Thus, you cannot be thinking simultaneously about what makes you unhappy and what makes you happy. You can use this human limitation to lift your mood by focusing your attention on thoughts that make you feel happier, or even on neutral thoughts. For example, you could think about your happiest moment, the last vacation you took, or your favorite food. You could also think about political or religious issues.

Creating a mental image, such as an image of your favorite place, is another form of distracting. Reading, doing crossword puzzles, and watching television are great distractions. Counting usually works well, too. You could count to 100 objects (cars, colors, tiles, whatever). If you really want to distract your mind from other thoughts, try counting backwards from 100 or saying the alphabet backwards. These take special concentration! Another distraction from depressing thoughts is to focus your thoughts on other people's lives. You could compare your situation to someone who has it worse than you by thinking about people you know or reading about disasters.

Distract from Your Depression by Engaging in Activities

Feelings relate to physiological states. The connections between how you think, feel, and act also have a physiological basis. Being upset corresponds with a certain physiological response. Distracting by engaging in other activities creates a different physiology in your body, which then affects your thoughts and feelings. Engaging in activities can also fill up your short-term memory with thoughts, visions, and feelings that are not associated with depression. Engage in activities such as going to the movies with a friend, going out for a nice meal, visiting the library, going shopping. Another way to distract with activities is to make contributions to others by doing volunteer work, helping someone out, or just doing something nice for someone. When you contribute to others you not only distract yourself but you get a good feeling from knowing that you've helped someone.

SOLVING PROBLEMS

Many people who are experiencing depression because of infertility are realistically and appropriately sad. They do not engage in the forms of thoughtless thinking that tend to worsen depression. Instead, they grieve naturally and deal with the many losses and potential losses involved with infertility. If your thinking is accurate and you view your infertility in a realistic manner, you need to get to the heart of the matter by solving the problem that is making you feel depressed. In this case, it is important to allow yourself to experience the natural sadness and mourn the losses that accompany infertility problems.

If you and your partner decide to pursue infertility treatments, another essential step in dealing with your depression is to do whatever is possible to solve your infertility problem. This may be learning about infertility and its medical treatments and getting involved in treatments. If the treatments fail to work after you have given them sufficient time to do so, then solving your problems may involve learning about and deciding on other options such as third-party reproduction, adoption, or child-free living. Taking positive steps to address the cause of your sadness is one of the best ways to improve your mood.

Utilize the form below on a daily basis to keep track of your automatic thoughts about infertility and help you come up with more rational responses.

Daily Record of Thoughtless Thinking (copyrighted 1999 by David Burns)[11]

Situation	Automatic Thought(s)	Cognitive Distortion(s)	Rational Response
Identify the event that has made you upset.	Write down the thoughts you are having and the interpretations you are making of this event.	Identify and list the types of cognitive distortions your automatic thoughts represent.	Utilize the techniques to combat thoughtless thinking to reevaluate your automatic thoughts and come up with more rational responses to the situation.

SECTION II SUMMARY

Infertility takes both a physical and emotional toll on a couple and can challenge the emotional resources of even ordinarily well-adjusted couples.

- The perception of lack of control, combined with societal expectations about parenthood, can lead to a reaction of surprise and shock when infertility is diagnosed.
- Initial denial of infertility can keep you from getting overwhelmed initially, but chronic denial can be dangerous to your emotional well-being and your relationships. Chronic denial can also keep you from getting medical treatments that could give you a baby.
- Stress and anxiety are commonly experienced during many phases of the infertility journey. It is important to remember that infertility causes stress, not the other way around.
- Guilt and negative self-image are often based on illogical thinking and inaccurate perceptions. It is important to identify such thoughtless thinking and replace it with more rational responses, using the techniques provided in this section.
- The experience of infertility can make you feel alienated from the fertile world and create the urge to withdraw from others. Resisting to the urge to isolate yourself can provide positive social support to help you get through your infertility.
- Infertility can be the source of many relationship difficulties and emotional rifts between partners. Infertility can also be something that strengthens your relationship and brings you and your partner closer together.
- Sadness and grief are normal, natural responses to infertility and its associated losses. However, normal sadness can turn into more serious depression if your perceptions and interpretations of infertility are based on irrational thinking.
- Depression can involve sadness, irritability, inactivity, feelings of worthlessness, guilt, difficulties in relationships, physical

symptoms (i.e., lack of appetite, weight loss or gain, problems with sleep, loss of libido, difficulties concentrating), and thoughts of death.

• If you have ongoing thoughts of suicide, it is imperative that you consult a doctor or mental health professional immediately.

• Infertility can trigger feelings of sadness and depression, including jeopardized hopes and dreams, losses and potential losses, and the pain associated with infertility treatment.

• There is a difference between the natural reaction of sadness that often accompanies infertility and the unnatural depression that is associated with thinking in an irrational manner about infertility. Sadness is normal; it is healthy to allow yourself to experience it and grieve your losses and potential losses. Irrational thinking is not normal and can lead to chronic depression.

• There is a connection between how you think, how you feel, and how you behave. Interpretations of neutral events based on irrational thinking will lead to negative feelings and negative behaviors. You can change how you feel by changing your thinking and your behavior.

• There is a connection between your mood and your level of activity. The less active you are, the worse your depression. The more active you are, the better you will feel.

• Engage in as many pleasant activities as you can. Use the Pleasant Activities and Weekly Activities schedules in this section to make plans to engage in those activities.

• Use activities to distract your thoughts from whatever is making you feel depressed.

• If your feelings of depression are based on accurate interpretations of your situation, then the best thing you can do to alleviate your depression is to tackle the problem at its heart.

III

Stress

Why It Is Not Enough To "Just Relax"

QUIZ: ARE YOU A STRESS CASE?

This quiz will help you identify the ways in which infertility affects your stress level. Answer the questions below as honestly as you can, with "yes" or "no" responses.

_____ 1. I feel very tense when I think about my fertility problems.

_____ 2. I often worry about whether I will ever have a (another) baby.

_____ 3. Thinking about my fertility problems is very nerve-racking.

_____ 4. Seeing signs of fertility (like pregnant women and babies) makes me very upset.

_____ 5. I am fearful about what a future without children will hold.

_____ 6. I feel very anxious when people ask me when I'm going to have a (another) baby.

_____ 7. Since my fertility problems started, I rarely feel calm.

_____ 8. I have sudden attacks of anxiety, with intense fear or discomfort and physical symptoms (e.g., pounding heart, sweating, chest pain, trembling).

_____ 9. I worry that my stress is causing my fertility problems or making them worse.

_____ 10. I don't know how to relax.

_____ 11. I worry about how to find meaning in life if I can't have a (another) baby.

_____ 12. I'm afraid that my partner will leave me because of our infertility problems.

_____ 13. I feel like infertility has left me with no control over my life.

_____ 14. When I feel overwhelmed by infertility problems, I just try to forget the whole thing.

_____ 15. I try not to let myself think about infertility problems much.

_____ 16. I try to avoid situations that could make me upset about my infertility, such as seeing pregnant women and going to baby showers.

_____ 17. When I'm upset about our infertility problems, I try to keep my feelings to myself.

_____ 18. My partner and I don't know how to go about solving our infertility problems.

_____ 19. The holidays are especially stressful.

SCORING THE STRESS QUIZ

The more "yes" answers you gave, the more likely that you are feel stress and tension related to your fertility problems, and the more likely this chapter can help you relax. Be sure to read through all the responses, even if you answered "no," so you can learn how to avoid some of the common tension traps faced by people with fertility problems.

Signs of Stress (Questions 1–7): The experience of infertility can turn even the calmest person into a "stress case." Chapter 7 will help you identify the signs of stress and learn how to reduce them.

Panic Attacks (Question 8): There is a difference between feeling stressed out and having a panic attack, which involves sudden and intense fear or discomfort and a number of physical symptoms. Chapter 7 will help you identify whether you are suffering from stress or having panic attacks.

The Chicken or the Egg? (Question 9): Chapter 8 offers techniques to decrease your stress and increase your ability to relax.

Relaxation Skills (Question 10): Regular methods of relaxation and coping with everyday problems may not be enough to deal with the intense emotional pain of infertility. Chapter 8 outlines a set of relaxation skills that you can use to deal with the severe stress associated with infertility.

Thoughtless Thinking (Questions 11–13): Thinking about your infertility in a distorted way can cause and worsen stress. Chapters 7 and 8 help you identify when you are engaging in thoughtless thinking and teaches you to tackle stress by changing the way you think about things.

Styles of Coping (Questions 14–17): People cope with the stress of infertility in different ways. Chapter 8 helps you identify your style of coping and learn healthy coping patterns that can diffuse stress.

Solving Problems (Question 18): Many people with fertility problems feel so overwhelmed by stress that their ability to solve problems goes out the window. Chapter 8 provides a series of tried-and-true problem-solving steps that allow you to tackle even the most challenging infertility problems.

Holiday Stress (Question 19): Holidays can be a source of stress for anyone, and an especially difficult time for people experiencing fertility problems. Chapter 8 shows you how to prepare for the holidays mentally and emotionally, reduce your vulnerability to painful holiday situations, and create more meaningful and pleasurable holiday traditions.

7

FIGHT OR FLIGHT

*Common Sources of Stress in Infertility
and How to Combat Them*

Ingrained in our physiology is the stress response, also known as the "fight or flight" response. This biological response occurs in situations in which you perceive danger and either may have to fight the source of danger or flee the situation. The stress response involves a number of physiological changes that help your body attack or get the heck out of there. These responses may include increased heart rate (pounding heart), increased blood pressure, increased blood flow to the muscles in the extremities and decreased blood flow to the digestive tract, as well as secretion of hormones that include epinephrine, norepinephrine, and steroid stress hormones called glucocorticoids. Thinking back to the days of cavemen, you can imagine that this fight or flight response  was crucial for survival. If, for example, the caveman was under attack by a lion, the stress response would direct blood flow to muscles to help him run away, the norepinephrine would help stimulate his brain cells, and the glucocorticoids would help his body make resources available for energy.

Unfortunately, the stress response can also be harmful to your health when the "dangerous" situation is constant. Modern day "lions" include traffic jams, demanding work situations, and, of course, the experience of infertility. Under conditions of constant danger, the stress response can result in cardiovascular disease, high blood pressure, digestive problems, damage to muscle tissue, and suppression of the immune system. Although glucocorticoids are associated with the secretion of sex steroid hormones such as testosterone, there is no conclusive evidence that stress *causes* infertility, which we will discuss in detail later in the chapter.

COMMON SOURCES OF STRESS IN INFERTILITY

While the idea that stress causes infertility has not been proven, it can be said with certainty that *infertility does cause stress.* A number of studies[1-4] have found that infertile patients had higher levels of stress and anxiety than the general population. Men and women experiencing fertility problems report many different sources of stress related to their infertility.

Emotional Distress

The diagnosis of infertility often evokes a range of stressful emotional reactions, including denial, shock, anger, and depression. Fears about normality, sexual adequacy, and even sufficiency as a human being are common. Individuals who have always had their hard work and competence rewarded with success may have their first experience with failure when they find they cannot conceive. This may challenge beliefs in one's ability to achieve highly desired goals through hard work.

The worst anxiety of all is the fear that I may never have children.

Without the prospect of having their own biological offspring, many couples report having to rethink their views about the purpose and meaning of life. These couples may also have to redefine their dreams to include a future without children.

Spiritual Concerns

The experience of infertility can also shake an individual's spiritual foundations. Many individuals question why God is punishing them, whether they are worthy as parents or even human beings, and what kind of a God gives babies to people who neglect or abuse them rather than to those who really want them. Insensitive comments such as "Maybe it just wasn't meant to be" can intensify these spiritual stressors.

We wondered if our fertility problems were God's way of telling us we wouldn't be good at parenting.

Social and Family Pressures

Another potential source of stress comes from societal and family pressures to reproduce. In many cultural and religious traditions, there is an expectation to propagate the species.

I feel so anxious at baby showers. I just can't stand to look at what I may never have.

Most people we've talked with about infertility have reported that they have at least one family member who constantly pressures them about when they plan to have a baby and why they haven't done so yet. Insensitive comments like "just relax" can also be stressful in themselves, since they imply that stress causes infertility and blame the victim. Many people report feeling jealousy, anger, and stress when confronted with other people's pregnancies. To avoid these negative interactions, some people with fertility problems tend to withdraw and isolate themselves socially. Unfortunately, they are cutting themselves off from potential sources of support that could reduce their stress.

Medical Treatment for Infertility

Medical treatment for infertility can be invasive, time consuming, painful, embarrassing, expensive, and thus, stressful. Simply going to the doctor can cause stress. In addition, many treatments involve close monitoring, often requiring women to go to the doctor every morning for up to two weeks per cycle. This requirement can negatively affect work schedules and may even threaten job security. People who are required to travel as part of their career  may be forced to turn down jobs and switch career paths so that they can be available for medical treatments during the time of ovulation. Women taking medications for infertility have reported side effects of fatigue, nausea, bloating, headaches, hot flashes, irritability, depression, and anxiety. The medical treatments can be embarrassing and involve a sense of loss of control. People have to expose intimate details of their private lives, as well as their private parts, to doctors.

I feel so lost in this IVF world. My life feels so out of control.

The choices involved in the medical treatment of infertility can be overwhelming, scary, and stressful. Many people report stress at having to choose which option to pursue, how long to engage in it, whether to switch to another option, and whether to quit treatment altogether. Choices involving moral and ethical questions about fetal reductions are excruciatingly difficult. Another stressful factor is the financial burden of medical treatments for infertility. Assisted reproductive technology is very expensive and can put incredible financial strain on people seeking treatment. It may also be stressful to decide whether to save money, spend money on infertility treatments, or spend money on other items such as vacations, home improvements, or a car.

Relationship Problems

Infertility, stress, and relationship problems are closely related, and their nuances are described more fully in Chapter 9. There are many potential sources of infertility-related relationship problems, which often result in feelings of stress and anxiety. These relationship stressors include differences between partners in personality styles, how they cope, how they think, and what they value. Another potential source of relationship distress involves differences in the beliefs and actions of the partner who carries the infertility factor and the partner who doesn't. Common gender differences in dealing with infertility can also be a source of marital strain.

My husband and I never seem to be on the same page.

Treatment decisions can be a source of stress for a couple when they disagree on a course of action. Everyday issues, such as having to inject a partner with infertility drugs or having to take daily basal body temperature readings, can also be distressing.

Physiological Causes of Anxiety[5]

Physiological causes of anxiety include taking stimulants such as caffeine, nicotine, and amphetamines, which can make people feel anxious and panicky. Even sedatives such as alcohol and marijuana can contribute to stress. Abruptly stopping sedative drugs (such as alcohol, tranquilizers, sleeping pills, and many antidepressants) can cause withdrawal symptoms, including anxiety. Furthermore, a number of medical conditions—including hyperthyroidism, hypoglycemia or diabetes, neurological disorders, and cardiovascular disorders—can be anxiety culprits. A thorough medical evaluation can help rule out and treat organic causes for your stress.

THE CHICKEN OR THE EGG: DOES STRESS CAUSE INFERTILITY OR DOES INFERTILITY CAUSE STRESS?

Many people worry that their stress may be causing or worsening their fertility problems. Thus, not only are they stressed and worried about infertility, they are also stressed about their stress and worried about their worry. Insensitive comments such as "Just relax and you'll get pregnant," feed the idea that stress causes infertility. The reality is that there is *no* conclusive scientific evidence that stress causes infertility.

Where did the idea of stress causing infertility come from? Back in the 1930s nearly half of all infertility problems were undiagnosed or untreated because of fledgling medical technology.[6-7] Because medical explanations could not be found, psychological explanations of infertility were offered to fill the gap. Many of these theories were based on Freudian or psychodynamic principles and explained infertility with arguments about subconscious disturbances in women. For example, infertile women were thought to have neurotic conflicted feelings about motherhood, their own mothers, or their status as an adult, which in turn caused their infertility.

Although most explanations focused on women, infertile men were thought to have overcontrolling mothers who expected rigid conformity to high moral codes, thus causing their sons to have sexual inhibitions, conflicting feelings about parenthood, and subsequent infertility. This model of infertility was popular until the 1980s, when advances in medical technology established a medical basis for the majority (90%) of infertility cases. More recent research indicates that less than 5% of infertility may be caused by emotional problems.[8]

There is some evidence that *extreme* stress can cause infertility, such as when women stop menstruating during famines or wars. However, thousands of women living in the exceedingly stressful conditions of war, poverty, and abuse get pregnant every day all over the world. Thus, there is little reason to believe that stress causes your fertility problems, even if your infertility is unexplained by medical factors.

THE TRUTH ABOUT STRESS AND INFERTILITY: WHY YOU SHOULD LOWER YOUR STRESS

Today, scientists believe that infertility causes stress. It is clear that the experience of infertility takes an emotional toll and wears thin the psychological resources of many individuals. However, this stress may *indirectly* relate to fertility problems if you are too stressed to have intercourse during the prescribed times of the cycle, if you are too overwhelmed to make effective treatment decisions, or if your distress interferes with medical treatments and compliance.

Relieving stress will help you in all aspects of everyday life and get you in shape to meet the emotional and physical demands of infertility. Some studies[9] have suggested that reducing each partner's stress levels can increase marital satisfaction. Depending on your type of infertility, the less stress you feel, the happier you will be in your relationship, making it more likely that you will have sexual intercourse, and get pregnant.

In addition, lowering your stress level can have positive effects on your ability to successfully handle and get through the medical treatment of infertility. The less stressed and overwhelmed you feel, the better you will be able to research and think through available treatment options.

Reducing stress will better equip you to handle the physical and emotional pain of infertility procedures, comply with your medical regimen, and follow through with your treatments. In fact, there is some evidence[10-13] to show that teaching infertile men and women to use the relaxation techniques described in this section helps to reduce levels of stress and boost pregnancy rates. Thus, it is critical that you learn how to reduce your stress. The following sections describe a variety of clinically proven stress-busting techniques.

LESS STRESS NOW: CLINICALLY PROVEN WAYS TO LOWER YOUR STRESS

Because the stress caused by infertility may *indirectly* contribute to infertility, it logically follows that reducing stress could help improve your chances of having a baby. At the very least, stress reduction techniques will help you better handle the emotional strain of infertility and deal more effectively with everyday stressors. Coping effectively doesn't mean you'll never feel stress again; it just means that you know how to keep it from overwhelming you so you can get on with your life.

A word to the wise: *You* are the only person who can reduce your stress. While the techniques provided in this chapter have been tested and proven to be effective in reducing stress and enhancing relaxation, it is *your choice* to study these techniques, practice them, and begin to apply them to the stressors in your life. The reduction in stress you experience will be directly proportional to the amount of effort you put into practicing these techniques. You may be tempted to skim through this chapter without practicing the techniques, but they won't work unless you intentionally put them to use in situations in which you feel stress. We have worked with many clients using these techniques and have watched them learn to combat their stress and anxiety. There are also data to prove that these techniques work on infertility-related distress! You have the choice of seeing whether these techniques work for you. But remember that if change is going to happen in your life, you are the one who must work to make it happen!

The Importance of Practice

Remember when you learned how to play your favorite sport? You probably weren't very good at first, but you improved with practice. Learning relaxation skills is just like learning to play a sport. You probably won't be too adept at it unless you keep practicing. Don't be too discouraged if your first attempts at practicing these skills don't result in complete relaxation. You will need to be your own cheerleader and remind yourself that practice makes perfect. The more you practice, the better you will be at eliciting the relaxation response.

It is very important that you practice these skills regularly and mindfully apply them to the stressors in your life. Reading about them in this book is like joining a health club and going through the orientation but not working out systematically. You can't expect to get in good physical shape by simply owning a membership to a gym. Similarly, you can't expect to reduce your infertility-related stress by simply reading this book. You must systematically practice the exercises in this book and look for opportunities to apply them to the infertility stressors in your life. For example, you can use these skills when you feel anxious about medical visits or results of pregnancy tests. You can also use them if you receive bad news about your test results.

TECHNIQUES TO PREVENT STRESS
Take Good Care of Yourself

The best way to combat stress is to prevent it from occurring in the first place. When you don't take care of yourself physically, your immunity plummets and your body becomes more susceptible to illness. Ever notice how you're more likely to catch colds from others when you're feeling run down physically? Just as with susceptibility to physical illnesses, you are more susceptible to emotional difficulties when you don't take care of yourself. When you are tired, hungry, or upset you have less resistance to negative emotions. Things that ordinarily wouldn't upset you can cause huge emotional reactions. Adding the stress of infertility to this emotional vulnerability makes you susceptible to feeling pretty miserable!

Researchers[14] at the University of Washington have identified a number of ways to reduce your emotional vulnerability. First, be sure to treat physical illnesses, which can lower your resistance to stress and other negative emotions. This relationship goes the other way, too, in that stress can make you more susceptible to getting sick physically. Eat a balanced diet. Eating too little or too much, as well as eating foods that don't agree with you, can make you more sensi-  tive to negative emotions. Try to eat the amount and types of foods that make you feel good, using the principle of moderation.

Stay away from drugs that can alter your mood, such as excessive caffeine or nicotine. Certainly, your doctor has already advised you to avoid alcohol and drugs. Make an effort to balance your sleep. Sleeping too little or too much can make you feel tired, irritable, or groggy. Find the amount of sleep that is best for you and stick with it. Napping may help, too. Create time for exercise in your schedule. Try to get at least 20–30 minutes of aerobic exercise at least 3–4 times per week. Exercise reduces stress and improves your mood.

Finally, engage in activities that make you feel confident, capable, and in control. The experience of infertility can threaten your self-confidence and sense of control over your life. You can balance this by doing things that make you feel good about yourself and increase your sense of control over your own life. For example, you can play sports you're good at, engage in hobbies you like, or take on business projects you know you can tackle successfully.

Knowledge is Power

Just knowing about the common reactions to infertility can help lower your stress. Learning about the experiences of others will make you understand that you are not alone and are not crazy for feeling the way you do. Reading this book is a great start to understanding common reactions to infertility. In addition, it may be helpful for you to join an infertility support group such as RESOLVE. Check the internet (www. RESOLVE.org) or your local phone book for information on this organization and contacts for local chapters.

Get in tune with your stress. The better you understand the things that make you feel stressed, the more you can prepare yourself to successfully handle, and even prevent, those situations from occurring in the future. For example, if you have to attend a family reunion, you may want to practice stress reduction techniques to deal with questions about when you're going to have a baby. It is also a good idea to use relaxation techniques when you're awaiting the results of a pregnancy test. Many people report that using relaxation skills helps them deal with the pain of medical procedures.

It is also helpful to catch your stress early on before it grows into full-blown anxiety. Learn to monitor the thoughts, feelings, and bodily sensations that accompany your stress. When you notice these coming on, you can use the coping skills described in this section to keep yourself from becoming more stressed out.

What if I Don't Feel Like Nurturing Myself?

You may not feel like taking care of yourself, especially if you feel guilty and believe you don't deserve nurturing. However, you must understand that the more you take care of yourself, the longer you'll be able to hang in there with infertility treatments. You'll also cope more effectively with the infertility experience. The thought that you don't deserve self care because of your infertility is a cognitive distortion (see Section II). Taking care of yourself will reduce your vulnerability to intense and painful emotions as well as to unproductive actions such as not complying with medical treatments.

Another cognitive distortion that can become a barrier to self-nurturing is the belief that if you suffer enough you will become pregnant, and that self-nurturance is not an option because you are supposed to be suffering. It is simply not the case that the more you suffer the more likely you are to be pregnant. Have all your fertile friends suffered? What about those who suffer and go through infertility treatments for years and years, and never get pregnant? Really think about how much water your theory holds, and then consider how much it is hurting you to maintain your erroneous belief.

Try nurturing your partner as well as nurturing yourself. This will not only prevent stress but can have positive effects on your relationship! Try a backrub, a candlelit dinner, walking together, or taking a weekend trip. See Section IV on relationship difficulties for more ideas.

CHANGE YOUR THOUGHTS: YOU FEEL WHAT YOU THINK

You may unintentionally be making your stress worse by the way you think about and react to your infertility. Psychologists[15-16] specializing  in the study of stress and anxiety have developed a theory to explain why some people experience stress. These psychologists believe that stress stems not only from difficult situations such as infertility but also from the way individuals perceive and evaluate the situation. If an individual believes that he or she does not have the resources to deal with the situation or that the situation will endanger his or her well-being, then the situation will be "stressful."

This is kind of like seeing the cup as half empty versus half full. Cognitive interpretations of neutral events affect how you feel and how you react. Telling yourself, "I can't handle this doctor's visit" will likely increase your level of stress and make you behave in ways that make the doctor's visit more difficult to handle. How you judge the situation affects what goes on around you. For example, some people who are stressed behave in ways that make the situation even more stressful, like avoiding the situation or stressing out others. The good news is that you can learn to evaluate situations and enhance your coping ability so that you feel less stress.

There are two ways you can effectively reduce your stress: Change the way you think about your stress and change your behavior. You must learn to interpret your environment, especially your fertility problems, in a more positive manner. If you perceive your infertility as something over which you have no control, you will increase your level of stress. If, on the other hand, you change your thoughts to view things in a more positive manner, your stress will decrease.

As we explained in chapters 5 and 6, much of how you *feel* results from how you *think*. Perceiving events that happen to us in a realistic manner will result in normal reactions. Seeing things in a negative, pessimistic, or distorted way will create more stress and anxiety. Please take time to review the sections on "Types of Thoughtless Thinking" and "Techniques to Counter Thoughtless Thinking" found in Chapter 6. Remember that the help you derive from this book will be proportional to the effort you put into it.

The automatic thoughts, images, and feelings you have when you are in stressful situations are just thoughts and inferences, not indisputable facts or truths! The way you process information is not infallible. It is subject to cognitive distortions. Examples of automatic thoughts include, "I can't handle this," "IVF treatments are futile," "I can't do anything right," "My life is meaningless if I can't have a baby," "I let my husband down," "It's all my fault," "My stress overwhelms me," "This is hopeless," and so on. Having fleeting thoughts of this nature is not necessarily a problem, but these thoughts can trigger increasingly negative thoughts and feelings, jeopardizing your ability to handle stress. This is a problem!

Before you can challenge your thoughtless thinking, you must first identify your cognitive distortions. One way to catch yourself when you are entertaining automatic thoughts is to notice when you use such words as "must, should, always, never." These are the red flags of all-or-nothing thinking. Challenge this black-and-white thinking by examining the evidence. Ask yourself whether these statements are really true—e.g., Are you really a *complete* failure because of your problems with fertility? If several attempts at IVF fail, does this really mean there is *no* hope? Such thoughts and feelings may seem real to you, but you don't have to buy into them. Be aware that you can reduce stress by challenging these automatic thoughts and feelings instead of fueling your stress by regarding them as absolute realities.

Another way to challenge automatic thoughts is to change your wording about how you think and feel about a situation. The chart below shows you several examples of how to change wording to reduce stress.[17]

Don't Say This	Say This Instead
I always mess up everything.	I occasionally have trouble doing some things.
Since our fertility problems, my partner never wants to have sex with me.	Since our fertility problems, my partner does not always want to have sex with me.
I must get pregnant this year.	I want to get pregnant this year.
I need to have a baby before I'm forty.	I prefer to have a baby before I'm forty.
I can't face my pregnant friends.	I would find it difficult to face my pregnant friends.
I can never get pregnant.	In the past, I have been unable to get pregnant.

One of the best ways to challenge your automatic thoughts is to examine the evidence. Observe your thoughts and analyze them as a scientist would. For example, if you notice yourself thinking, "This infertility is taking over my whole life. I'll never be able to get over it," you can ask yourself how much you really believe that your stress affects your entire life. Think of other times when you felt really stressed but your life didn't fall apart. List examples of stressful times when you were able to pull yourself together. You probably can come up with many examples, right? Given this, it is inaccurate to say that the stress of infertility is ruining your whole life and that you will fall apart.

Another example involves the thought, "My life would be meaningless if we can't have a baby." Ask yourself if having a baby is the *only* road to a meaningful life. Are there other things in your life that give you meaning? Won't those things still be available even if you don't have a child?

Another example: "My husband won't want to be with me if I can't bear a child." Challenge yourself by asking if you really know this is how he views things. What is your evidence for this assumption? It is probably true that he would be disappointed and even depressed, which are natural responses, but that does not necessarily mean he wouldn't want to be with you.

Still another example is the thought, "This is all my fault! If I didn't have that abortion in my teens I would have been able to get pregnant now." Challenge yourself by asking if there is another possible reason for what happened. What do experts like your physician say about this? How do you know that the abortion caused your current fertility problems?

An additional way to challenge your thoughts before you decide what to believe is to imagine that you are a member of a jury who has to judge whether the thought is accurate enough for a guilty verdict. As a responsible member of a jury, would you convict someone based on an assumption and without thoroughly analyzing the facts? It's likely that very few of your assumptions would stand up to the standard of "guilty without a reasonable doubt." So why condemn yourself to a bout of anxiety and/or depression based on unsubstantiated thoughts or feelings when you wouldn't do this to someone on trial?

The table below shows common forms of thoughtless thinking that lead to increased stress and anxiety, as well as rational responses to these automatic thoughts.

Daily Record of Thoughtless Thinking[18]

Situation	Automatic Thought(s)	Cognitive Distortion(s)	Rational Response(s)
Getting results about a failed IVF attempt.	We're never going to have a (another) baby. There's no hope.	Jumping to conclusions and over generalization.	One failed attempt does not mean that this will be a never-ending pattern. We are dealing with probabilities, not certainties, in either direction. In the past, we have been unable to have a baby. We would love to be able to conceive in the future.
Thinking about your fertility problems during sex.	I can't have a good sexual relationship if my sperm/eggs are infertile.	All-or-nothing thinking, mental filter, and magnification.	Having a good sexual relationship does not depend on ability to reproduce. It depends on love, communication, and skill—which I have. Many couples that never have children have a satisfying sexual relationship.
You're at a baby shower, where your friends and family members keep asking when it is going to be your turn to have a shower.	These people are so rude! They should know better. I can't handle this pressure.	Labeling and mislabeling, should statement, jumping to conclusions.	They are not trying to be rude, they just don't know any better. Maybe if I talk to them about how I feel they will stop pressuring me. It would be nice if they knew better and stopped pressuring me about having a baby. This is a lot of pressure, but I can use coping skills to get through this shower.

ASSIGNMENT 7.1: CHALLENGE YOUR AUTOMATIC THOUGHTS

To determine your automatic thoughts and the meanings and predictions you assign to them, ask yourself the following questions: When was the last time that I felt stress or anxiety about my fertility problems? What thoughts were running through my head the last time I was feeling stressed? What did I think would happen in that stressful situation? What did I picture would happen? What was I saying to myself in that situation?

Challenge your automatic thoughts by asking yourself: How do I know that will indeed happen? What is my evidence for that happening? What is the evidence for my conclusion? Is there evidence that contradicts this conclusion? Are there alternative explanations for this situation?

Situation	Automatic Thought(s)	Cognitive Distortion(s)	Rational Response(s)

Schedule "Worry Time"

Some people find it useful to limit the time they allow themselves to spend worrying about their fertility problems. Schedule 20–30 minutes each day to think about your infertility and con-sider possible solutions to your fertility problems. During this time, you are not allowed to think about anything else. If you notice yourself thinking about other matters, direct your attention back to your infertility. If you find yourself thinking about your infertility outside of your worry time, briefly write down your concern on a pad of paper and tell yourself that you will think about it during your worry time.

Scheduling worry time can help you think about your infertility in a constructive manner. It can also help you develop a sense of control over your stress and your life rather than feeling like infertility has taken over your existence. Worry time works well not only for people who tend to think about their fertility problems excessively but also for those who tend to avoid or deny their fertility problems.

8

COPING WITH STRESS
How to Act the Part

Some people make their stress worse by the way they deal with it: They increase the tension in their bodies, dwell on their problems, and take no action or ineffective action to solve their problems. Such behavior feeds the body's stress response and increases your anxiety level. Using a variety of coping skills can effectively reduce your stress. Most people already use coping skills regularly. However, when you feel like you're stretched beyond your limits, you typically forget to use these coping skills.

Before adopting new ones, however, it is important for you to remember the coping skills that already have worked for you. You know yourself best, and what used to work will most likely work again for you. So, think about what kinds of things help you relax and get through difficult situations. These might include doing deep breathing exercises, working on projects, and talking with friends—i.e., adding pleasant events to your life. On the flip side, it is also useful to think about things you've done in the past that have *not* helped relieve your stress. These things will be unlikely to help you with extremely stressful situations and are better avoided. For example, walking is a coping skill that works for many people but makes some feel their anxiety more intensely because they think about their stressful situation while walking.

ASSIGNMENT 8.1: LIST YOUR COPING SKILLS

In the blanks below, list the coping skills you have used in the past to lower your stress and deal successfully with difficult situations.

_____

_____

_____

_____

Now list the coping skills you have tried, but that did not work to reduce your stress:

_____

_____

_____

_____

WHY SHOULD I LEARN MORE RELAXATION AND COPING SKILLS?

Coping skills are like tools in a toolbox. Different situations call for different coping skills, just as different jobs require different tools. The more skills you have available in your "toolbox," the more likely you will be to cope successfully with whatever situation comes your way. The goal of this chapter is to give you a set of coping skills that cover a range of potentially stressful situations. Having a variety of coping skills to draw on will offer you greater protection from the effects of stress. You will need to experiment with using different skills in different situations to determine which skills are best in which circumstances.

It is also important to note that different skills work best for different people. For example, men and women tend to utilize different coping styles. Women cope by seeking support and sharing their feelings with others, looking up information about infertility and its medical treatments, and focusing on solving their infertility problems. Men tend to busy themselves with other activities or try to avoid thinking about their infertility problems. Allow your partner to react and cope in whatever way works for him or her, even if it is different from yours. Just because your partner reacts and copes differently than you does not mean that he or she doesn't care or has gone off the deep end.

Relaxation Skills: Deep Breathing

Deep breathing is one of the simplest and quickest, yet most effective, forms of relaxation.

I use deep breathing exercises a lot during the two-week wait between ovulation and when I expect to get the results of the pregnancy test. They really help me to get through this most stressful time.

Deep breathing is also called diaphragmatic, or "belly," breathing. Your breath should come from deep within your lungs (in your diaphragm near your belly) instead of higher in your chest. Find a quiet, comfortable spot. It is best to start by lying down on your back. Now put one hand on your belly and the other hand on your chest. Concentrate your attention on breathing. Breathe in and out, gently and evenly. As you take a deep breath in, imagine that your stomach is a balloon being filled with air. This will bring the air into the lower half of your lungs, near your diaphragm. You will notice that the hand on your belly is rising. The hand on your chest should remain relatively stable. Gently and slowly exhale, noticing that the hand on your belly goes back down.

Some people find it even more relaxing to repeat the words, "I am breathing in peace" as they inhale and the words, "I am breathing out stress" as they exhale. Continue to inhale and exhale in this manner for 10 breaths. With each breath notice that you are feeling increasingly relaxed. Now let your breathing slow down and become automatic, but still work to release all the tension in your body. When you are ready, bring your attention back to the room. Once you have mastered belly breathing, you can do it sitting in a chair or even standing up. We suggest that you practice deep breathing every day, especially in situations that you anticipate will be stressful.

Relaxation Skills: Progressive Muscle Relaxation

A number of researchers have found that teaching infertile men and women a variety of relaxation skills can reduce stress by a significant amount[1] and increase their potential to conceive.[2-4] Progressive relaxation training was developed in the 1930s by a physiologist named Jacobson and has been modified more recently[5-6] to make it simpler and more effective. Basically, progressive relaxation training consists of learning to tense and then systematically relax various groups of muscles throughout your body while paying very close attention to the feelings associated with both relaxation and tension.

I use progressive muscle relaxation before and during each doctor's appointment. It helps me to feel much more relaxed and able to get through the painful procedures.

How Progressive Muscle Relaxation Works Researchers have found that the body responds to perceived stressors by activating the sympathetic branch of the autonomic nervous system, which increases muscle tension via the fight-or-flight response. Progressive relaxation works by reducing sympathetic nervous system activity and by activating the parasympathetic nervous system, which helps you to calm down. Because relaxation and tension are incompatible states, you can get rid of tension and create a less painful infertility experience by inducing the relaxation response. You can also use relaxation skills to unwind and regain a feeling of control over your life after stressful experiences.

This training can help only if you learn to be sensitive to muscle tension in your body. You can benefit by these exercises when you experience  symptoms of stress, including muscle tension, rapid/shallow breathing patterns, jitters, moodiness, panic, fatigue, depression, faintness, forgetfulness, difficulties in concentration, increased heart rate and blood pressure, excessive sweating, gastrointestinal upset, difficulties sleeping, and feelings of being overwhelmed. If you experience *many* physical symptoms of stress, you should consult your physician and get a thorough medical evaluation to rule out a possible organic basis for your stress, such as metabolic, neurological, or cardiovascular disorders. With medical approval, you can then begin relaxation training.

The basic technique of progressive relaxation training involves tensing and releasing muscle groups while focusing your attention on the differences between tension and relaxation. This allows you to notice even the smallest amount of tension in your body. You will also learn to recognize and produce the sensations associated with relaxation. These exercises should not cause pain or discomfort. If you have preexisting injuries in certain muscle groups, you can substitute or omit the tensing and releasing of those muscle groups.

Progressive relaxation training involves a number of steps that build on one another so that by the final step you will be able to relax simply by counting to ten. Read through and practice the following steps to learn how to elicit your relaxation response and reduce your anxiety.

Step 1: Learning Progressive Muscle Relaxation   The first step is to learn the techniques of progressive relaxation. Get into a comfortable position in an area that is quiet and free from distracting noises or interruptions. Find a comfortable chair, preferably one that reclines and provides adequate support for your head and spine. You may use pillows to help you get comfortable in the chair. As you lie in the chair, make sure that your head is centered on the mid-line of your body. Close your eyes so that your eyelids and forehead are smooth. Make sure that your lips are slightly parted and that your tongue is resting gently in your mouth. Do not move your throat and do not attempt to talk during this exercise. Keep your shoulders lowered and even. Do not move except to breathe rhythmically. Breathe slowly and regularly. Curl your fingers in a relaxed position and point your toes away from each other at a 45 to 90 degree angle. If you are wearing any uncomfortable articles of clothing, such as tight belts, buttoned collars, or cuffs, remove or loosen them.

Start with five deep breaths in and out before moving to the progressive muscle relaxation procedure. Gradually let your breathing slow down to its regular pace. When you are comfortable and breathing regularly, tense and relax each of the muscle groups in the order described below. Tense the muscle group for five to seven seconds, noticing the sensations that the tension produces. Then, release the tension quickly, paying close attention to the differences in the sensations produced by relaxation and those produced by tension. Allow the muscle group you are focusing on to relax for 30 to 40 seconds before you move on to the next muscle group.

Muscle Group	Method of Tensing
1. Dominant (i.e., right if you're right-handed) hand and forearm	Make a tight fist
2. Dominant upper arm	Push elbow down against chair
3. Nondominant hand and forearm	Same as dominant
4. Nondominant upper arm	Same as dominant
5. Forehead	Raise eyebrows as high as possible
6. Upper cheek and nose	Squint eyes and wrinkle nose
7. Lower face	Clench teeth and pull back corners of mouth

8. Neck	Pull chin toward chest and try to raise chin simultaneously. Don't bring your chin all the way down to your chest, as you could pull a muscle.
9. Chest, shoulders, and upper back	Pull shoulder blades together
10. Abdomen	Make stomach hard
11. Dominant upper leg	Tense muscles on upper side and lower side of leg
12. Dominant calf	Point toes toward head
13. Dominant foot	Point toes downward, turn foot in, and curl toes gently
14. Nondominant upper leg	Same as dominant
15. Nondominant calf	Same as dominant
16. Nondominant foot	Same as dominant

It may be helpful to make a tape recording of your own voice guiding you through these steps so you don't have to read while you're trying to relax. An added benefit is that you will associate the feelings of relaxation with the sound of your own voice. Simply refer to the sixteen muscle groups as you dictate the steps into the recorder. For example, for the first muscle group you can instruct yourself by saying, "Tense the muscles in your dominant hand and forearm by making a tight fist. Hold the tension and notice what it feels like. Hold it." Wait five to seven seconds and then say, "Okay, now relax the muscles in your dominant hand and forearm. Let the muscles be quiet and without tension. Notice the difference between the muscles when tense and when relaxed. Focus your attention on the sensations in the muscles being relaxed. Keep your breathing slow and regular as you continue to let the muscles relax, relax, relax." Let all the tension go all at once, not gradually. Wait 30–40 seconds and repeat the tense-release-relax procedure with the same muscle group. Then repeat this procedure with the next muscle groups.

As you practice this technique, be sure not to hold your breath, which may cause muscle tension and impede relaxation. Rhythmic, relaxed breathing is an important component of this exercise. When you are finished with all sixteen muscle groups, continue to notice the sensations of relaxation by allowing the muscles to stay relaxed. When you are ready to end the exercise and turn your attention to your daily tasks, count backwards from five to one, gaining increasing awareness of your surroundings with each number. For example, you can record the following instructions, "Five: gently move your feet and legs. Four: Move your arms and hands. Three: Move your head and shoulders. Two: Open your eyes. One: You should now be alert, refreshed, and ready to resume normal activities." Be sure to practice this exercise at least twice a day for 15 to 20 minutes each time. Regular practice is the only way to master the skill of relaxation.

Step 2: Relaxation Using Seven Muscle Groups The next step is to combine muscle groups. Once you have practiced the sixteen-muscle-group technique to the point where you can achieve deep relaxation with two or fewer tense-release-relax cycles, you can shorten the relaxation exercise to a seven-muscle-group procedure by combining muscles from the original exercise. The tense-release-relax technique is the same, but now you will tense and relax the following combined muscle groups simultaneously:

- Dominant hand, forearm, and upper arm
- Nondominant hand, forearm, and upper arm
- All muscles in the face
- Neck
- Chest, shoulders, upper back, abdomen
- Dominant upper leg, calf, and foot
- Nondominant upper leg, calf, and foot

Step 3: More Relaxation Using Four Muscle Groups Next, you will combine even more muscle groups. Once you have practiced the seven-muscle-group technique to the point where you can achieve deep relaxation with two or fewer tense-release-relax cycles, you can shorten the relaxation exercise to a four-muscle group. The tense-release-relax technique continues, but now you will tense and relax the following new muscle groups simultaneously:

- Both arms and both hands
- Face and neck
- Chest, shoulders, back, and abdomen
- Both legs and feet

Step 4: Relaxation through Recall This step will teach you how to achieve a state of relaxation simply by recalling the feelings associated with the previously learned relaxation techniques. Thus, instead of actually going through the tense-release-relax procedure with each muscle group, you will now focus your attention on the four groups of muscles in the last procedure. Start with the first muscle group in the four-group procedure. Say to yourself, "Okay, relax," while remembering the sensations in the muscles as the tension is released and the muscles begin to relax. Tell yourself to relax while you recall the relaxation sensations for the next 30–40 seconds. Repeat this step until the first muscle group feels relaxed, then continue with the second muscle group, the third, and finally the fourth. When you are first learning this technique, you may have to reinstitute the tense-release-relax procedure until the muscle group feels relaxed. Be sure to practice this relaxation-by-recall exercise throughout the week.

Step 5: Relaxation through Recall with Counting   The next step combines recall with counting. Once you are able to achieve relaxation by recall, you will add a counting procedure to increase the depth of your relaxation. The idea is simple. In addition to the relaxation-by-recall procedures, you count slowly from one to ten, telling yourself to relax more deeply with each number. It is best to time the counting with your breathing, one number at every exhalation.

Step 6: Relaxation through Counting Alone   The final step involves counting alone. In the last step, you learned to associate feelings of relaxation with the counting procedure. Drop the relaxation-by-recall procedures and focus on relaxation while you simply count to ten. Remember to tell yourself to relax more deeply with each number and to time the counting with your breathing, one number at every exhalation.

If your thoughts tend to stray from noticing your sensations during the exercises, don't become angry with yourself. The ability to focus your attention requires lots of practice. Refocus your attention by listening to the sound of your voice on the recording. If this doesn't work, try to focus on a mental image of a relaxing scene such as a beach scene. Another alternative is to focus on a physical sensation, such as the feelings in your throat as the air goes in and out during breathing.

Coping Skills

Coping through Distraction   Because the experience of infertility has the potential to cause pain in so many areas of your life, you may find that you are always thinking about your fertility problems and what the prospect of not having your own child will mean to your life. Many people struggling with infertility complain of feeling that it has taken over their lives, that they can think of little else, and that their lives have become defined by their infertility. While it is important to think constructively about your fertility problems and how you can solve them, it is unhealthy to dwell on your problems *all* the time. The coping skills below will teach you to distract yourself temporarily from your pain and give yourself a break from infertility problems. Occasional distraction will also help bring back some balance to your life. It is important to note that distraction coping skills are not meant to solve your problems. However, a break will help you to bear your pain more effectively. Distraction coping skills are to be used when you cannot make changes in your situation and must survive painful emotions.

The rationale behind these distraction techniques, developed by researchers[7] at the University of Washington, is that the human mind cannot think about two different things at once. If you occupy your mind by focusing attention on distractions, you cannot also dwell on what bothers you. The idea behind distraction coping is to temporarily divert attention away from your pain. There are a number of different ways to distract, as described below.

Distract through Activities   Think about and engage in activities—particularly pleasant activities—you enjoy, such as exercise, social events, eating out, work, computer games, hobbies, going to concerts, or even cleaning. Use the blanks below to write down a number of activities you can engage in next time you want to use the distraction coping skill.

Distract through Contributing to Others   Contributing to others refocuses your attention away from yourself and your problems. It also can increase your sense of self-worth and self-respect, as well as add meaning to your life. Another positive of this coping strategy is that the person you help also benefits. You can contribute by volunteering time at your favorite agency, making something for another person, or surprising someone with a thoughtful gift. In the blanks below, write

---

ASSIGNMENT 8.2: MY DISTRACTING ACTIVITIES

_____ _____ _____

_____ _____ _____

_____ _____ _____

ASSIGNMENT 8.3: WHAT I PLAN TO CONTRIBUTE

_____ _____ _____

_____ _____ _____

down a number of ways you can cope by contributing to others. Be as specific as possible. List what you will do, for whom you will do it, and when you will do it.

Distract through Comparisons   When you think about your infertility problems, you are probably dwelling on how bad you have it and maybe that nobody has suffered as much as you. The reality is that there is always someone out there who is worse off. Sometimes comparing yourself to others who are less fortunate or who are coping less well can help put your problems in perspective. Comparisons also can highlight what you have going for you, allowing you to be thankful for what you do have instead of focusing on what you don't have. You can distract by comparing yourself to those worse off than you, reading about disasters, or even watching soap operas.

Distract with Opposite Emotions   Since you cannot simultaneously feel happy and sad, anxious and relaxed, you can replace your painful emotion by generating an opposite emotion. If you are sad or depressed, do something that sparks feelings of happiness, such as watching comedies, listening to upbeat music, or reading humorous books. If you are anxious, use the relaxation skills detailed in this chapter or listen to soothing music. In the blanks below, write down a number of things you can do to create an opposite emotion.

Distract with Other Thoughts   If you focus your attention on thoughts other than infertility, you will fill your short-term memory with these new thoughts and edge out your old painful thoughts. Since how you think affects how you feel, thinking about pleasant things will improve

---

ASSIGNMENT 8.4: CREATING OPPOSITE EMOTIONS

_____   _____   _____   _____

_____   _____   _____   _____

ASSIGNMENT 8.5: THOUGHTS I CAN
DISTRACT MYSELF WITH

_____   _____   _____   _____

_____   _____   _____   _____

your mood and decrease your stress. It doesn't really matter what other thoughts you choose to focus on, as long as they do not make you feel bad. Be sure that the other thoughts you choose can captivate you and capture your full attention. You can distract with other thoughts by counting to ten, saying the alphabet (even backwards), reading, writing, working puzzles, and so on. Fill in the blanks in Assignment 8.5 with a list of things you can think about that will capture your attention from what is bothering you.

Distract with Self-Nurturing   It is easy to get caught up in the stressful nature of infertility and forget to nurture yourself. However, failing to nurture yourself will increase your stress and worsen your infertility experience. Some people with fertility problems, especially those who believe that their infertility is a punishment for some past sin, don't believe that they deserve self-nurturing. Others believe that if they suffer enough, they will be rewarded with a baby. Buying into these irrational beliefs and not taking care of yourself is very costly, whereas self-nurturing has many potential benefits.

Using your five senses is one way to nurture and soothe yourself and reduce stress. Self-soothe with vision by studying nature around you, looking at art in a museum, looking at pictures in a magazine, enjoying a ballet or other performance, or gazing at the sunset. Self-soothing through hearing could involve listening to beautiful music, singing or humming your favorite tune, listening to the sounds of nature, or learning to play a musical instrument. Your sense of smell can also be used to self-soothe: Use your favorite perfume or cologne, light a scented candle, make baked goods, or notice the scent of fresh rain. Soothe yourself with your sense of taste. Eat something flavorful or special while really noticing its complex flavors. Self-soothe through touch by taking a bubble bath, petting your cat or dog, getting a massage, hugging someone, putting clean sheets on your bed, or relaxing in a comfortable chair.

In the blanks below, write down the different ways you can use your five senses to soothe your stress.

ASSIGNMENT 8.6: USING MY FIVE SENSES TO SELF-SOOTHE

_____ _____ _____ _____

_____ _____ _____ _____

_____ _____ _____ _____

ASSIGNMENT 8.7: MY PLEASANT IMAGES

_____ _____ _____ _____

_____ _____ _____ _____

_____ _____ _____ _____

Distract with Imagery   Another way to relieve your stress of the moment is through your imagination. You can imagine very relaxing scenes—a tropical island, a beautiful river, or a snow-capped mountain. Imagine that you are coping well with your situation, that all your painful emotions are draining out of you. Be careful not to imagine things that will increase your anxiety. In the blanks above, write down a number of things or events or places you could imagine that would help reduce your stress.

Distract with a Vacation   Just as taking a vacation to a place like Hawaii can help get your mind off the problems back home that stress you out, so can taking a vacation from infertility treatment give you a little break from related worries.

Coping Through Prayer   Millions of people around the world report that faith and prayer help them get through the most difficult times. It may be helpful for you to turn your troubles over to God or your Higher Power and ask for strength to bear the pain of infertility. If you participate in a religious community, you may find it a great source of support during this difficult time.

Coping By Creating Meaning   By suggesting that you create meaning out of your fertility problems, we are in no way suggesting that your infertility was meant to be. Rather, we have found that many people are helped by finding meaning, purpose, or value in their pain. Sages have said, "What does not kill me, makes me stronger." Concentrating on spiritual values can help you create meaning, as can focusing on whatever positive aspects of your infertility you can find.

> *My faith teaches that we must not complain to God about what He has withheld from us. Rather, we must praise Him for what He has given us, and He has been very, very good to us.*

The idea here is that when life hands you lemons, make lemonade. For example, some couples have found that their infertility experience brings them closer together as they communicate feelings, gain a deeper understanding of each other, share their pain, and increasingly rely upon each other. Some have found that their infertility experience has made them more sensitive to the pain of others and has allowed them to more effectively understand and help others.

Coping Through Facing Your Feelings When it comes to handling painful emotions, many people believe that the best way to cope is to avoid the painful situation. They refuse to think or talk about it, deny the problem, avoid anything that may trigger painful thoughts or feelings, or escape situations where there may be reminders of the problem. The problem with avoidance is that it simply does not work. Paradoxically, trying to avoid a painful situation can intensify the painful thoughts and feelings around that situation.

Years of research and countless studies have shown that the more people try to avoid and shut off emotional pain, the more it comes back to haunt them. This holds true with the experience of infertility. Research[8] analyzing the effectiveness of coping skills with infertile males and females has shown that the more an individual used avoidance and escape to deal with fertility problems, the higher their levels of tension, anxiety, depression, anger, confusion, and general mood disturbance were likely to be. These researchers also found that trying to cope through distancing oneself from infertility problems or reining in feelings about infertility was also associated with poor psychological health. Other researchers[9] found that members of an infertility support group who used avoidance strategies had more negative psychological symptoms than those who had active coping styles that allowed them to confront their infertility and use problem-solving skills. For all these reasons, it is of the utmost importance for you to get in touch and deal with your infertility-related thoughts and feelings.

It is important to accept your infertility difficulties and the impact that they can have on your life. Avoiding problems associated with your infertility will ensure that your infertility-related emotional pain will continue. Accepting your infertility problems and dealing with your feelings will eventually make the painful feelings less intense and more bearable. Research has shown that some of the most successful and effective treatment programs for reducing emotional pain involve learning to experience, tolerate, and accept the pain.

Loss and grief provide an example of the importance of acceptance. Pathological grieving, or grieving that never ends, can result from denying the loss or avoiding cues related to the loss. When a loved one dies, it is vital to emotional well-being that loved ones accept the loss and allow themselves to experience any feelings that the loss may evoke. Similarly, infertility can be described as a form of bereavement in that couples grieve the loss of a potential child. The losses and potential losses associated with infertility must be accepted, just as the loss of a loved one must be accepted.

There are a number of ways for you to use emotion-focused and acceptance coping strategies.

Write it out. There is a whole body of research showing that writing down your thoughts and feelings can be beneficial to your mental health. Taking the time to search your mind and your heart for what your infertility experience means to you and putting this into words can help clarify your thoughts and feelings. Refer to Assignment 6.1 in Chapter 6 to help you with this. In addition, some people find it helpful to record their infertility-related thoughts and feelings in a diary or journal.

Talk with others. Talking with others about your thoughts and feelings is another way to deal with the pain of infertility. Confiding in someone you know will be understanding and caring helps you discharge your feelings and provides a source of support and comfort. Talking with your partner can also help increase the emotional intimacy in your relationship through mutual sharing of feelings and emotional validation. Chapter 10 on relationships discusses how partners can validate one another by discussing their feelings. Many infertile men and women also find it useful to talk with others who are experiencing infertility.

I am so thankful for my friends on the internet bulletin boards. They're always there to hear me vent when I'm angry, support me when I'm depressed, assure me when I'm feeling afraid, and restore my hope when I feel like throwing in the towel.

Infertility support groups, such as RESOLVE, can be a safe place to talk with others about your infertility experience. There are also online bulletin boards for infertility, such as can be found at www.RESOLVE.

org. When seeking support, we discourage you from buying into the belief that only others with fertility problems can understand your situation. In our experience, infertility does not necessarily make someone a good source of support. There are many people with no fertility problems who are incredibly understanding, and there are some people with fertility problems who are unsupportive.

Coping By Solving Your Problems Sometimes a major source of stress in infertility is indecision or not having a plan of action for resolving infertility problems. Another commonly reported stressor is the choices and decisions involving assisted reproductive technologies, adoption, or remaining child-free. Even a skilled decision maker can feel overwhelmed by these choices, which often encompass emotional, moral, and financial issues. For these reasons, we suggest that you follow the tried-and-true steps[10] presented here in your decision-making process:

Step 1: Identify the Problem. Define the stressor or stress reaction as a problem to be solved. Focus on *one* problem at a time. The more specific you can be in identifying the problem, the more successful you will be at solving it. For example, don't identify the problem as "I'm not happy." A more specific problem would be, "We have been trying to get pregnant for a long time. We now use the pills to stimulate ovulation, but they haven't been working."

Step 2: Select a Goal. Set concrete, realistic goals by stating the problem in behavioral terms and by delineating steps necessary to reach each goal. It is not realistic to expect that you will definitely get pregnant, and that it will happen immediately. Examples of goals that are not concrete would be, "I want to have a baby," or "I want to be happier." A more realistic and concrete goal would be, "I want to start trying a form of assisted reproductive technology."

Step 3: Generate Alternatives. Come up with a wide range of alternative solutions. It is important to seek information about available alternatives. Read books, search the internet, talk with doctors and counselors, and chat with others who have gone through similar experiences. If you want to try assisted reproductive technology, list all of the possibilities, including IVF, GIFT, and ZIFT.

Step 4: Consider the Consequences. Evaluate the pros and cons of each proposed alternative, and rank the solutions from least to most practical and desirable. With assisted reproductive technologies, it is important to consider such factors as success rates, the emotional and physical toll, time and convenience of treatment, finances, and moral and religious concerns. It may be helpful for you to imagine yourself living with each of these alternatives and noticing how you feel, what would be required of you, and what you enjoy/don't enjoy about each alternative. It is also helpful to think about how you would cope with the consequences of each alternative, considering coping skills that have been effective in the past and the new skills you've learned in this book. The more you research and think through the potential consequences, the better you will be prepared mentally, emotionally, and physically to handle the consequences of your decisions.

Step 5: Make a Decision. Decide which alternative you wish to implement. It may be a good idea to start with the most acceptable and feasible solution.

Step 6: Implement the Decision. Put your decision into action. Break your plan into small, manageable steps and follow through. It is important to realize that although some failures may occur, you should reward yourself for having tried. Make contingency plans for the future. For example, you may want to decide how long to pursue a particular form of treatment before switching to an alternative.

Step 7: Evaluation. Evaluate whether the alternative you chose worked. Consider possible disappointments and setbacks as necessary feedback to restart the problem-solving process. Reconsider the original problem in light of the attempt at problem solving. If your solution worked, you can stop and enjoy the fruits of your labor. If it didn't work, go back to the alternatives step and start the cycle over from there.

Coping With the Holidays[11]   Holidays can be stressful for anyone, even when things are going well. There tend to be many social demands, financial pressures, and expectations for everyone to be happy. Many holiday celebrations, such as Christmas and Chanukah, are centered around family and children.

The holidays just represent our childlessness and remind us of the family we don't yet have.

For the couple with infertility problems, holidays can be painful reminders of happiness you don't feel and what you don't have. Family gatherings may be occasions when long-lost family members ask about when you plan to have a baby or make insensitive comments about your fertility. You can deal with holiday stress, like other sources of stress, by using the coping skills that have been described throughout this chapter. These include strategies to identify and challenge cognitive distortions you may have around the holidays, deep breathing, muscle relaxation exercises, coping through distraction, prayer, dealing with feelings, and going through the problem-solving steps.

Knowing that the holidays have this potential for pain, we urge you to use the following tips to prepare yourself to deal with holiday stress and create a more enjoyable holiday experience.

Be Gentle With Yourself. Given the potential for stress during the holidays, it is important not to be too hard on yourself for feeling anxiety, sadness, or other intense emotions. Acknowledge your pain and give yourself permission to have these natural and normal reactions.

Reduce Your Emotional Vulnerability. Earlier in the chapter we talked about the importance of taking good care of yourself to reduce your vulnerability to intense negative emotions. This principle holds true especially during the holidays. Being hungry or tired can lower your threshold so things that ordinarily wouldn't make you upset can cause you to go over the edge. Avoid this emotional vulnerability by making sure to eat and sleep appropriately, exercise regularly, and treat your physical illnesses.

Stock Up On Emotional Strength. Knowing that the holidays can take a huge emotional toll, try to stockpile your emotional strength. Pamper yourself, engage in relaxing activities to balance the hectic holidays, do things that make you feel more confident, and draw on support from friends and loved ones. Practice as many of the coping skills in this chapter as possible during the holidays.

Be Prepared. Try to predict the difficult situations that will come up and develop a game plan for dealing with them. For example, create coping plans for dealing with friends and family who question your fertility, announcements about others' pregnancies, and being around babies and children. Imagine yourself using these coping skills to successfully handle stressful situations.

Bolster Your Relationship. Be sure to spend extra quality time with your partner, since the holidays can take a toll on your relationship. Because you know you will be making many "relationship withdrawals" during difficult times, be sure to balance these with lots of "relationship deposits." The more work you put into feeling close to your partner, the more you will be able to draw upon that closeness when painful situations arise during the holidays.

Choose Holiday Activities Wisely. Be selective in choosing holiday activities. If you predict that a certain gathering will be too difficult, then decline that invitation. You do not have to attend every holiday gathering to which you are invited. Celebra-tions with lots of children, pregnant women, or intrusive family members may be just too hard to handle right now. You are going through an incredibly difficult time, and it is okay to take care of yourself by not going to a party.

Minimize the Pain. If you have to attend a holiday gathering that you predict will be painful, try to structure your time and activities to minimize the pain. Try showing up just before dinner is served, staying for a short time, or arranging to be in the company of people you feel comfortable with.

Smart Shopping. Shopping during the holidays is a stressful experience for everyone, but you may feel especially distressed by seeing all the children and pregnant women in the malls. Try shopping early, using catalogues, or ordering gifts through the internet.

Create a Party Made to Order. Create your own holiday gathering. Invite only childless couples or people you know won't hassle you about not having a family. This will help you create holiday cheer you feel comfortable with. Furthermore, if you time it right you won't have to go to one of the other parties you're dreading. Hosting a gathering will also help you and your partner develop a sense of family tradition, even without children of your own.

Do Something Special for Yourself. Holidays are not only about giving to others. They are also about giving to yourself. You can create a more plea-surable holiday experience by doing something special for yourself, like buying yourself a present, getting a massage or facial, going on a fishing trip, and spending time with loved ones.

Do Something Special for Others.   Helping others not only distracts your attention from yourself, it can help you create and pass along holiday cheer. There are many occasions and opportunities to do special things for others during the holidays. These include volunteering your time and talents to help those less fortunate, helping with community or church activities, and making gifts for others.

SECTION III SUMMARY

- Sources of infertility-related stress include intense emotions, spiritual concerns, social and family pressures, medical treatments for infertility, and relationship problems.
- There is no conclusive evidence that stress causes infertility. So, you don't need to contribute to your stress by being worried that you're stressed.
- While stress does not cause infertility, it may *indirectly* relate to fertility problems by interfering with your normal love-making routine, rendering you unable to make effective treatment decisions, or interfering with pursuing and complying with infertility medical treatments.
- Lowering your stress level will guard against the indirect effects of stress on fertility, as well as improve your everyday mood and help you better handle the physical and emotional pain of infertility.
- You can prevent stress and vulnerability to other painful emotions by taking good care of yourself. This includes eating and sleeping properly, exercising regularly, treating physical illness, and doing things to improve your self-confidence.
- Learning about infertility, medical treatments, and common emotional reactions to infertility can help lower your stress.
- Thoughtless thinking can create stress or make it worse. Learn to identify forms of twisted thinking and use strategies to challenge your cognitive distortions.
- Deep breathing is one of the simplest and quickest, yet most effective, forms of relaxation.
- Progressive muscle relaxation can help ease stress-related physical tension in your body.
- Coping through distractions can help you take a break and bear your pain more effectively.

- Prayer and involvement in religious activities can be effective coping skills.
- Many infertile couples are helped by finding meaning, purpose, or value in their pain.
- Accepting and dealing with your feelings is an essential coping skill. Journaling your feelings or talking about them with others can help you do this.
- Solving your infertility-related problems through effective decision making can help reduce stress. The problem-solving steps described in chapter 8 can help you sort through alternative solutions and implement a course of action.
- You can learn to prevent and deal with holiday stress, and create a more pleasurable holiday experience, by implementing the coping skills described in this chapter.

IV

Couple Trouble
Infertility and Your Relationship

QUIZ: IS INFERTILITY TAKING A TOLL ON YOUR RELATIONSHIP?

This quiz will help you identify the ways in which infertility is affecting your relationship. Answer the questions below as honestly as you can, with "yes" or "no" responses.

_____ 1. I am not as happy as I used to be in my relationship with my partner.

_____ 2. Infertility has taken a toll on our relationship.

_____ 3. Sometimes I worry that my partner and I will separate or divorce because of infertility.

_____ 4. I feel so overwhelmed by my own experience of infertility that it is difficult for me to support my partner.

_____ 5. I tend to view infertility as *my* problem instead of my partner and I regarding it as *our* problem.

_____ 6. My partner views infertility as mainly my problem.

_____ 7. My partner is not as involved as I'd like him/her to be in dealing with our infertility.

_____ 8. I would be willing to make some changes in how I behave in my relationship *if* my partner would also be willing to change his/her relationship behavior.

_____ 9. I believe that if I fail to provide biological offspring then I have failed as a husband/wife/partner.

_____ 10. I feel like less of a man/woman because of infertility problems.

_____ 11. My partner and I have different levels of motivation and interest in infertility treatment.

_____ 12. My partner has such a different reaction to our infertility than I do that it is hard for me to understand him/her.

_____ 13. My partner and I have different ways of coping with infertility problems.

_____ 14. My partner and I don't spend enough time together.

_____ 15. My partner and I don't do nice things for one another the way we used to.

_____ 16. I don't feel I can talk about my experience of infertility with my partner.

_____ 17. When we talk about our infertility, it always seems to end in an argument.

_____ 18. I feel like my partner doesn't understand my experience of infertility.

_____ 19. My partner and I don't agree on infertility treatment decisions.

_____ 20. My partner and I have a hard time solving problems that come up in our relationship.

_____ 21. I feel hopeless in dealing with the problems infertility has caused in my relationship.

_____ 22. Infertility is negatively affecting my sex life.

SCORING THE RELATIONSHIP QUIZ

If you answered "yes" to any of these questions, then this section can be beneficial for you and your relationship. Be sure to read through all the responses even if you answered "no" so you can learn how to avoid some of the common relationship traps faced by couples with fertility problems.

General Relationship Problems (Questions 1–4): The experience of infertility and its medical treatment can highlight the differences between partners and cause relationship problems even in ordinarily happy couples. Chapter 9 will enhance your understanding of the common sources of infertility-centered relationship problems.

Responsibility for Infertility (Questions 5–7): Many couples perceive infertility as the problem of whoever carries the infertility factor. Chapter 9 highlights the importance of partners collaborating to deal with infertility and tend to the relationship.

Who Changes First? (Question 8): Many partners feel so burned out or hurt that they start to play the "If you do X, then I will do Y" game. Both partners must make an individual commitment to making the relationship work. The relationship skills detailed in this section can foster communication and compromise with your partner.

Thoughtless Thinking (Questions 9–10): Twisted thinking (refer to Chapter 6) can make you feel stressed or depressed and negatively affect your relationship. Cognitive distortions can also become self fulfilling prophecies. This section discusses cognitive distortions as a source of relationship distress.

Gender Differences (Questions 11-13): Men and women have characteristically different ways of reacting to and coping with infertility, which can cause conflict in a relationship. The section will make you aware of the differences between you and your partner so that you can recognize and adapt to one another's coping styles.

Quality Time (Questions 14-15): Like other big strains on a relationship, infertility can cause you and your partner to drift apart. This section will help you develop techniques for spending quality time together and bringing you closer together.

Communication (Questions 16-18): Infertility is a very personal topic, and it can be especially difficult to share your feelings with your partner and feel understood. Chapter 10 offers tips on how to be a good listener, how to validate your partner's feelings, and how to express both positive and negative feelings to your partner.

Solving Problems (Questions 19-20): Discussions about solving infertility problems can lead to hurtful arguments. Chapter 10 breaks down the problem-solving process into easy-to-follow steps and offers useful tips to deal successfully with infertility-related problems.

Feeling Hopeless (Question 21): It may seem that relationships strained by the infertility experience will never get back to the way they were before the problems began. This chapter will teach you and your partner to create positive relationship experiences that rekindle the flame and intimacy in your relationship.

Sexual Problems (Question 22): Previously spontaneous and romantic sex may feel more like a chore if treatment involves sex on schedule. Infertility also tends to affect people's self-image as sexual and desirable beings. Chapter 10 offers tips on improving your sexual relationship.

9

COUPLE TROUBLE
Recognizing Relationship Pitfalls in Infertility

One very important way for you to handle infertility-related relationship problems is to understand that they are normal. Overcoming relationship hurdles requires that you be aware of the common sources of relationship problems that arise because of infertility. This chapter covers many aspects of relationships and offers a variety of tried-and-true methods for increasing relationship satisfaction.

Before we focus on how infertility can affect relationships negatively, we would like to point out that many couples find that the experience of infertility brings them closer together.

I feel that we are closer to one another now than we would have been had we not experienced infertility. I think that any time you have to experience painful, difficult experiences together you come out stronger as a unit and as individuals. Everyday I am appreciative that we have each other.

I can honestly say that infertility made my husband and I closer. I felt like the only person who could really understand me was my husband. We felt like we had to protect each other from outside stresses and just take care of each other. We were in this together—all the ups and downs.

This whole experience made us realize that we do have a family, children or no children.

I think that going through all the treatments has made our relation-ship stronger. It has made me realize how profoundly I love my wife as a whole person. This wholeness is much greater than the sum of her parts, reproductive or otherwise. Going through the treatments has made me appreciate my wife for who she is, not whether she and I can reproduce ourselves or not.

COMMON INFERTILITY-RELATED RELATIONSHIP PROBLEMS

We can't tell you how many times we've observed couples having dis-agreements over infertility-related situations. In addition to the relation-ship problems you and your partner may have had before your fertility problems become apparent, many aspects of infertility can create new problems or make your original problems seem worse. The following list of common infertility-related relationship problems will help you understand the source and nature of your difficulties and affirm that you and your partner are not alone in confronting these difficulties.

Individual Differences

Nobody marries his or her identical twin, so you and your partner surely will have differences in personalities, coping styles, the way you think, values and beliefs, and depth of desire to have your own biologi-cal children. These differences can cause problems.

Personality Styles[1]   Personality style includes patterns—e.g., the way you explain things, whether you tend to attribute problems to yourself or others, the extent to which you persevere in the attainment of goals, whether you are passive or aggressive in pursuing your goals, and how compliant you are. Personality style clashes between partners can con-tribute to conflict. For example, if one partner tends to be assertive and the other passive, this difference could play out in the way you pursue infertility treatment. It is common to equate a personality style like aggressiveness with the level of caring about having a baby. However, it is not necessarily the case that the partner who is more aggressive in pursuing infertility treatment cares more than the partner who is pas-sive. You must be careful not to misinterpret the situation and to see it for what it is—a reflection of personality differences.

Coping Styles   Everyone copes with stress differently. Some people may deny or avoid the problem; others may try to distance themselves by keeping busy with other things; still others may put all their energy into directly tackling the problem and finding a solution. Problems can arise when coping styles clash. For example, if your style is to work on finding a solution to the problem while your partner's style is to keep distracted, you could easily become very angry with your partner and perceive his or her behavior as not caring about having a baby. As with personality differences, it is very important to see differences in coping styles as just that and avoid the temptation to misinterpret them as evidence of how much your partner cares.

Thinking Styles   Thoughtless thinking also can negatively affect relationships, especially when people start to feel and act as if their cognitive distortions are true. A partner who feels worthless if he or she cannot impregnate or become pregnant may offer the other partner a divorce. Because he or she feels undeserving of a relationship, the partner carrying the infertility factor may make problems worse so that the other partner eventually does leave.

> *I had fantasies about leaving my husband so he could remarry a fertile woman.*

Values and Beliefs   You and your partner may differ in values and beliefs about relationships, marriage, family, and assisted reproductive options. These values and beliefs may be associated with religion, culture, class, gender, or individual differences. Even partners who share the same religion and culture may differ in

---

ASSIGNMENT 9.1

In what ways do the individual differences between you and your partner show up in your relationship when it comes to your fertility problems?

_____

_____

In what ways does learning about these individual differences help you better understand your partner and his or her behavior?

_____

_____

the extent to which they adhere to values and traditions. People from different backgrounds place varying value on marriage, family, work, recreation, and so on.

Reactions to Infertility

Remember the common reactions to infertility discussed in Chapter 4? It is very unlikely that you and your partner will have exactly the same reactions at the same time or that you will experience them to the same degree. You may experience depression while your partner feels anger; you may seek support from others while your partner wants to isolate; or you may hope that the infertility experience will bring you closer together while your partner sees it as something that could tear you apart. Hormonal medications can make the situation worse by creating intense, fluctuating emotions. Because both you and your partner are experiencing powerful emotions, you may find it difficult to support one another.

Carrier of the Infertility Factor   Statistics indicate that in about 70% of cases, one partner has been diagnosed as carrying the infertility factor. When one partner carries the medical diagnosis of infertility, it is tempting to perceive infertility as the problem of that person, rather than seeing it as a *couple* problem. When partners fail to address infertility as an issue that faces them both, the following problems can arise:

The partner who carries the infertility factor:

- May be in denial, which may frustrate the other partner. It is important to realize that this denial may mask underlying feelings of fear, guilt, depression, confusion, and so on. It is better to address these underlying feelings using the communication and validation skills described later in this chapter than to confront the denial itself.
- May fear that the other partner will abandon them or stay in the relationship resentfully.
- May feel guilty for letting the fertile partner down.
- May feel guilty if the other partner has to endure the bulk of the medical treatments.
- May feel responsible for the couple's problems and not feel entitled to express negative feelings about the medical procedures.
- May volunteer divorce because he or she believes that the purpose of marriage is to procreate or thinks the fertile partner wants to find a new partner who is also fertile.

- May pick at the faults of the other partner in order to not feel he/she is the only one with faults.

My wife is always apologizing for being a "dud," but I always remind her that this is our problem and that she would be enough for me even if we couldn't have a baby.

My husband hates all the drugs I have to take and can't stand that I'm going through all of this because of him. He would much rather adopt, but I can't give up my dream yet.

My husband already feels so bad about our infertility being male-factor. I worry that I might make him feel worse if I complain about anything.

I went so far as to tell my husband to divorce me, leave me so that he could have a life just like he always dreamed, with a real family. I loved him more than life itself, and still do, and I just couldn't ruin his life just because I was inadequate as a woman. He would not hear of such nonsense, and he just held me closer and loved me more. He is a saint!

The partner not carrying the infertility factor:

- May have difficulty asking for support from the other partner, especially if the other partner is the one medically responsible for the infertility.
- May feel anger towards the partner who does carry the infertility factor, then feel guilty for having this anger.
- May feel resentful at having to undergo medical procedures. This is particularly true if the male carries the infertility factor and the female has to bear the brunt of the medical procedures. In this case, the male may feel guilty for being spared the medical procedures.

Our issue is severe male factor infertility. I'm totally healthy, knock on wood, and never in a million years thought I'd have to deal with this. I've had a very hard time accepting this and have blamed him and resented him more often than I care to admit. I try to keep as much as I can inside, though it comes out at times, usually after we find out a friend or family member is pregnant, or after a negative beta. I feel extremely guilty for having these feelings toward him, and love him dearly.

Decisions

There are many decisions to be made surrounding the issue of infertility. Partners have to decide whether to tell others about infertility, who to tell, how to deal with infertility in social situations, and how to handle intrusive family members. They also have to make treatment decisions, what methods to pursue, how long to pursue them, whether to switch to another method, and when, if ever, to end treatment that is not working. When ART doesn't work, some couples must make decisions about adoption.

Religious and cultural differences between partners can make these decisions especially difficult. Another factor that can make decisions even more difficult is if one partner has children from a previous marriage and the other partner does not. These situations are further complicated because they involve choices about how money is spent. Partners may have different values about spending versus saving or may argue about whether to spend money on more attempts to get pregnant versus spending on a car or a trip.

Everyday Issues

Everyday issues involving infertility can be a source of conflict. These issues include anxiety and discomfort about having to inject a partner with infertility drugs, having to take daily basal body temperature readings, using home ovulation predictor kits, having sex on schedule, having to go to the infertility clinic every morning for tests and blood work, having to schedule activities around infertility treatments, and having to put major life decisions on hold until the effects of treatment are determined.[2]

Infertility forces people to face huge issues regarding fundamental beliefs and dreams. The possibility of not having biological children may involve redefining your relationship, the future, your ideas about the meaning and purpose of life and marriage, and your ideas about what it means to be a male/female. This can be especially difficult for people from religions or traditional cultures that strongly associate having biological children with the concepts of marriage, family, masculinity/femininity, and the purpose of life.

Gender Differences

Researchers[3-9] have found differences in how men and women respond to their infertility, the level of psychosocial distress they experience, the skills they use to deal with their distress, and how the stages of medical treatment affect them. These gender differences can create relationship conflicts.

To help you and your partner understand the nature of *potential* sources of conflict in your relationship, this section describes typical gender differences in a number of  areas, our ideas about why these gender differences exist, and tips showing how you and your partner can deal with these gender differences. It is important to note that not all men and women follow these patterns or react in ways that are consistent with gender stereotypes. For example, men have the capacity to be sensitive and emotional, and women have the capacity to hide their emotions.

A number of studies exploring gender differences in response to infertility have concluded that women were more distressed overall by the experience of infertility and its medical treatment. Specifically, women scored higher than men on measures of anxiety, sexual adjustment, drop in self-esteem, and depression.

Women are initially more affected than men by the diagnosis of infertility. This is likely due to differences in the way women and men are socialized. In general, society places a stronger link between the value of a woman and motherhood than on the value of a man and fatherhood. Men can more easily attain value in areas that are independent of fertility, such as education, career, and material successes. Thus, the diagnosis of infertility may carry stronger implications for the woman than it does for the man.

General Reactions

- Men may feel helpless or useless with respect to infertility, especially since they are used to applying logic to solve problems. They are more likely to label their feelings as frustration or anger, whereas women tend to label their feelings as sadness or stress. This difference likely stems from the ways men and women have been taught to label their feelings, as well as gender differences in the social acceptability of certain feelings.
- Men may feel isolated by the experience of infertility since they do not talk about their feelings in the same language as their female partners. Men may have the same reactions as women, but they are socialized to be more reserved about expressing them. They are taught that it is not "manly" to have or express deep emotions, so they try to hide them by denying, avoiding, or distracting their attention from their feelings.

- Women tend to have a greater drop in self-esteem throughout the process of infertility. Because of gender differences in socialization, women's self-image is likely to be more negatively affected. Infertility attacks their sense of competence and completeness more so than it does for men.
- Women tend to be open about their problems and to seek comfort and support from others. Men tend to try to solve problems on their own because they want to appear competent and problem-free. Men may become upset when their female partners tell others about their problems. However, this leaves the female partner with little social and emotional support.

My wife always seems to want to talk about infertility. Since our infertility is male-factor, talking about it just feels like rubbing my failure in my face. I feel like if I complain about infertility then I'm both a failure and a whiner.

- When infertility is detected, women are more likely to take the blame and to attribute the problem to some failure of their own biological system or some past behavior they perceive as a transgression. Even if it has been determined that the male carries the infertility factor, studies show that women still tend to take the blame. Men, on the other hand, are more likely to externalize and blame others.
- Women tend to engage in more problem-focused and escape coping techniques while men tend to employ denial, distancing, and avoidance coping strategies. Women may interpret this lack of emotional display as not caring. Women may also come to resent their male partners for not sharing their feelings and instead becoming absorbed in other areas of their lives in an effort to distract themselves.

I was so angry at my husband for being able to carry on his normal life while I was the one making all the phone calls and visits to the doctor's office, reading books on fertility, and searching the web for information.

My husband says he would be fine not having a biological child and adopting. He seems to have accepted the situation better than I have, which, of course, makes me frustrated and resentful that he could be so "at peace" while I'm so nuts!

- Men are more likely to compartmentalize their feelings about infertility. They are also more likely to distance themselves from the problem or engage in self-control behaviors. Men try to be strong for their wives because it is difficult for them to see their wives in such pain. Men want to fix the problem and may withdraw when they find they can't. This withdrawal can make wives feel abandoned or rejected.

- Women tend to be more sensitive than men to infertility-related triggers such as seeing pregnant women, commercials with babies, and so on. They also tend to become more distressed than men by hearing comments from others about their infertility or reminders of their childless state, such as finding out about a friend's pregnancy.

- Women tend to express emotions while men want to solve the problem. Again, this is likely due to socialization. This difference can cause problems if the woman wants to share her feelings and be validated. The woman may not want to talk about solutions while the man may feel useless if he can't address solutions.

- Women tend to be more dedicated to the goal of having children and to the pursuit of medical treatments in order to do so. This is probably tied to socialization, as well as to the fact that the woman typically undergoes the bulk of medical treatments for infertility, even if the man carries the infertility diagnosis. Because medical treatment for infertility tends to focus on the female, men may feel excluded from the treatment process. This problem is easily addressed by both partners attending treatment appointments together.

- Men tend to adapt better to failed infertility treatments and to the idea of never having a biological child of their own. A life without biological children has less powerful implications for a man, who can create meaning and purpose in other areas of his life, than for a woman, who is socialized to believe that motherhood equals meaning and purpose.

When we ran out of money for IVF, I was like, "OK, let's go the adoption route." It seemed pretty logical to me but my wife got angry and accused me of not caring about having a biological child.

- Women report a greater decrease in sexual satisfaction than men with extended infertility treatment. This is probably because women are more likely the subjects of medically invasive and intrusive treatment, which can make them feel much less "sexy."

It is very important to note that despite the gender differences we've highlighted, there are many similarities in how men and women respond to the diagnosis and treatment of infertility. Both men and women have painful emotional reactions to the diagnostic process, both experience infertility as a blow to their self-esteem and sense of control, both must find strategies to cope with infertility, both must contend with the ups and downs of treatment, and both view infertility as a threat to their life pursuits and goals.

Table 9.1 summarizes typical gender differences with respect to infertility. The information in this table has been adapted from a number of studies comparing varying reactions to infertility based on gender differences.

ASSIGNMENT 9.2

In what ways do you and your partner fit the above gender stereotypes when it comes to your fertility problems?

_____

_____

_____

In what ways do you and your partner act differently from the gender stereotypes?

_____

_____

_____

In what ways does learning about these typical gender differences help you better understand your partner and his or her behavior?

_____

_____

_____

Table 9.1 Summary of Gender Differences

Issue	Women	Men
Overall	More distressed	Less distressed
Initial reactions	More affected	Less affected
Emotional reactions	Overwhelmed if they can't solve problem	Helpless or useless if they can't solve problem
Labeling feelings	Label feelings as sadness or stress	Label feelings as frustration or anger
Self-esteem and self-image	Greater drop in self-esteem; attacks self-image	Self-esteem and self-image less affected
Expression of emotions	More likely to express emotions	More likely to hide emotions
Telling others	More likely to disclose to others	More likely to be private
Isolation	Less isolated because they seek support	More isolated because they keep private
Attributions	Blame self	Blame others
Coping styles	Problem-focused and escape coping styles Generalize fertility failure to overall failure	Denying, distancing, distracting and avoiding styles Compartmentalize feelings about infertility
Source of support	Turn to partner and others	Turn to partner
Sensitivity	More sensitive to infertility-related triggers	Less sensitive to infertility-related triggers
Communication	Talk about problem	Fix problem or else withdraw
Seeking treatment	More active and committed to treatment	Less active and committed to treatment
Involvement in treatment	Feel involved in treatment	Feel isolated from treatment
Failed treatments	Adapt less well to failed treatments and prospect of childlessness	Adapt better to failed treatments and prospect of childlessness
Sexual satisfaction	Greater decrease with extended lengths of treatment	Smaller decrease with extended lengths of treatment

Tips for Dealing with Gender Differences[10]

Understand Gender-Specific Reactions and Coping Strategies   A little knowledge can go a long way to help you and your partner understand one another's responses to infertility. Work on understanding how gender differences affect your communication and how you interpret your partner's behavior. Instead of blaming, assuming your partner does not

care, or has become an emotional mess, try to understand where your partner is coming from. Remember that most couples experience these difficulties.

Support Your Partner   Human beings tend to believe that others think, feel, react, and cope the same way they do. Based on this assumption, partners may offer, and expect in return, the same kind of support they themselves would find helpful. For example, since men prefer to focus on problem-solving during communication, they may become frustrated when their partner wants to keep talking about feelings and becomes upset at their attempts to offer solutions. When a man talks about his feelings regarding infertility with his female partner, he may misinterpret her failure to offer solutions as her not listening or caring. Instead of assuming, try asking how your partner thinks, feels, and wants to be treated. You can also do your partner a favor by explaining your thoughts and feelings, as well explaining as how you would like to be supported.

> *I realized I had been expecting my husband to think and feel and react as I had been, but this wasn't good for him or for our relationship. We finally sat down and explained to one another how we were feeling and what we wanted. After that, things between us got a lot better.*

Accept and Change   Dealing with gender differences involves a balance between accepting and understanding your partner's differences, on the one hand, and trying to change your response, on the other

hand. For example, consider that women tend to be more visibly distressed while men tend to avoid or distract themselves from the problem. Conflicts can arise in the relationship if the woman interprets the man's avoidance as not caring and the man interprets the woman's emotions as being out of control. An ideal solution would be for each partner to allow the other to react and cope in his or her own way, without misinterpreting it or considering it to be some sort of disordered behavior. The solution would involve the woman balancing her emotional response with the rational responses described in Chapter 4, limiting the display of her emotions, and turning to other sources of comfort, such as friends and other relatives. The ideal solution for the man would be to get more in touch with his emotions regarding infertility and make a greater effort to communicate his feelings to his partner.

When my husband and I used to talk about infertility, I would complain and cry while he would try to fix the problem. I told him that I didn't need him to resolve the problem, and he felt relieved by this. I told him that I wanted him to cry and be sad with me, and admit that he really wanted a baby too. I also think he felt relieved by this because he had been trying to hold back his emotions to protect me. Now when we talk about infertility, we share our feelings and validate one another. If he feels less talkative, I understand that he's probably doing it for my benefit. It took us a while to come to this understanding, but it really saved us!

Communicate   Couples should talk constructively as often as possible about their thoughts, feelings, motives, differences, and goals. Limit the amount of time you spend talking about infertility issues. Setting limits will make the talkative partner more concise, and the less talkative partner more willing to listen—and maybe even more willing to talk. It will also allow time for you to rebuild your relationship using the skills described in Chapter 10. In addition, it may be useful for you to set limits on how long you and your partner will engage in infertility treatments before you decide to quit or seek another alternative for having a child.

We used to talk on and on about our infertility. These discussions seemed to go nowhere and ended in my husband throwing up his hands and leaving the room. I found that when we limited out infertility talks to 20 minutes, my husband was open to talking and our discussions were much smoother.

We believe that a couple should never let their perfectly legitimate quest to have their own biological child get to the point where it consumes their marriage and turns into a manic desire to perpetuate one's own DNA at whatever cost. Couples should set limits, be ready for the possibility of failure, and keep an open mind about adoption.

10

BUILDING A STRONGER RELATIONSHIP

Relationships can be difficult, even without the added strain of infertility. Add the many potential sources of infertility-related relationship problems, and conflicts are assured. The difference between couples who are happy and those who are not is not an absence of argument but *how* they argue and patch things up after the argument. The way you handle conflict and differences will impact on the degree of satisfaction with your relationship.

Infertility may cause you to blame or attack your spouse or emotionally disconnect from the relationship. You may feel these responses are justified, given the intensity of your feelings or the lack of your partner's understanding. However, such responses will not help you to have a happy relationship and will keep you from getting the support you need from (and need to give to) your partner during this difficult time. You and your partner need to join forces against your common problem of infertility. The skills taught in this chapter can help you express your feelings and obtain the support you desire from your partner. Instead of suffering separately in silence, you can help each other deal with the painful emotions of infertility.

Half the battle in handling conflict is to learn about common responses to infertility, become educated about infertility treatments, and function as active partners in the treatment process. The other half of the battle involves spending quality time together, learning positive communication skills, and working together to solve problems. This chap-

ter describes ways to make an ally of your partner and achieve the validation and support you both require.

The skills covered in this chapter are based on years of research from the University of Washington.[1] Researchers there have conducted countless studies analyzing the types of couple behaviors that make relationships work, those that contribute to failed relationships, and ways to achieve greater satisfaction in a relationship.

One word of caution before you read on. Even though the couples skills taught in this chapter are clinically proven, they do not work overnight. Change takes time and mastering the skills will require continued and consistent practice. Be patient with yourself and with your partner in this process. Once you start spending quality time together, talking openly, and working through problems in tandem, you will notice that you and your partner will feel closer to one another, allowing you to join forces to overcome infertility.

COUPLE KINDNESS[2]

Couples with fertility problems often get so caught up in dealing with their infertility that everything else, including their relationship, has lower priority. Because infertility is such a strain, couples pull from and take a lot of energy out of the relationship. The problem is that when the energy gets drained from the relationship, without any new energy being put in, the relationship wastes away. A relationship is like a bank account that needs to have balance between withdrawals and deposits. Infertility makes couples take out many "withdrawals" from their relationship, including time, energy, patience, and compassion. Because couples are so busy dealing with the strains of infertility, they very often forget to make "deposits" back into the relationship. Infertility causes a deficit of time, energy, patience, and compassion. This deficit needs to be replaced.

When the relationship balance is out of whack, partners often tend to feel emotionally distant from one another and become increasingly unhappy with their relationship. The more distant and dissatisfied they feel, the less they want to work to make their relationship better. You can see how this might lead to a vicious cycle: You feel distant from your partner so you stop trying, and because you stop trying you become even more distant.

Fortunately, there is a simple solution to this problem: making regu-lar deposits into your "relationship account." This means spending time together, doing nice things for one another, taking breaks from talking about infertility, engaging in activities unrelated to infertility that enhance your closeness as a couple, having sex for pleasure versus for reproduction, and so on. We call these "couple kindnesses." This section details how you and your partner can put these into practice in your relationship.

The Connection Between Couple Kindness and Relationship Satisfaction

Research has shown that most couples feel closer to one another and more satisfied with their relationship when they spend quality time together and lavish couple kindnesses on one another. When couples feel closer and happier in their relationship, they have greater motivation to work hard to tackle their more difficult relationship problems. Couple kindness should become a regular part of your relationship.

We were so focused on our infertility that we forgot about one another. Once we started to spend some quality time together it became clear that we already had a family— each other— and that we had to focus on nurturing this family, too.

How to Know What Makes You and Your Partner Feel Close

The best way for you and your partner to understand what makes the other happy is to talk about it openly. It would be nice if our partners automatically knew what we wanted, but most of us are not married to mind readers. It is really not fair to expect our partners to know our changing needs at all times. Some of you may be reluctant to make specific requests of your partner because you fear that she or he will comply with your request only out of obligation, which will detract from compliance with the request.

As common as this attitude is, it is also a huge disservice to your partner! You are putting your partner in a no-win situation. You blame your partner for not knowing what you want but you're not willing to tell him/her how to improve. Is this fair? It is important to remember that even if you specify what you want, your partner still has the power to decide whether or not he/she will comply with your request. At least then your partner can focus efforts on things that please you and stop wasting effort doing things that do not. Furthermore, isn't there something special about a partner who is willing to comply with your request even if it is something they would not have thought of doing on their own?

When you and your partner talk about the types of things that make you feel closer to one another and happier in the relationship, consider

ASSIGNMENT 10.1

Talk with your partner about what makes him or her feel closer to you and happier in the relationship. Make a list of the things your partner describes. Pick one or two items from this list and carry them out each day for at least the next two weeks to complete your couple kindnesses.

_____

_____

_____

_____

behaviors and activities that fall into the following categories: compliments, affection, sex (for fun, not for procreation), time spent together, time spent alone, recreational activities, projects, hobbies, household tasks, financial decisions, work or school, personal appearance, personal habits, and communication.

For example, under the compliments category you might tell your partner that it makes you feel happy when he or she compliments you on your cooking, your appearance, or your breakthroughs at work or school. You could tell your partner that you really enjoy when he or she dresses in a certain way, does his or her hair in a particular way, or wears your favorite cologne or perfume.

How to Communicate Requests

It is important to remember a few guidelines when you and your partner request couple kindnesses from one another.

- Be assertive in communicating your requests, but don't be demanding.
- Use phrases such as "I would like you to…," "I would appreciate it if you would…," or "Would you please…"
- Use language that is specific. Don't say, "I'd like you to spend more time with me." Instead, try, "I would like you to take me out for dinner on Saturday night."
- Use language that is neutral and not threatening. Saying "You never tell me I look good anymore" is not the best way to get your partner to start complimenting you. Instead, try saying, "It makes me feel so good when you compliment me on how I look. Would you please compliment me more often?"
- Remember to focus on the kinds of things that make you feel happy and closer to your partner. Save the things that make

you feel unhappy and distant for the skills that will be taught later in the chapter.

- Make sure your requests are not expensive in terms of time, money, or emotional resources.

Another approach is to come up with a list of things you think your partner would enjoy. These things should also be low cost in terms of cost, time, and emotional resources required to carry them out. They should have no negative emotional history associated with them—i.e., they should not be the subject of repeated arguments or previous disappointments in the past.

In order for the couple kindness technique to work, both partners must take responsibility. The giver must be aware of the recipient's needs and provide the behaviors that the recipient finds pleasing. The recipient must notice what the giver is doing and reward the giver's efforts by verbalizing how thankful they are. If your partner is going out of his or her way to do nice things for you, and you fail to notice or express your appreciation, your partner will most likely stop doing those nice things. Criticizing your partner's couple kindnesses is a sure way to get him or her to stop doing even the couple kindnesses that you do like. Your dual responsibility is to be both a good giver and a good receiver! You might leave written notes of gratitude for your partner saying, "I appreciated it when you called me at work to tell me you were thinking of me."

In addition to maintaining the giver–recipient aspect of couple kindness, it is also important to engage in activities that are mutually pleasing to both partners. For example, engaging in sexual activity can be a mutually pleasing activity. Engaging in companionship activities is also important to your relationship. Companionship activities include

---

ASSIGNMENT 10.2

Make a list of the things you think your partner would enjoy. Pick one or two items from this list and carry them out each day for at least the next two weeks to complete your couple kindnesses. Notice the effect that it has on your partner and on your relationship satisfaction. If you find that something you thought would make your partner happy is not working, modify your list.

_____

_____

_____

_____

ASSIGNMENT 10.3

Make a list of the things you and your partner find mutually pleasing. Together, pick one or two items from this list and carry them out each day for at least the next two weeks to complete your couple kindnesses.

_____

_____

_____

_____

---

mutual projects and recreation like walking, hiking, camping, playing tennis, golf, etc. The best way to decide on mutually pleasing activities is to compare lists after each partner has made his or her own list. You can participate in activities that used to please both of you while you were dating. And you can try shared activities that are new to both of you, such as golf or dance lessons.

Using Couple Kindness as Prevention

Some couples have patterns of "down times" in their relationship. They may be certain weekdays, weekends, holidays, etc. Down times tend to be a reality for couples engaged in infertility treatments such as IVF, where great hope is followed by great loss if the treatment fails. If you can identify the down times in your relationship and anticipate when they are likely to come up, you can try to counter them with a surge in couple kindness activities. For example, when you're about to get the results of an IVF procedure, you can plan to a number of pleasurable activities with your partner. Engaging in couple kindnesses can help cushion the blow of bad news and improve your overall relationship and sense of closeness with your partner.

FOSTERING BETTER COMMUNICATION WITH YOUR PARTNER

The skills listed here will teach you to connect with your partner when you try to discuss difficult topics such as infertility.

Communication Skills

Most people assume that good communication skills somehow come with being in a long-term relationship. Individuals figure that because they get along just fine at work or with friends they have good communication skills. They also regard their partners as capable of clear communication in a relationship. However, the abilitiy to listen empathically, communicate your understanding to your partner, validate your partner's feelings, and express your own feelings does not come magically or easily. These skills can be more difficult in the context of a relationship in which emotions run high. Infertility further complicates communication. Even ordinarily happy couples struggle with how to talk about their feelings regarding infertility.

Researchers[3] who have studied the components of effective communication have put together a series of communication skills to help couples understand one another and express their feelings more clearly. These skills have been shown to be clinically effective in helping couples achieve happier relationships. Study the skills detailed here and think about how they can apply to your situation. Most important, you must practice them as often as possible. As with any other skill, you will need to practice until you become a professional. This will require patience; changes in communication patterns take time.

Listening   Listening is more than just hearing. It encompasses actions that do not involve words. These nonverbal behaviors include:

- Bodily orientation toward your partner, not toward the TV or anything else;
- Undivided attention, not trying to listen while you're doing or thinking about something else;
- Eye contact with your partner as he or she is speaking; and
- Alertness to the content of discussion, not falling asleep or spacing out.

Reflecting   This means conveying your understanding of what your partner is saying. Often, half the battle is to let your partner know that you understand his or her perspective, even if you don't agree. Reflection does not mean responding to the content of your partner's remark, agreeing or disagreeing with it, getting defensive, or trying to fix the problem. Reflection is verbally showing your partner that you understand what he or she has said. Reflection is akin to paraphrasing what your partner said in your own words, but with the additional and necessary component of conveying empathy.

Conveying empathy means including a comment about the emotional state that may be underlying your partner's words. For example, your partner might say, "I found out today that my best friend is pregnant. I feel happy for her, but why hasn't it happened for us? They haven't even been trying for very long, and it just doesn't seem fair!" A nice reflection would be, "Sounds like you're having some mixed feel-ings about her pregnancy. I imagine you might feel happy yet jealous and angry. Is this right?" Such reflection conveys sensitivity to both the content and the emotions behind what your partner is saying. Rather than assign feelings to your partner, reflection makes an educated guess and then checks it out. Thus, good reflections should involve the follow-ing components:

- An accurate paraphrase of the content of your partner's comment.
- Your best guess of the emotions associated with your partner's comment.
- An emotional inference conveyed as a possibility, not as a fact.
- A question about whether the reflection is accurate.

A good reflection should avoid the following components:

- Assigning feelings to your partner's comments, especially with-out checking them out with your partner.
- Reading something into the comments that your partner did not intend.
- Using reflection as an opportunity to contradict or discount what your partner said.
- Using reflection to manipulate and/or control your partner.
- Negatively evaluating the comment or the emotion.

Validating Expressing validation for your partner's comments involves conveying your understanding and giving the comments legit-imacy. Psychologists[4] have defined a number of levels of validation:

- The most basic forms of validation include paying attention to your partner, reflecting his or her comments, and verbalizing the feelings you think are associated with the comments.
- You can also validate your partner's feelings by understand-ing them in terms of your partner's history. For example, your partner might come from a religious background where rais-ing children is an important part of life. You can validate your partner's pain and fear at the prospect of not being able to have children by saying, "It makes sense to me that you would feel that way given your religious background. Everyone in your religious community has big families, and they are always talk-ing about how important family is. It sounds like you feel sad

that you can't be a part of that and fearful of how you can make sense of life without children."

- Other forms of validation include understanding your partner's behavior, given the situation in which it occurred. For example, if your partner is at a family reunion with lots of children and relatives badgering him or her about when you are going to have babies, natural reactions would include anger and sadness. You could validate by saying, "Of course you would feel angry; anyone in that situation would be really frustrated."
- The highest level of validation involves mirroring the feelings expressed by your partner. You not only validate their feelings but tell them that you understand and share his or her reaction. These expressions of validation include saying, "I would have felt/said/done the same thing," or "I'm upset about that, too." For example, when your partner gets news of a failed IVF procedure and shares his or her sadness with you, you can simply say, "I know; that makes me feel sad, too."

It is important to note that validation does not necessarily mean agreeing with the comment. You should strive to understand and validate your partner's feelings, even if you don't feel that way yourself. For example, if your husband came from an adopted family that gave him a good life, he might feel very strongly about adopting. You can validate his desire to create a good life for a child just as his adoptive parents did for him, even if you fundamentally disagree with the idea of adopting a child of your own.

Sharing Feelings   Talking about personal feelings can be an important part of a satisfying relationship. This involves being extra mindful of what you and you partner are feeling, putting words to the feelings, conveying them to your partner, and hopefully receiving validation for expressing these feelings.

Offering Positive Expressions   Relationships in distress tend to be marked by lots of negative expressions and lack of positive expressions. Making statements that convey affection and caring are very important. Although initial stages of couples' relationships are full of such remarks, they tend to drop off over time. Some people just assume that their partner knows how they feel, so they think they don't need to say it anymore. However, it is wonderful under any circumstances to hear your partner verbalize his or her affection and caring for you. It may be as simple as saying, "I love you," "I was thinking about you today," "I missed you," etc.

Giving praise and compliments to your partner is also very important. Take time to notice something nice about your partner or his or her behavior, and verbalize this. You can also express appreciation for something your partner has said or done—how he or she makes you feel better, has made your life happier, or made you a better person. You can express respect for a quality your partner has or convey how much you admire who he or she as a human being. Making these positive statements is a win–win situation for everyone. Positive expressions will make your partner happier. The happier your partner is, the nicer he or she will be to you, and the more likely he or she will be to reciprocate such statements. This will improve the relationship and make you happier also.

Expressing Negative Feelings   Although it is initially more effective to focus on the expression of positive feelings when your relationship is in trouble, there may be circumstances in which it would be beneficial to express negative feelings. The question to ask yourself before you express a negative feeling such as anger or irritation is, "Will this make our relationship better?" If the negative expression will serve only to make you feel better by helping you vent and will make the relationship suffer, then it is probably better left unsaid. Expressions of negative feelings are most likely to be effective under the following circumstances:

- When they specify the cause of the negative feeling (i.e., "I'm angry with you for not making time to come with me to the doctor's appointment," instead of "You're such a jerk! Why don't you ever support me?").
- When the cause is stated as specifically as possible (i.e., "I'm hurt because you don't seem to understand what having a baby means to me," instead of "I'm pissed off because you just don't understand me").
- When the statement is specific to one behavior or occasion (i.e., "I'm angry at you for missing last week's RESOLVE meeting" instead of "You never come to any meetings or support me in the RE treatments").
- When the statement does not include a put-down or judgment (i.e., "You jerk," or "You're lazy").
- When the statement does not include a demand (i.e., "You better not miss another doctor's appointment with me").
- When the statement does not include a threat (i.e., "If you miss another appointment I'm going to leave you").

ASSIGNMENT 10.4

Schedule a time this week for you and your partner to practice the communication skills you've learned so far in this chapter. Take turns practicing being a good listener (with reflection and validation) and a good speaker (expressing both positive and negative emotions). Start by discussing a topic of mild to moderate difficulty in your relationship. Once you've mastered these skills, you can move on to more challenging issues, such as infertility.

We will practice our communication skills on _____ (day/date) at _____ (time.)

HOW TO SOLVE RELATIONSHIP PROBLEMS[5]

Solving problems that come up in relationships seems easy enough to many people. After all, most successfully employed individuals solve what seem to be insurmountable problems all day long. However, your problem-solving skills at work don't always translate so easily at home. In fact, many couples have great difficulty finding mutually agreeable solutions when it comes to relationship woes. This can be especially true in the case of infertility, since it taps into so many other areas of emotions, hopes, goals, and lifelong desires.

All relationships involve conflict from time to time. Good relationships are marked by the ability to resolve disputes in a manner that is acceptable to both parties. Disputes generally involve one partner making a complaint about the other partner's behavior and requesting a change in that behavior. Resolution requires collaboration and compromise on the part of both partners. It may involve making sacrifices about what you want or even sacrifices of your personal freedom. When such compromises and sacrifices are mutually agreed upon, they end up making  both parties happy. So, even the person who makes the sacrifice is happier? Yes, because your sacrifice will make your partner happy, he/she will be likely to act in ways that make you happy, thus creating a satisfying relationship.

Before you start practicing these steps, keep in mind that problem solving will most likely feel awkward at first. You may find it rote, difficult, and complex. You may also find it very different from how you usually handle situations, but that's probably a good thing. If your regular patterns aren't effective, it's better to stay away from them and take a new approach.

The focus of this section will be on the *process* of solving problems and coming to agreements that require change. Some couples can solve problems, but the process they have to go through to do so may leave one or both parties feeling frustrated, angry, resentful, or like they've been manipulated. For example, some couples get into a rut in which one partner escalates an argument and the other partner gives in just to get the escalating partner to stop. Some couples start arguing about one problem and get side tracked with other problems, often throwing everything but the kitchen sink into the argument.

The Best Setting for Problem Solving

Problem solving is not a task that can be done anywhere or at any time. To achieve the best possible results, you need to create optimum conditions for problem solving. Typically, the best time to work on solving a problem is when you and your partner are alone, are not tired/sick/hungry/etc., are not likely to be bothered by distractions, and have enough time to talk over the problem thoroughly and go through the steps of problem solving. However, avoid spending more than an hour talking about a problem to ensure that you don't get tired or burned out. Many relationship experts[6] in the area of infertility recommend spending no more than twenty minutes discussing infertility-related problems. If you go through the steps correctly, it should take no longer than twenty minutes to solve problems.

Although it may be tempting to talk about the problem when it occurs, this generally is not an optimal time since it is likely that you and/or your partner will be highly emotional. People don't tend to think most clearly when emotions run high. It is better to wait until both parties have had a chance to calm down and think about the problem. Some couples have a "24-hour rule" for the maximum amount of time they have before re-engaging the discussion. You might adapt a similar rule for a cooling-off period that makes sense for you and your partner. The more proficient you become at problem solving, the closer you can schedule your problem-solving discussions to the actual arguments.

The best place for problem-solving discussions is one in which you will have comfort and privacy, such as in your home. Avoid talking in public places where others might hear your conversations, such as in relatives' homes or restaurants.

What's Your Problem-Solving Attitude?

Do you see arguments as a power struggle, with the person who compromises the loser and the person who gets his or her way the winner? Do you see your partner's problems with the relationship as his/her problems and your problems with the relationship as your problems? If you start problem-solving discussions in this frame of mind, you will likely not be effective. Instead, try to remind yourself that because you and your partner share a relationship, there is no "winner" or "loser" in an argument. The person who "gives in" may be facing a short-term sacrifice, but in the long run everyone will benefit from the compromise.

All problems that come up in a relationship are *shared* problems. There is no "my" problem or "his/her" problem. If one partner is unhappy, it will likely affect how good a partner he or she is, which will affect the relationship and the other partner adversely. Starting your problem solving in a frame of mind in which you realize that all problems are mutual and that problem solving requires collaboration will allow you to come up with mutually satisfying resolutions.

How to Solve Problems: Tips from Pros Who Know

The following tips are offered to help you and your partner breeze your way through problem solving. These tips are based on years of studying couples and analyzing the types of behaviors that lead to successful problem resolution and satisfied relationships, as well as the types of behaviors that lead to destructive arguments and unhappy relationships. As with the other skills taught in this chapter, the problem-solving skills below have been tested and proven to be clinically effective in helping couples solve their relationship problems and create happier relationships.

The first thing you need to remember is that there are two separate phases of problem solving: the problem-definition phase and the problem-solution phase. During the problem-definition phase, the goal is for you and your partner to agree on a clear and specific definition of the problem. The goal of the problem-solution phase is to come up with a solution agreed upon by both partners. These phases must be kept separate. This means that you must avoid trying to get at solutions during the problem-definition phase and avoid further analyzing the problem during the problem-solution phase. This distinction between phases is very important because it has been found that problem solving can become destructive if the phases overlap.

Tips for the problem-definition phase:

Tip 1: Always compliment before you complain. Start off with something positive when bringing up a problem. Your partner will be much less likely to become defensive or counterattack if you begin by saying what you do like about your partner and his or her behavior. We like to remember this tip with the song, "A spoonful of sugar helps the medicine go down." People are much more likely to comply if they know their efforts are being noticed and appreciated. Compliments and praise are very powerful in creating and maintaining behavior change. Furthermore, the two of you will be much more likely to be in a collaborative mode if you start off by accentuating the positives. Compliments and expressions of appreciation will go a long way toward setting the stage for an effective problem-solving discussion.

Tip 2: Be explicit when describing the behavior that upsets you. State your concerns in terms of specific behaviors and examples of those behaviors. Instead of making a generalization such as "You don't care about me anymore," be precise in describing what your partner does or doesn't do that makes you feel not cared about such as, "You haven't come to the last four doctor's appointments with me." The more explicitly you state the problem, the clearer your partner will be about what upsets you. Being specific will also reduce the chances of having one of those arguments when you fight about everything but the kitchen sink.

Tip 3: Avoid labels and judgments. In addition to making your partner defensive, using labels will confuse the matter. Telling your partner he or she is "emotionally unavailable" is both a label and a judgment. Your partner will not know what exactly he or she did or said to make you think this. It would be better to say, "After we came back from Michelle's baby shower and you didn't talk about your feelings, it was hard for me to understand what was going on with you."

Tip 4: Avoid exaggerations and extreme words. The following words are best deleted from your vocabulary during problem-solving discussions: always, never, all, none, etc. Using these words will only make your partner defensive and sidetrack your discussion so that it involves situations that are contrary to your criticism instead of being a collaborative discussion about the specific situation in question. Furthermore, it will likely make your partner feel invalidated about occasions when he or she has not behaved in the manner you are criticizing.

Tip 5: Address the behavior, not your partner's personality. In describing the problem, be sure not to attribute it to personality traits of your partner. Confine it to specific behaviors. For example, instead of calling your partner "selfish," state that it hurts your feelings when they don't want to go to RESOLVE meetings with you. Behaviors are much more likely to change than are personality traits.

Tip 6: Tell your partner how you feel. When you express your feelings be sure to make a clear connection between the problematic behavior and how it makes you feel. Your reaction was triggered by a specific behavior. Making this connection will help you communicate what your partner does to make you feel a certain way. Try using the phrase, "When you _____, it makes me feel _____." For example, you might say, "When you aren't willing to talk about our infertility it makes me feel alone in this problem."

Tip 7: Fight your pride and acknowledge your role in the problem. Most couples' problems are the result of an interaction between both partners. Even if your partner's behavior is what upsets you, your behavior may unintentionally set the stage for your partner's response. Consider what you did to contribute to the problem and confess to your role in it. Owing up to your responsibility is much more effective than pointing fingers and blaming your partner. Admitting your role will make your partner less defensive and will prime him or her to do the same, ensuring that the two of you collaborate against the problem, instead of against one another.

Tip 8: Don't be a "Chatty Cathy." Be as brief and concise as possible when defining the problem. Don't get stuck in the trap of spending the majority of your problem solving discussion trying to define the problem, giving umpteen examples of it, dredging up related problems from years ago, or trying to answer the all-too-philosophical question of "why" it happens. Spending too much time on the problem will take away from time necessary to talk about the solution. The longer you spend on problem solving discussions, the more tedious and aversive they will become, and the less likely you will be in the future to engage in problem solving.

Tip 9: Avoid getting defensive during the problem-definition phase. When your partner brings up a problem, you may be tempted to defend yourself. This is not effective in the problem-definition phase. The fact that your partner perceives it as a problem, even if you disagree, makes whatever it is a problem in your relationship. One form of being defensive is to talk about your good intentions. Again, the bottom line is that your partner finds your behavior problematic, even if your intentions were the best. Thus, it *is* a problem.

Tips that apply to both the problem-definition and problem-solution phases:

Tip 1: Stay away from the kitchen sink! Limit yourself to discussing only ONE problem at a time. While problems often are interrelated, tackling more than one problem at a time will confuse matters, overwhelm you, and sidetrack your attention from the matter at hand. Pretty soon you will be arguing about the details of some other dilemma instead of discussing the original problem. Sidetracking can take the form of being defensive, counterattacking, bringing up examples from the past, talking about the involvement of others not directly related to the issue, etc. If you notice you and your partner straying to a different issue, you can say, "That's important too, but let's finish talking about X first before we talk about that."

Tip 2: Use your listening skills, reflect, and validate. Before you respond, it is crucial that you have an accurate understanding of what your partner said. The best way to do this is to paraphrase what you understood and ask if you got it right. Paraphrasing will force you to listen carefully so that you can accurately summarize your partner's comments. Only when you paraphrase and your partner tells you that you're on target should you respond to what was said.

Tip 3: Don't be a mind reader. Avoid making conclusions about what your partner thinks or wants, what his or her true motivations are, what he or she will do in the future, etc. You may think you know your partner well enough to do this, but there is a possibility that you could be wrong. Nobody likes to be told what they think, want, etc. Instead, focus on the facts, including what you have observed with your own eyes and ears.

Tips for the Problem-Solving Stage:

Tip 1: Look to the future. Once you've finished with the problem-definition stage, close the door behind you, lock it, and don't look back. Your focus now should be on solutions that are future-oriented. This means no more talking about definitions or examples of the problem that are oriented in the past. The main question to ask at this point is, "What can we do to make this problem better and/or keep it from occurring again?" Brainstorm with your partner and generate as many different solutions as possible. Let your imagination run free; don't allow yourself to be limited by any constraints at this stage of problem solving. Even absurd solutions are welcome. As you think of different alternatives, write them down. Once you have as many solutions on your list as you can think of, go over them and eliminate those that would not be possible or are not reasonable. This leaves you to consider how you could implement the remaining reasonable solutions.

Tip 2: Think "how" not "why" as you generate solutions. Trying to figure out why your partner is not as affectionate as you'd like or why your partner is so emotional is not an effective use of problem-solving time. Instead, focus on how your partner could do things differently or how you can learn to understand and accept your partner's behavior, or a compromise between these alternatives. The bottom line is that regardless of the answer to the "why," the "how" to make it better will be the same. Insight is nice, and often interesting, but it is not necessary to the problem-solving process. So skip to the "how." You can figure out the "why" when things are better.

Tip 3: Compromise, compromise, compromise. When generating solutions, it is very important for *both* partners to compromise. The best types of solutions occur when both partners give a little, even if the solution obviously calls for change on the part of one partner only. So, when you are about to ask your partner to change some aspect of his or her behavior that bothers you, start by offering to change some aspect of your own behavior. Another way to come up with a compromise is to look for solutions that both you and your partner are willing to implement and those that you both are unwilling to implement. Agreeing on these commonalities will help you collaborate and compromise in your problem solving.

Tip 4: Less is more, really. If you expect your partner or even yourself to make a 180-degree change overnight, you're only setting yourself up for failure. When people feel overwhelmed by, or fail at, change, they will be less likely to commit to making more changes. Change is not easy for anyone. It generally happens very gradually and requires patience. Thus, when you are working to generate solutions that require change, be sure to avoid asking for sweeping changes. Consider what you'd like your partner to do differently in an ideal world versus what you would be willing to accept for now. Ask for the latter. You can always ask for more later. For example, perhaps your partner has never come to a RESOLVE meeting with you and you want him or her to come to all the meetings. Asking your partner to change from being unsupportive to being 100% supportive is a bit much. It would be more effective to ask him or her to come to one meeting per month. Your partner will be much more likely to comply with a request for change they feel is not too big.

Tip 5: Realize that not all solutions to problems involve change. Some very effective solutions center around accepting the status quo—understanding where your partner is coming from, why their behavior and your acceptance is important to them, and validating that even if you don't agree. Acceptance is just as powerful and profound a solution as change.

Tip 6: Talk about the pros and cons of each solution you generated. Consider the consequences that each solution would have on you, your partner, and your relationship. Be sure to include both short-term and long-term consequences. Weigh the pros and cons and select the best possible solution.

Tip 7: Spell it out. Once you agree on a solution, be sure to spell out in the most clear and specific language what each partner has agreed to do differently, when they have agreed to act differently, and how often. The more specific you are, the less likely you will be to argue over interpretations.

For example, a poor solution would be, "We will try to save more of our monthly salary to pay for infertility drugs." To make this solution more specific, try, "We will set aside 15% of each of our salaries every month and create a fund to be used solely for infertility treatments." Another poor solution would be, "Howard will be more understanding of Julie's feelings." You need to specify what Howard will do differently to be more understanding, such as, "Howard will use his communication skills of listening, reflecting, and validating when Julie talks about her feelings. He will also refrain from trying to 'mind read' or judge her feelings during these discussions." Yet another poor but all too frequently used solution is to say, "Sean will try to be more supportive of Kristen's feelings about their infertility treatments." What the heck does this really mean, anyway? It is far better to spell out what, exactly, Sean will do to demonstrate his support of Kristen. Try, "Sean will initiate at least two discussions per week, on Wednesday and Sunday nights, on how Kristen is feeling about the infertility treatments. He will also attend at least one appointment per month with her." Be sure to write down these agreements and place them in locations where they'll serve as reminders for you to implement the agreements.

Tip 8: Shower praise on your partner for honoring the agreements. Be sure not only to notice that your partner is behaving differently to honor the change agreement, but to compliment him or her on the changes. You can simply say, "I noticed that you made arrangements to come to the RESOLVE meeting with me, and I really appreciate it." You can also let your partner know how the new behavior makes you feel better, such as, "It really helps me to feel close to you when you open up to me." The more you notice and compliment your partner's new behaviors, the more likely your partner will be to feel appreciated and continue to engage in these new behaviors.

Summary of Problem-Solving Tips

Problem-definition phase:
- Always compliment before you complain.
- Be explicit when describing the behavior that upsets you.
- Avoid labels and judgments.
- Avoid exaggerations and extreme words.
- Address the behavior, not your partner's personality.
- Tell your partner how you feel.
- Fight your pride and acknowledge your role in the problem.
- Be brief and concise when defining the problem.
- Avoid getting defensive.

Problem-definition phase and problem-solution phases:
- Discuss only one problem at a time.
- Use your listening, reflection, and validation skills.
- Don't be a mind reader.

Problem-solution phase:
- Focus on solutions.
- Think "how," not "why," as you generate solutions.
- Compromise, compromise, compromise.
- Start with smaller requests for change.
- Realize that not all solutions to problems involve change.
- Talk about the pros and cons of each solution you generated.
- Spell out the agreement.
- Shower praise on your partner for honoring the agreement.

Practice Your Relationship Techniques

Now that you have studied some state-of-the-art techniques to improve relationship satisfaction, it is time to put them to work in your own relationship. We hope that you have been practicing all along, but just in case you haven't, here's your big chance. The techniques in this book won't do a thing for your relationship unless you practice putting them into action. You are reading this book because infertility is taking a toll on your relationship and you want to learn new ways to make your relationship better. You can either put this book away now and continue to suffer through the unfortunate problems in your relationship, or you can take advantage of these clinically proven methods for improving your relationship. It is up to you to decide what to do with these relationship techniques.

ASSIGNMENT 10.5

Your homework is to use the couples skills described above to discuss the infertility-related problems in your relationship. You may want to start with smaller problems and work up to the larger problems as you and your partner gain more practice using the skills. When you look at the list, your first thought will probably be, "I don't even want to go there!" While this is understandable, we can promise you that you will have to address these issues at some point during the course of infertility. It is far better to address them up front, while you and your partner are getting along, rather than while you are arguing over them. You can tackle them slowly, one by one. Following is a list of some of the larger issues. Practice talking about these issues as they apply to you and your partner:

- What the following mean to you: fertility, infertility, parenting, childlessness, adoption, masculinity, femininity, marriage, and life. Don't just define these terms. Be sure to cover the emotional or deeper associations, connotations, implications, and potential consequences of each term. What did you grow up learning about these issues? What messages did you receive, and continue to receive, about these issues? How is your meaning of these words affected by your infertility?
- How much each of you wants to have children, and your thoughts about having your own biological children versus using a third-party donor or adopting.
- Your thoughts, feelings, and reactions regarding fertility problems.
- Your thoughts and feelings about who is carrying the infertility factor and who is undergoing the bulk of medical treatment.
- How you and your partner can negotiate the different ways you cope with infertility.
- Decisions about who to tell and how much to tell others about infertility, as well as how to handle friends and family members.
- Decisions about treatment, including what treatment options to pursue, how long to pursue them before switching to another type of treatment or stopping, when to quit treatment, feelings about third-party reproduction or adoption, and so on.

- Decisions about the invasiveness level of infertility procedures you and your partner are willing to tolerate, as well as the possible side effects of each treatment.
- Decisions around the possibility of multiple births, selective reduction of fetuses, and caring for multiples.
- Financial decisions, including how much money to spend on infertility treatments, when to stop spending, how to pay for the treatments, and whether and how much to tap into savings, go into debt, or borrow.

Nobody can change for you. You must make an individual commitment to work as hard as possible to make the relationship better, regardless of what your partner is or isn't doing. If change is going to happen in your relationship, you're the one who has to start trying. Even if your partner is less supportive than you'd like, you have a responsibility to give all you can. We certainly hope you choose to implement the techniques taught in this chapter. There is no reason for couples to suffer unnecessarily when there are ready-to-use methods available to help them. After working with many couples, we know that relationship change is not easy. But, it is possible!

SEXUAL RELATIONS

Most couples with infertility experience problems in their sexual relationship. The experience of infertility can put a damper on sexual relations that previously felt passionate, romantic, and spontaneous. Instead, sex can become very mechanical and can feel like a chore.[7] If you are experiencing problems in the bedroom, you are certainly not alone. Researchers have found that 80% of men experience erectile difficulties at some point in their lives, and that high levels of stress can interfere with sexual functioning. According to a recent study,[8] men experience periods of erectile difficulties in 80% of the cases attributed to male-factor infertility. This research also found that women with ovulatory problems experienced poor body image, feelings of inadequacy, and decreased sexual desirability. Almost half of women polled in another study said that infertility had caused a change in their sexual functioning.[9]

These sexual problems can be frightening and can negatively affect your relationship. However, it is very important to note that while sexual problems such as erectile difficulties and loss of orgasm are very common during infertility, they are generally temporary and short-lived.

The sexual problems usually go away once the emotional distress of the infertility experience has been reduced or eliminated.

Sexual Problems versus Sexual Dysfunction

There is a difference between temporary sexual problems and more longstanding sexual dysfunction. Sexual problems include a temporary lack of sexual desire, erectile difficulties in males, and loss of orgasm in females. These sexual problems are very common in infertile couples and are usually short-lived. Sexual dysfunction involves sexual problems that are persistent and recur over longer periods of time. Sexual dysfunction includes waning or absent sexual desire, disorders in sexual arousal, erectile disorders, orgasmic disorders, premature ejaculation, and sexual pain disorders. All of these can also occur on a temporary basis (and often do with infertility); they are not considered dysfunctional unless they are persistent and recurring. While sexual dysfunction has been implicated in infertility, researchers[10] have found that only 2.6–5.0% of infertile individuals actually have any evidence of sexual dysfunction. Thus, the suggestions offered in this chapter focus on sexual problems, not sexual dysfunction.

If your sexual problems are persistent, have recurred for long periods of time, or preceded your infertility diagnosis, we recommend you seek counseling with a therapist who specializes in sexual dysfunction. In addition, there are many self-help books that can help you overcome your dysfunction. Lonnie Barback has written an excellent book on this topic entitled *For Each Other*. For male sexual dysfunction, we recommend *The New Male Sexuality: The Truth About Men, Sex, and Pleasure* by Bernie Zilbergeld. For female sexual dysfunction we suggest either *For Yourself: The Fulfillment of Female Sexuality* by Lonnie Barback or *Becoming Orgasmic: A Sexual and Personal Growth Program for Women* by Julia Heiman and Joseph Lopiccolo.

Common Causes of Sexual Problems in Infertility

Sexual problems are typically the effect rather than the cause of infertility. Couples often experience mild and temporary sexual problems stemming from various aspects of the infertility experience, as described below.

Sexual Problems Related to Medical Treatment The medical aspects of treatment for infertility can really dowse the flames of romance. Demands for sex on schedule, having to monitor basal body temperature, performance anxiety, side effects of fertility medications, and painful medical procedures are all notorious for destroying a couple's sex life. Most couples report tremendous frustration at having to engage in sex on the doctor's schedule. It is very common for couples to want to make love when they are supposed to be refraining from sex. When couples are supposed to be having sex, they often aren't in the mood or experience performance anxiety. Decreased sexual desire and pressures to perform can lead to sexual problems such as lack of lubrication in women and erectile difficulties in men. Demands for sex on schedule can make women feel like nothing more than "egg donors" and men feel they are wanted only for their sperm.

Keeping a schedule for sex is another common cause of sexual problems. Couples often argue over who should be responsible for monitoring fertility indicators such as basal body temperature and who should be in charge of initiating sex during the fertile times of the cycle. Often the partner who carries the infertility factor will feel responsible for this but at the same time will feel resentment at having to take this responsibility. This can cause further sexual problems and can negatively affect the couple's relationship. Many couples have resolved the argument on responsibility by putting the basal body temperature chart in a place where both partners will see it, thus sharing the responsibility.

Another sexual problem commonly experienced by infertile couples is the association between sex and the pain of medical treatments for infertility. Women may feel that they are being "poked" by their partner during sex just as they are "poked" by the doctor during medical examinations and treatments. Men may experience guilt and subsequent erectile difficulties from having to engage in something as pleasurable as masturbation to do "their part" while their partner must endure physically painful procedures. Pain in sexual organs resulting from medical treatment, as well as side effects of fertility medications, can also interfere with sexual functioning. In addition, having doctors and nurses (and even some nosy family members) inquire about the details of your once private sex life can negatively affect sexuality. All of this can result in the mere thought of sex becoming a painful reminder of your infertility.

Sexual Problems Related to Emotional Aspects of Infertility The emotional aspects of the infertility experience can also interfere with sexual functioning. Common emotional reactions include depression, stress, anxiety, and grief, all of which have negative effects on sexual functioning. Emotional distress and libido typically do not mix well. In fact, most couples respond to the definitive diagnosis of infertility with a period of intense grief in which they do not engage in sexual relations.[11] This lack of sexual desire may stem from feelings of sadness and anxiety associated with grief or from a negative self-image related to carrying the infertility factor. If you or your partner are experiencing sexual problems connected with grief, it is important to allow yourself to grieve

and to respect one another's wishes to forgo sexual relations until both partners are ready. If one partner is grieving while the other partner is ready to resume sexual relations, masturbation can help relieve sexual tensions.

Conquering the emotional aspects of infertility can help you regain your libido and return to a more satisfying sex life. Resuming sexual relations will also maximize your chances for getting pregnant. The techniques described in Chapters 5 and 6 can help improve your mood, and the coping skills discussed in Chapters 7 and 8 can help reduce your stress and anxiety. The skills explained in Chapter 12 will allow you to better understand and cope with your grief.

Sexual Problems Related to Relationship Difficulties Sometimes sexual problems emanate from existing difficulties in the couple's relationship, such as unrealistic expectations about sex, failure to distinguish between sex and reproduction, lack of communication, or gender differences. Western societies glorify sex, and the media shows images of passionate and steamy sex that they would have you believe is an everyday occurrence. Most couples do not live up to this ideal, but hold unrealistic expectations that they should. The reality is that there is no "right" way to have sex and no "correct" number of times to have sexual intercourse. Every couple is different. The only thing you "should" do is what feels pleasurable to you balanced with what is optimal for your fertility if you want to conceive. Resist the urge to compare your sex life with others or with what you believe is the ideal.

Because sex is required for reproduction, the two concepts become so closely associated that most infertile couples forget the difference. Sexual problems among infertile couples often result when partners start viewing sex solely as a means of reproduction and stop seeing it as a natural expression of their love for one another. Under these conditions sex often becomes mechanical and routine. If this is the case for you, then your sex life can be revived by making a distinction between task-oriented sex (sex for conception) and pleasure-oriented sex (sex for love and fun). Researchers[12] have found that helping couples differentiate between task-oriented sex during the fertile days of the menstrual cycle and pleasure-oriented sex during the rest of the cycle helps couples practice sex on schedule more reliably while maintaining their sexual pleasure and satisfaction. Other couples have found relief from their sexual problems after taking a break from keeping basal body temperature charts and engaging in scheduled sex, or taking a vacation from infertility treatments altogether. Some couples even use birth control during these breaks to eliminate the possibility of sex for conception, allowing them to focus fully on sex for pleasure.

Sexual intimacy is closely related to a couple's emotional intimacy. Relationship difficulties such as communication problems, lack of trust, and disagreements over finances often result in emotional distance between partners. Partners who do not *feel* close to one another or who are upset with one another often do not want to *be* close to one another. This is especially true for women, who are more apt than men to equate emotional and sexual intimacy. If relationship problems are the cause of your sexual difficulties, we urge you to use the communication and validation skills described earlier in this chapter to talk with your partner specifically about your sexual difficulties and sexual desires and preferences. The emotional closeness you gain from such communication can rekindle the flames in your sex life.

My wife doesn't seem to understand how important sex is to me, because I don't think it's as important to her. For me, sex and love are just about equal. When she doesn't want to have sex with me I feel like she doesn't care about me.

Differences in how men and women view love and closeness can also fuel sexual problems. Women often feel emotional closeness in the relationship when they communicate well with their partner, receive tenderness and support, and are told that they are loved. On the other hand, men often feel wanted and loved when their female partner shows sexual interest in them and when they are making love. Sex is just as important to men as emotional closeness is to women.

The problems come about when partners project their own ideas about what constitutes loving behavior onto their partner and act accordingly to what they *think* the other partner wants. For example, women may try to make their husbands feel loved by striving to communicate intimately with them, being supportive, and constantly reminding them that they are loved. Men may try to convey their love by showing interest in sex and initiating lovemaking. A partner who does not see his or her efforts returned in the way they are given may misinterpret this as lack of love and caring. Instead of guessing, we recommend that you and your partner talk about your ideas of loving behavior and share with one another *how* you would like to be loved and cared about.

Sex just feels like a cruel joke to me now. At first it was so sexy to be trying to conceive a baby together. But now, after months and months of disappointments, sex just represents failure. Whenever my husband wants to have sex with me, all I can think about is failure.

Other common gender differences can result in sexual problems. For example, the male partner may conclude that the female partner is not interested in sex because she is moody and depressed. If he doesn't initiate sex based on this interpretation, the female partner may perceive this as his not wanting to have sex because her infertility problems make her unattractive. Another common scenario involves the female partner misinterpreting the male's erectile difficulties as a sign that he does not care for her or does not want to have a baby. The reality is that temporary problems in sexual functioning are common and generally have nothing to do with sexual attraction, caring for one another, desire to have a baby, or commitment to infertility treatments. Understanding these common gender differences can go a long way to help you overcome your sexual problems.

After talking with my husband, I finally realized that his desire to have sex was as strong as my desire to have a baby. This realization helped me to stop being so irritated with his sexual advances and understand that he is a normal man.

Tips to Improve Your Sex Life and Maximize Your Fertility

- Remember that it is very common for couples with infertility to experience sexual problems. These sexual problems are usually temporary and will go away once the emotional distress of infertility is reduced.
- Share the responsibilities for monitoring fertility during the cycle and initiating sex during the fertile times of the cycle. The woman can monitor the fertility signs while the man tracks them on a chart. Put the chart in a place where both of you can see it.

- Although most couples do best when sharing the responsibility for keeping track of fertility, some men are unable to function sexually when the demand is too great. For some men, knowing that it is "show time" creates too much pressure for them to "perform." These men may be better sexual partners if they do not know when the woman is ovulating. However, they must be willing to engage in sexual intercourse frequently enough to "catch" the fertile window.

- If your sexual problems result from feelings of sadness, stress, anxiety, or grief, address this emotional distress by using the skills taught earlier in this chapter to increase the emotional intimacy in your relationship. Talk with your partner about your sexual concerns and desires. Increasing emotional intimacy can enhance your sexual relationship, which can in turn maximize your chances of having sex during the fertile times of the cycle and getting pregnant.

- Challenge any unrealistic ideals you may have about how sex should be and how often it should occur. Use the skills described in Chapter 5 to challenge any thoughtless thinking you may have about your sexuality. Don't compare yourself to any ideals regarding masculinity/femininity or the desire for, frequency, or variety of sex. There is no right amount of sex. You need to focus on what makes you and your partner comfortable and what maximizes your fertility.

- Because you are most fertile during ovulation, it is critical that you have intercourse on schedule during this time. Even if sex seems mechanical and you feel like you are just going through the motions, be sure that you don't miss this fertile window. You can use the less fertile times of the month to focus on sex for pleasure versus sex for reproduction.

- If you find that having to engage in sexual intercourse on schedule is taking too big a toll on your relationship, we recommend that you take a break from trying to conceive, especially if there are no age-related fertility factors. If you decide to take a break, you may even want to use birth control so there is no chance that you will be hopeful of conception. During your break, focus on the joy and pleasure of sex for its own sake.

- If typical gender differences are at the root of your sexual problems, try to understand these differences and see the situation from your partner's perspective. Strive to show your partner love in the ways he or she would like to receive it. For women, pleasing your partner may mean showing him that you are interested in him sexually because you find him attractive, not just because you need his sperm during the fertile time of the cycle. For men, pleasing your partner may involve opening up emotionally, being supportive of her emotional reactions, and reminding her how much she is loved. Talk with your partner about how he or she feels and would like to be loved, instead of relying on stereotypes.

- Remember that having sex is not solely for reproduction. Sex can also be a natural expression of your love for one another.
- Remember that making love is not just sexual intercourse. Making love can also involve such activities as holding one another, massaging, kissing, and oral sex.
- Try adding a variety of pleasurable acts to your lovemaking, such as kissing, cuddling, touching and petting, oral sex, massaging, and different sexual positions. These can make your lovemaking more romantic and less mechanical.
- Create a romantic mood by lighting candles, playing romantic music, showering together, wearing sexy lingerie, wearing perfume or cologne, using body lotions, or using sex toys.
- Try different sexual positions or changing the location and time you have sex. Variety can spice up your sex life.
- Read sexual "how to" guides, which can teach you many techniques to heighten your sexual pleasure. You can easily find these in bookstores.
- If your sexual problems persist, consult with your doctor and get a complete physical to rule out any physical problems. If problems still continue despite a clean bill of health, you may want to seek the help of a counselor who specializes in sex therapy.

ASSIGNMENT 10.6

Using the tips above or your own ideas, list what you plan to do this week to spice up your sex life and maximize your fertility.

_____

_____

_____

_____

_____

_____

_____

SECTION IV SUMMARY

- Remember that relationship problems are very common in couples experiencing infertility. Each partner must make an *individual* commitment to work as hard as possible to make the relationship better, regardless of what the other partner is or isn't doing.
- Understand that differences based on gender, culture, and religion may be underlying your relationship problems.
- Infertility is a couple issue, even if only one partner carries the infertility factor.
- Attend as many doctor appointments and RESOLVE meetings together as possible.
- Consider infertility as an "external adversary" against which you and your partner must join forces. This is much better than considering one another as the enemy.
- Resist the urge to pull away from your partner during this time. You are in this boat together and need to understand and support one another.
- Focus on your strengths and your partner's strengths.
- Remember that the experience of infertility brings many couples closer together and makes their relationship stronger.
- Talk to one another regularly about your thoughts, feelings, and reactions to infertility.
- Thoughtless thinking can cause problems in your relationship. Refer to Chapter 8 to counter your relationship-related cognitive distortions.
- Make regular deposits in your "relationship bank account" by spending quality time together that is not related to infertility and by using the couple kindness skills delineated in this section to do kind things for one another.

- Avoid dangerous communication patterns and use the roster of communication skills in this section to effectively listen to and validate one another.
- Use the problem-solving skills given in this section to deal with any differences you may have.
- Consider couple therapy if you still have problems after practicing the skills in this chapter.
- If you are experiencing sexual problems related to your infertility, make use of the tips provided to improve your sex life and maximize your fertility.

V
Infertility
The Mourning After

QUIZ: ARE YOU MOURNING?

This quiz will help you identify the extent to which you are affected by infertility loss, the stage of grief you are in, and how well you are coping with your grief. Respond to the statements below as honestly as you can with a "yes" or "no."

_____ 1. My partner and I have always dreamed about what our child would look like and fantasized about how our lives would be changed by having a baby.

_____ 2. I feel that infertility has taken control of my life.

_____ 3. My fertility problems still shock me, even though I received my diagnosis months ago.

_____ 4. I cannot accept my fertility problems.

_____ 5. Hearing of others' unwanted pregnancies or abortions fills me with anger.

_____ 6. I have tried to make "deals" with myself or God (or a Higher Power) in which I promise some sort of good behavior in the hope of being rewarded with a baby.

_____ 7. I feel sad or depressed after acknowledging each new infertility loss.

_____ 8. My sadness/depression is getting in the way of my ability to function from day to day.

_____ 9. I have accepted my infertility, and I feel hope for the future.

_____ 10. My partner and I hardly ever seem to be in the same emotional place at the same time.

_____ 11. Since my fertility problems started, I haven't been eating well, sleeping well, or exercising.

_____ 12. I try not to let myself feel sad or cry about my infertility.

_____ 13. I don't know how to cope with my infertility losses.

_____ 14. My fertility problems have left me feeling like the world is no longer fair or just.

_____ 15. I feel that my infertility losses have darkened my view of the world.

_____ 16. People around me don't know how to help me through my grief.

SCORING THE QUIZ

The more "yes" answers you gave, the more likely you are to be suffering from "mourning sickness," and the more likely that this chapter can help you survive your infertility losses and grief. Be sure to read through all the responses, even if you answered "no," so you can learn how to avoid some of the common trouble spots faced by those grieving their infertility losses.

Infertility loss (Questions 1–2): The experience of infertility can involve many losses that must be acknowledged and grieved over to successfully get through the emotional crisis. Chapter 11 discusses infertility losses and the normal course of grief, while Chapter 12 offers ways to cope with your grief.

Stages of emotional reactions in infertility (Questions 3–9): The actual and potential losses surrounding infertility tend to create a series of highly charged emotional reactions. Chapter 11 will help you identify the stage of grief you are currently in, and Chapter 12 will supply you with skills to cope with your grief.

Gender differences in grieving (Question 10): If you answered "yes" to this question, you are not alone! Most couples are rarely "on the same page" emotionally in dealing with infertility-related loss. Chapter 11 spells out typical gender differences in grieving and give tips on how to deal with these differences.

Taking care of yourself (Question 11): In the midst of the many emotional reactions involved in infertility, some people stop taking good care of themselves. This section teaches you the importance of self-care during grief and shows how it can be an important coping skill.

Permission to grieve (Question 12): Couples report many reasons for bottling up their feelings about infertility, which is one of the worst things you can do. For better or for worse, the only way to get through the grieving process is to allow yourself to experience and deal with all of the emotions that accompany loss.

Coping with grief (Question 13): Sometimes the grief can feel so overwhelming that it is hard to know how to cope. Chapter 12 offers a number of skills that can help you deal with your grief.

Cognitive distortions (Questions 14–15): Some aspects of grief can be based on irrational thoughts and perceptions. This section will help you identify and challenge these cognitive distortions.

Increasing your positive social support (Question 16): Many people don't know what to say or how to be supportive when it comes to infertility. Chapter 12 provides tips for helping others grieve their infertility losses. You can use these tips to help your partner or friends with infertility, or give it to people around you so they can help you grieve.

11

COMMON SOURCES OF LOSS
AND GRIEF IN INFERTILITY

The experience of infertility can involve many losses, including the loss of what could have been were it not for your fertility problems. Barbara Menning, the founder of RESOLVE, argues that the most common, appropriate, and necessary reaction to the diagnosis of infertility is grief.[1] To successfully get through the emotional crisis of infertility, both actual and potential losses must be acknowledged and grieved. This chapter discusses these losses and describes the normal course of grief.

LOSSES AND POTENTIAL LOSSES IN INFERTILITY[2-6]

The nature of losses and potential losses is widespread because infertility affects so many areas of a couple's life. Below we describe some of these losses.

Loss of Your Dream Child

Many people have ideas and dreams about the child they want. Little girls grow up playing with baby dolls, which represent the qualities and characteristics of a dream child.

> As far back as I can remember, I've always put myself in the motherhood role. I used to play with dolls, I watched my younger brothers and sisters, and I babysat for most of the families in the neighborhood.

Men may dream about teaching their kids how to play ball and may want their sons to follow in their footsteps. As they prepare for marriage, many couples talk at length about the type of children they want and the type of parents they plan to be. The dream child becomes a symbol of the love, unity, and oneness of the couple's relationship, as well as a symbol of their future together. This dream child inherits the best qualities and characteristics of each parent and will grow up to become the best at whatever he or she chooses. The realization that infertility may not allow a couple to have this dream child can be a tremendous loss that must be grieved.

Loss of Experience

Infertility can threaten a couple's ability to have a biologically related child and go through the experiences involved in pregnancy, labor, delivery, and breastfeeding. The couple feels unable to participate in conversations about these topics with other parents—e.g., comparing labor stories at baby showers. This loss of potential experiences must be considered and grieved.

> *Every Thanksgiving I have to listen to my cousins and in-laws talking about problems with their kids while the guys are watching football. I feel so left out.*

Loss of Control

Most people are used to feeling in control of their lives. When they want something, such as an education or job, they work hard to get it. In addition, most people feel they have control over their bodies. If they want to get in shape, they will work out and diet until they are satisfied with their appearance. People even feel that they have control over their ability to have a baby. They use birth control or other methods of family planning until they feel ready to have a baby. So, for most people, it comes as a huge shock to find that they have no control over their fertility. They can't believe that all the effort, intelligence, connections, and sincerity that helped them reach goals in other parts of their lives does not apply here.

The feeling of being out of control may also show up during the course of infertility treatment. Medical treatment for infertility requires you to expose many aspects of your personal life, as well as your body, to infertility specialists and their medical staff. Furthermore, the course of medical treatment, which involves hope often followed by loss and despair, can make you feel out of control emotionally.

> *Up until this point, I have been able to have some sort of control over my life, and now I am spiraling out of control in this IVF world.*

You may also be required to have once-spontaneous sexual relations on the doctor's schedule, and go to appointments regularly. Use of fertility medications can make you feel out of control emotionally.

Loss of Self-confidence

Loss of control can affect your self-confidence. Much of self-confidence comes from knowing that you can achieve your goals. Infertility can feel like a failure to achieve the goal of having a biologically related child. Men with infertility often feel less than masculine, and women with infertility often report that they don't feel feminine. It is not uncommon to hear people with infertility refer to themselves as "defective," "unattractive," or "inadequate." This loss of self-worth and self-esteem must be worked through in the process of grieving.

Loss of Relationships

The experience of infertility can certainly take its toll on a couple's relationship. Even couples that ordinarily get along well and solve problems collaboratively can have their relationship strained by infertility. The partner who carries the infertility factor may live in fear that the fertile partner will abandon him or her and act in ways that make this fear a self-fulfilling prophecy. Depressed, stressed, or emotionally overwhelmed partners may withdraw from one another. People with fertility problems may also withdraw from others, including family, friends, and the fertile world in general.

Infertility can also jeopardize the strength of your faith and affect your relationship with God. You may have doubts about why a loving God does not allow you to have a baby, especially when you have tried so hard to be a good person. You may wonder why this is happening to you while hundreds of other couples are having unwanted babies. You may question the fairness of your infertility and why bad things happen to good people. You may have worries about the meaning and purpose of life now that your ability to have a child is threatened.

The losses affecting relationships—whether with your partner, family, friends, or even with God—must be dealt with in order to move through the process of grief in infertility.

Loss of Status or Prestige

We live in a society where couples, especially married couples, are expected to have children. These expectations are especially prominent among certain ethnic and religious subcultures in our country. Parenting often confers the official status of adulthood, as well as social prestige.

Even though I am older than most of my cousins, my family doesn't really consider me an adult since we don't have children yet.

Being unable to meet these expectations can deprive a couple of the sense of normalcy, fitting in, or of status and prestige in the community. As with other losses, these must be acknowledged and worked through.

Loss of Security

Infertility can jeopardize your sense of security in many areas. We've already addressed how it can affect your sense of self-worth and self-confidence, your relationships, your sense of control over your life, your belief in the fairness of the world, and your faith in God. In addition, medical treatments for infertility can affect your job security since you will likely need time off to go to appointments. If your job involves traveling, you will have to make arrangements to be around during the fertile times of the cycle.

I grew up in a very poor family and promised I would not allow that for my future children. So my wife and I decided to wait to have children until we were financially stable enough to ensure them a life without want. Ironically, the waiting probably caused the infertility, and the cost of fertility treatments is now threatening the financial security we waited so long to achieve.

The cost of medical treatments can also affect your financial security. Many couples have to sacrifice vacations, nicer houses or cars, and other luxuries in order to pay for infertility treatments. The loss or potential loss of these sources of security must be acknowledged and grieved.

Miscarriage

Certainly the loss of a fetus through miscarriage can be intensely painful. Pregnancy brings hopes and dreams about how your life will be different with the addition of this dream child. These hopes and dreams can give you a strong sense of attachment to the fetus. For women, who experience the physical sensations of the fetus growing inside their bodies, the sense of attachment can be even greater. Thus, when the fetus is lost through miscarriage couples often report feeling "devastated."

ASSIGNMENT 11.1

List all the infertility-related losses you and your partner have had to deal with. Acknowledging these losses is the first step in coping with your grief.

_____

_____

_____

_____

Unfortunately, our culture does not recognize miscarriages in the same way we recognize deaths of people who have been born, even if the death involves a baby who is only days old. Couples mourning the loss of a pregnancy often do not receive the benefits of increased community and family support, rituals such as funerals or memorial services, flowers, condolences, or prayers. However, *pregnancy loss is real,* and the grief can be just as great as that experienced after the death of a human who has lived with us for many years.

REPEATED GRIEF

The losses described above are likely to be experienced and re-experienced on many occasions when dealing with infertility. You may experience grief on learning of your diagnosis of infertility and realizing that you may not be able to conceive without the help of medical technology. The losses and potential losses of a dream child, of the pregnancy/birth experience, of self-confidence, and control are prominent areas of grief.

In addition, you may feel grief when the woman starts her period each month you didn't get pregnant, and when you experience failed ART attempts, fetal losses, and miscarriages. What was in your body may not have looked like a baby yet, but it was a baby to you. Depending on your definition of when life is created, there may be special issues of grief involved with fetal losses and miscarriages. Couples who believe that a life is created when the sperm meets the egg may experience just as much grief at learning of a fetal loss during IVF as when a term baby is lost. Couples who believe that a life is created when vital organs begin to function in the fetus will feel tremendous loss after a miscarriage later in the pregnancy. Couples who have repeated miscarriages may also experience anticipatory anxiety of another loss with each new pregnancy.

After repeatedly unsuccessful attempts at becoming pregnant with your own egg and sperm and trying to carry a baby in your own womb, you may experience grief at having to turn to a donor. Using donor eggs or sperm, or both, may involve the loss of a dream child that is fully biologically related to you. Not being able to carry a pregnancy to term and having to use a gestational carrier instead can involve the loss of experience, control, self-confidence, relationship, and social status.

> *I cry every time I think about how handsome, kind, and intelligent my husband is, because I know that he will not be able to pass along his genes to our baby.*

After realizing that pregnancy will be impossible and deciding to stop the pursuit of pregnancy, you will most certainly experience grief. Loss of the dream child, of experience, relationship, control, security, and status may be involved in this grief. At this point many couples begin to consider adoption or child-free living, which also involves a number of losses.

There may be grief when learning of problems in the adoption process. This is especially prominent when the birth mother changes her mind and decides to keep the baby you were hoping to adopt. Many couples form a relationship with the birth mother and keep in contact with her during pregnancy. In these cases, and in cases in which the adopting couple actually has the baby for even a short amount of time before the birth mother changes her mind, the losses are often incredibly painful. Such losses can make a couple leery of the adoption process, of trusting another birth mother, and of forming another emotional attachment with the adopted baby for fear of adoption loss.

> *After everything we had been through with IVF failures and miscarriages, we thought we deserved a "break" with the adoption process. We had the birth mother over for dinner every week and paid for all her medical expenses. When she decided to keep our son, we were devastated. We weren't ready for another loss.*

After all other options have been exhausted and proven unsuccessful, a couple may have no choice but to remain child-free. When this is the case, a tremendous sense of grief will ensue, since it will involve all of the losses described above.

STAGES OF GRIEF IN THE INFERTILITY CRISIS

The multiple losses involved in infertility tend to create a series of emotional reactions in the infertile couple. Dr. Kubler-Ross,[7] an expert on death and dying, explains that the typical reaction to the loss of a loved one involves the following five stages: denial, anger, bargaining, depression, and acceptance.

Specialists in infertility[8-10] have adapted these five stages to the types of losses experienced in infertility, although there are a number of differences between the death of a loved one and the losses involved in infertility:

- Grieving the death of a friend or family member involves memories, whereas grieving the loss of fertility involves unfulfilled hopes and potential.
- When a loved one dies, there is an end point. Infertility seldom has a natural ending point.
- Death involves an irreversible loss, one with closure. However, infertility involves alternating between periods of hope and loss.
- Death of a loved one is a public event that often brings together friends and family to support one another. Infertility, on the other hand, is a private event that often lacks support of friends and family and any public marker of the loss. No such support is available each month upon menses.
- Infertility is stigmatized, and family and friends who are potential sources of support may feel uncomfortable talking about such topics as sexuality. Death of a loved one has no such stigma.

Before describing the stages of grief, it is important to note that these stages are not always experienced by all grievers; nor are they always experienced in the order in which they are presented. The roller coaster nature of infertility treatments, with alternating hope and despair, leads many couples to jump back and forth between the stages. Furthermore, Menning[11] points out that the feelings involved some stages are based on reality and a rational reaction to the pain of infertility. However, other feelings are often based on irrational thinking and cognitive distortions.

Surprise and Denial

Most couples expect to be able to reproduce easily and at the time of their choosing. Few are prepared for the diagnosis of infertility. Thus, the initial emotional reaction experienced by most couples diagnosed with infertility is one of shock and surprise.

I never imagined that I could have such a problem having a baby. It seems to come so easily to everyone else.

The next reaction to infertility is often denial. Most couples cannot believe that the experience of infertility is happening to them. Denial is most pronounced in cases where tests reveal that the infertility is absolute or untreatable. Denial can express itself in many forms—unwillingness to go to the doctor for an infertility workup, blaming your partner for infertility, shopping from doctor to doctor in search of one who will give you a better diagnosis, insisting that the test results were a mistake, denying wanting a child, discounting the importance of the loss, becoming a workaholic in order to get your mind off your infertility, or continuing to buy supplies and furniture for a new baby.

Initially, denial serves an important role. It keeps the infertile couple from being overwhelmed with all the painful emotions that infertility can produce. However, chronic denial is very unhealthy. It can interfere with movement through the stages of grief and thus inhibit successful resolution. Because denial often results in sadness and isolation, prolonged denial can hurt your relationship with your partner and with other potential sources of support. It can also keep you from getting the medical help you need.

One method of reducing denial is to read and educate yourself about infertility. Many people report that their infertility is easier to accept once they learn how common it is.[12] Reading books such as this one, researching infertility on the internet, and talking with others who have fertility problems are ways in which you can educate yourself about infertility.

ASSIGNMENT 11.2

What was your first reaction to learning of your infertility diagnosis?

Are either you or your partner in the denial stage of the grieving process?

If so, what kinds of things did you/your partner do in an effort to deny infertility?

How is denial affecting your relationships with your partner, friends, family members, and the fertile world? Do you believe that this is healthy for you?

Anger

Anger also can follow recognition of a loss.[13] Couples receiving the diagnosis of infertility often are angry because they feel "cheated" out of the fertility they had always taken for granted.[14] Many couples feel that their personal justice has been violated.[15] Some infertile individuals feel angry at life in general or at God for being unjust and threatening their belief that life is predictable and fair.[16] Couples with fertility problems also report anger towards insensitive acquaintances, friends, and family members. In addition, because infertility treatment involves giving over control of your body and your reproductive destiny to a doctor, couples in medical treatment for infertility often report feeling a loss of control. This loss of control and sense of helplessness typically lead to anger.

> *Everything makes me angry. I am angry at my body because it has betrayed me, even though I have worked so hard to take care of it. I'm angry at my husband because he seems so calm while I feel like I'm falling apart. I'm angry at my friends and family because they just don't seem to understand and always say hurtful things. I'm angry at my boss because he won't let me take time off to see a specialist. I'm angry at my co-workers who announce their pregnancies with "we weren't even trying." I'm angry at insurance companies because they won't pay for infertility, even though they pay for Viagra. I'm angry at drug-abusing, child-abusing teenagers who get pregnant at the drop of a hat but don't even want babies. I'm angry at God for letting me down.*

The way in which anger is expressed varies from person to person. Sometimes this anger is directed at the infertility doctor or the fertile partner. Other targets of anger include people who seem to have babies without effort, people who mistreat their children, or people who have abortions. At other times, the anger is directed inward. Some people blame themselves for their fertility problems, attributing their infertility to past behaviors they believe to be "sins" or "transgressions," such as premarital sex or abortions.

In some cases the anger is rational, and appropriately focused. These cases include anger over the multitude of losses in infertility, the inconvenience and pain involved in medical treatments, and the insensitivity of people regarding your infertility. Venting this rational anger can help clarify your feelings and have a cathartic effect. Experiencing your anger is, in fact, *necessary* to get through this stage of grief. Your anger will likely melt away as you allow yourself to confront it or share it with people you trust. We recommend that you either talk about your frustrations and anger with a trusted friend such as your partner or that you write out your thoughts and feelings in a journal. Many people with fertility problems also report finding relief from infertility support groups or from seeing counselors on an individual basis.

In other cases, however, the anger may be irrational and directed at inappropriate targets such as abortion rights activists, people who abuse their children, and even at your own past behaviors. This inappropriate anger is most likely masking underlying feelings of intense sadness, pain, and grief that have yet to be acknowledged.[17] It is important to experience and vent this inappropriate anger so that you can get to the root of the problem and work through the remaining stages of grief.

Anger directed at oneself because of past thoughts and behaviors believed to be sinful is also problematic. These include thoughts or actions involving masturbation, promiscuity, premarital sex, infidelity, incest, same-sex experiences, or abortions. In cases where the anger is directed inward, we encourage you to examine the validity of your conclusions. You may be engaging in thoughtless thinking that has no scientific or medical validity. Please refer to Chapter 2 for further information on the scientific causes of infertility.

ASSIGNMENT 11.3

What kinds of things about the infertility experience make you angry?

_____

_____

_____

_____

How do you express your anger?

_____

Is your anger rational or irrational? How so?

_____

_____

_____

Bargaining

The third stage of grief is bargaining. Bargaining typically involves trying to make a "deal" with God or some Higher Power in which you promise to modify your behavior in the hope of being rewarded with a baby. For example, some couples spend a great deal of time and energy researching infertility treatments and talking with reproductive endocrinologists, hoping that through this effort alone they will be rewarded with a pregnancy. Others vow to improve their physical health by changing their diet and exercising, hoping that then they will be blessed with a baby. Still others may offer good behavior, such as promising to be a perfect parent or volunteering at some organization, in return for having a child. We have heard of couples depriving themselves or placing themselves in emotionally or physically painful situations, such as volunteering for painful or experimental treatments, in expectation of atoning for their sins and receiving forgiveness in the form of a baby.

> *I volunteered for six months in our church's daycare center. I guess I was trying to prove to God what a good parent I could be.*

Bargaining is most likely an effort to postpone the infertility that couples believe to be a punishment from God. It may also be an effort to exercise control over a situation that feels out of control. While bargaining is normal and understandable, it typically represents magical and illogical thinking. All the volunteer work in the world is unlikely to unblock tubes, get rid of fibroids, cure endometriosis, or improve sperm count. We suggest you refer to Chapter 5 to see if your bargaining is based on rational thinking. Bargaining efforts not based on logic are likely to fail, which tends to lead to depression.

ASSIGNMENT 11.4

Have either you or your partner tried to make any "deals" in order to improve your fertility? What have you offered in return for fertility?

_____

_____

Is your bargaining based on logical or irrational thinking? How so?

_____

_____

_____

ASSIGNMENT 11.5

If you haven't already done so, set aside some time to acknowledge sadness over your infertility-related losses. Think through how the losses have made you feel, what they mean to you, and how they could affect your life goals.

Sadness and Depression

Sadness is commonly associated with grief. Acknowledging the many losses involved in infertility can lead to intense feelings of both grief and sorrow. It is important to note that sadness is a normal and natural reaction to infertility. Allowing yourself to acknowledge your losses and experience your sadness will most likely diminish your pain over time and help you to move through this stage of grieving.

I've never cried so much or so easily in my life.

However, while sadness is normal, it can turn into a more serious depression if you are reading some illogical meaning into your infertility diagnosis or are otherwise engaging in thoughtless thinking about your infertility. For example, inaccurate perceptions such as "My infertility means that I'm a failure" or "I deserve this because of my abortion" can turn natural sadness into an unnatural depression. Depression is different from grief and sadness because it interferes with your ability to function in everyday life, including at school, work, and in relationships. Chapters 5 and 6 offer information on combating depression by identifying thoughtless thinking and challenging your inaccurate perceptions.

Acceptance and Resolution

Once the other stages of grief are successfully navigated and the painful feelings are acknowledged and worked through, the final stage of acceptance and resolution is reached. Acceptance of infertility and of the losses associated with infertility does not mean that you stop experiencing feelings of denial, anxiety, anger, isolation, guilt, or depression. Rather, it means that the feelings are no longer experienced with the same intensity. You may notice a return of energy, faith, self-esteem, and sense of humor.[18] Instead of being preoccupied with infertility, it is now only one part of your identity.

We finally realized that "reproducing" did not have to mean passing along our genes. We could "reproduce" by passing along our good

---

ASSIGNMENT 11.6

Do you remember a time when your emotional reactions to infertility were more intense? If so, how are your emotional reactions different now?

_____

_____

_____

What other identities do you hold in addition to being infertile?

_____

_____

What positive lessons have you learned from your infertility experience?

_____

_____

_____

---

qualities and characteristics to the children around us or even to an adopted child.

Focusing less energy on grieving your infertility will allow you to invest more energy in other aspects of your life. You will begin to make plans around your infertility that allow you to get on with your lives.[19] As you develop a new identity that incorporates your losses, you will redefine how you wish your future to be and weigh the options of ARTs, adoption, or remaining child-free.[20]

GENDER DIFFERENCES IN GRIEVING

As discussed in Chapter 9, men and women tend to respond to infertility in different ways. These gender differences also show up in the grieving process. Consider the story of Mike and Marcella. When they learned of their third IVF treatment failure, Marcella was devastated. She felt as though her lifelong dreams and goals of having a family were shattered and wondered what she had done to deserve this. She felt betrayed by her body and believed she had let Mike down. She worried if Mike would still want to be with her. Worse yet, Marcella was paralyzed by her depression and anxiety. The fertility medications she was taking made her emotions even more intense.

Mike could not understand why Marcella, who was ordinarily fairly level-headed, was now "freaking out." He hated to see her in pain and set out to fix the problem. She wanted a baby very badly, so he was going to find a way for them to have one. He carefully researched other medical treatments. He, too, felt sadness over the IVF failure and fear that he would never be a father, but he was careful not to let these feelings show because he wanted to protect Marcella. Marcella saw Mike's emotionless attitude as a lack of caring about having a child of their own. She wanted him to validate her sadness and fear, but instead she saw him as being too "cool" in his search for other treatments. When Mike approached Marcella to tell her about the alternative treatment options he had found, Marcella cried and told him she just couldn't take another loss.

Wanting to protect Marcella from such loss and fearing for her health, Mike responded by suggesting that they quit infertility treat-

ments and look into adoption. Marcella was outraged and hurt. She wondered how he could give up so quickly on having their own biological child. Marcella saw this as more evidence that Mike did not care. Mike was confused by Marcella's anger. Why was she so upset that he had suggested quitting treatment? He was just trying to protect her, but it seemed that everything he did made her feel worse. He hated the frustration, the sense of helplessness, and that everything he did was wrong in her eyes, so he backed off the whole infertility issue. Marcella was now convinced that Mike did not care. She stopped sharing her feelings about infertility with Mike.

The gender differences in Mike and Marcella's story are not uncommon. On the whole, women tend to experience infertility loss more emotionally and intimately than men. Men tend to see infertility as a problem that needs to be fixed. In setting out to solve the problem, men may gain a sense of control over a situation that feels out of control. Society's mandate that men be in control extends to emotional control. Men are expected to "be strong" and "keep a stiff upper lip." They are also taught to be the protectors of the family. If they show their sadness or fear over infertility, they not only are considered weak but also have failed to protect their families.

The story of Mike and Marcella illustrates the importance of being aware of and dealing with gender differences. In looking for and suggesting alternative infertility treatments, Mike was only trying to live up to societal expectations that he be the "fixer." By suppressing his emotions he was striving to remain strong so he could support Marcella and continue to work on their dream of having a family. He suggested quitting infertility treatments not because he did not care, but because he did. He wanted to protect Marcella (and himself) from having to go through another loss. He also was thankful that she was alive and wanted to protect her from the physical risks of another cycle of treatment.

DOS AND DON'TS OF DEALING WITH GENDER DIFFERENCES IN GRIEVING

Don't Expect Your Partner to React Like You Do

Because you are in touch with your own thoughts and emotions, you may expect those around you to think and feel the same way. If they don't, you may judge them as being wrong. However, you must remember that people's thoughts and reactions are partly based on how they have been raised and what society has taught them. You and your partner have been raised differently, so it is likely that you will react differently. Neither of you is necessarily right or wrong; you are just reacting as you have been taught to react.

Don't Expect Your Partner to Be in the Same Emotional Stage As You Are Given gender differences and individual differences between you and your partner, it is almost certain that the two of you will not experience the same emotional reaction at the same time. You may be hopeful while your partner is feeling hopeless. Your partner may be angry when you are feeling depressed. You may be actively searching out new treatment options just as your partner seems ready to quit. Sound familiar? While it may be frustrating that your partner seems to be on another planet, we have found that the different emotional reactions can complement one another and balance each other out. For example, the  partner who is feeling hopeful can help uplift the one who feels hopeless, while the one who feels hopeless can keep the other partner from having unrealistic expectations. Try to use the differences between you and your partner to your advantage.

Don't Judge Your Partner

When you see your partner behaving in a way that you don't understand, it is easy to apply a label (usually negative) to it. Given typical gender differences, men find the emotional reactions of their partners to be "too much" or "too hysterical." They tell them that they are "overreacting," "freaking out," or "losing it." Women, on the other hand, label their partner's lack of emotional displays as "not caring" or "apathetic." It's easy, but very destructive, to label. Applying negative labels to your partner will not further you understanding or closeness. Instead, it will create distance and resentment between you. Instead of using labels, we encourage you to talk through your emotional reactions in an effort to understand where your partner is coming from. This will enhance closeness.

Do Understand Gender Differences

Chances are that your partner is acting the way he or she has been taught by society to behave. Realizing that your partner is acting in a gender-stereotypical manner can go a long way to help you and your partner understand one another's different reactions to infertility-related loss.

Do Talk with Your Partner about Your Reactions

You can help your partner understand and support you more effectively if you explain what you are feeling, where you are coming from, and how you would like to be supported. In return, you can best help your partner by asking the same questions. Couples with whom we've worked refer to these talks as "getting on the same page." Limit the amount of time you spend discussing your reactions. Setting time limits for infertility-related talk can make the more talkative partner more concise and the less talkative partner more willing to listen—and maybe even more willing to talk.

Do Compromise

Dealing with gender differences involves compromise and balance between acceptance and change. On the one hand, you can ask your partner to understand typical gender differences and accept some degree of difference between the two of you. On the other hand, you can try to change your behavior so that your partner can more easily deal with it. Consider the story of Mike and Marcella, in which Mike feels that Marcella is "freaking out" emotionally and Marcella feels that since Mike is too "cool" emotionally he must not care. A compromise in this situation would involve both partners making an effort to understand and accept each other's different emotional reactions. It would also involve both partners making an effort to change. Marcella could try to limit her display of emotions and Mike could try to be more in touch with his emotions and share them with Marcella.

ASSIGNMENT 11.7

How have you and your partner coped differently with infertility-related loss? Do these differences fit with gender stereotypes?

_____

_____

_____

_____

_____

How can you and your partner use the tips given in this chapter to deal with the gender differences in your relationship?

_____

_____

_____

_____

_____

Plan some time this week to talk with your partner about how you can accept and resolve your gender differences. What day and time do you plan to do this?

_____

_____

_____

_____

_____

12

SURVIVAL STRATEGIES
FOR COPING WITH GRIEF

A variety of strategies are available to help you cope with your pain, mourn your losses, and move through the stages of grief. It is important to remember that all people cope and mourn differently, and that there is no right or wrong way to grieve. In addition, coping skills work more or less effectively depending on the persons and situations involved. The roster of coping strategies provided here should allow you to find at least one or two that will be of help.

THE BASICS OF COPING
Take Good Care of Yourself

Because grief can take a toll on your emotional and physical well-being, it is important for you to take especially good care of yourself during the grief process. You will need to be in the best shape possible to handle the stress of grief and loss. Taking good care of yourself will also reduce your vulnerability to more intense emotional reactions, as discussed in Chapters 5 and 6.

Taking proper care of yourself involves treating any physical illnesses. Remember that your physical well-being is connected to your emotional well-being. Very often the last thing you want to do when you're grieving is to eat, but you need a balanced diet to keep up your energy and allow you to cope effectively. Stay away from drugs that can alter your mood, such as excessive alcohol, caffeine, or nicotine. Sleeping too little or too much can make you feel tired, irritable, or groggy. Find the amount of sleep that is best for you and stick with it. Napping may help, too. If you

---

ASSIGNMENT 12.1

List the things you will do this week to take good care of yourself:

_____

_____

_____

---

still have problems sleeping, pick up a copy of *No More Sleepless Nights* by Peter Hauri and Shirley Linde at the bookstore.

Try to get at least 20–30 minutes of aerobic exercise at least 3–4 times per week. Exercise can naturally reduce stress and improve your mood. Engage in activities that make you feel confident, capable, and in control. The experiences of loss and grief can threaten your self-confidence and sense of control over your life. You can balance this by doing things that make you feel good about yourself and more in control. For example, play sports you're good at, engage in hobbies you enjoy, or take on business projects you know you can tackle successfully.

Give Yourself Permission to Grieve

In our experience of working with people who are grieving, we have come across many situations and beliefs that interfere with the ability to fully experience the emotions related to grief. It is easy to get so caught up in infertility assessment and treatment that you don't allow yourself room to have or express your feelings about the situation. Some people try to avoid their feelings of grief for fear that if they allow themselves to experience them, they will become overwhelmed by their pain, lose control, and never be able to recover. While it is true that allowing yourself to experience grief may be very painful, we have never witnessed anybody lose control or be unable to regain their composure.

Another obstacle that we have seen couples run into is the thought that they don't deserve to grieve because they believe they caused their own infertility, or that if they suffer in silence that they will be rewarded with a baby. The reality is that everyone deserves to experience the emotions related to grief. The losses of infertility are just too great to be left ungrieved. There is no scientific evidence that any amount of suffering will lead to a successful pregnancy.

Problems with grieving can also arise when only one partner carries the infertility factor. It is not uncommon for the person who carries the infertility factor to feel that he or she can't express negative feelings about infertility to the other partner, especially if the other partner is undergoing the bulk of the infertility treatments. We have also encountered instances in which the person who does not carry the infertility factor fears that bringing up the topic of grief or expressing negative emotions would be tantamount to "rubbing infertility in the face" of the partner who does carry the infertility factor. Unfortunately, keeping your mindset from your partner can easily lead to feelings of isolation and estrangement. This silence can become a breeding ground for resentment or the perception of not caring.

We strongly encourage you to allow yourself to experience your emotions related to grief and share them with your partner. You simply cannot "escape" your grief. Jim Miller[1] writes that "the best way to handle your feelings is not to 'handle' them but to feel them." If you feel sadness, allow yourself to cry. Crying goes hand in hand with grief. Sometimes a good cry can go a long way to cleanse and heal you. However, you don't need to force yourself to cry. Some people in grief don't feel the need to cry, and this is all right, too. On the other hand, if you feel like laughing, allow yourself to laugh. Research has shown that laughter is quite therapeutic in the grieving process.[2] Don't get stuck thinking that you are not allowed to be happy while grieving or that happiness would betray your losses. If you feel angry, allow yourself to express your anger in a safe way. You can try venting to a trusted person, screaming in your shower (or in the woods, or your car), hitting your pillow, or throwing a temper tantrum on your bed (carefully).

I get together with some of my infertile girlfriends for "venting sessions." We compare stories about relatives announcing their accidental pregnancies at family reunions, co-workers complaining about their children, and crack-abusing women who get out of prison because of morning sickness. By the end, we all feel better and even joke about how we have to be teenagers again and develop a drug habit in order to get pregnant.

ASSIGNMENT 12.2

List the ways you will give yourself permission to grieve:

_____

_____

_____

SPECIFIC COPING STRATEGIES
Talk with Others You Trust

One of the best things you can do for yourself as you grieve is to talk about your feelings with someone you trust. Talking with others will help you clarify and experience your grief-related feelings. The listener can help validate your feelings and support you through your grief. Talking with others will also help relieve some of the pressure you may be feeling, give you a new perspective, and help you keep in contact with others. Be sure to select a listener who is sensitive, caring, and validating. It is best if this listener is your partner, since the two of you are in the same boat and in the perfect position to help one another.

If it is too difficult to talk with your partner even after you have tried the communication strategies outlined in Chapter 10, try talking with a trusted friend or family member. We also recommend talking with members of a support group, such as RESOLVE. You can participate in support groups either in person or online. Infertility support groups can be especially helpful because they consist of people who are likely in very similar situations. These people can validate your reactions and feelings and teach you how they have successfully coped with infertility and grief. Infertility counselors and therapists can also be a great source of help, especially if support groups are not for you, if your grief is particularly intense or long-lasting, or if you are experiencing thoughts of suicide.

Keep a Journal

Writing down your thoughts and feelings related to infertility and grief is another way to get in touch with and confront your emotions. Your journal should focus on your innermost thoughts and feelings about infertility and its losses as you pass through the stages of grief. Try to be as honest with yourself as possible, even though it may be painful. This journal is for your eyes only, so don't worry about censoring your most private thoughts and feelings.

ASSIGNMENT 12.3

List the people you can talk with about infertility and the times this week you plan to talk with them:

_____

_____

_____

Turn to Religion or Your Spirituality

Some couples with infertility report finding strength, support, and guidance through their religious or spiritual beliefs and/or through their religious community. If you are religious, we recommend that you study scriptures, pray, meditate, and/or talk with your clergy about your feelings. Members of your religious community may also provide a source of support. Many people are not interested in organized religion, but have a sense of spirituality. Others find peace in being at one with nature or through performing acts of kindness to people in need. Whatever your convictions, religion and spirituality can help you find consolation and maybe even meaning in your losses.

Creative Outlets

Creative endeavors can help you express your grief and memorialize what has been lost. Centuries of poetry, art, music, and monuments attest to the healing power of creative outlets. Creatively expressing grief can involve translating feelings into words or art. In addition, creative expressions can help improve your mood. Creative outlets include writing (poetry, songs, stories, and letters), drawing, painting, performance art (singing, choreographing a dance, playing an instrument, composing music, listening to music, watching videos, and acting), quilting, sewing, gardening, cooking, building, or woodworking, among many others.

Create Rituals

When someone dies there are many bereavement rituals around the death, such as funerals and memorials. These rituals help the bereaved move through the stages of grief by legitimizing the grieving process, making the loss tangible, mobilizing social support, and providing closure.

> *Whenever I start my period and my husband hears me crying, he comes into the bathroom and gives me a big hug, pants around the ankles and all. I love this man!*

Unfortunately, our society does not offer any such rituals for couples struggling with the losses of infertility or with miscarriages. However, you can create your own rituals to help you mourn your infertility losses. In addition, a number of rituals have been suggested by infertility specialists:

The "Bed and Chocolate" Ritual [3] This ritual was used by a couple to cope with the grief that began each month when the woman started her period. The ritual consisted of her calling her husband with news that she had started her period, leaving work, and crawling into bed at home. Meanwhile, her husband would leave work early, pick up some chocolates and videotapes, and join her in bed. This ritual helped the couple share a comforting experience even when they could not find the words to console each other.

The Imaginary Funeral Exercise Arrange a funeral or memorial service for your infertility losses or your lost baby(ies). You can create this service in your mind or aloud with your partner. Consider who you  would like to be present at the service, how you would feel, and what you would like to be said. Some couples also find it useful to write a eulogy around the hopes and dreams they had for their potential child, as well as the types of parents they hoped to be.

Burial of a Symbol Another ritual involves actually carrying out the imaginary funeral exercise described above. You can buy a doll with the physical characteristics you hoped your baby would have, dress it in the baby clothes you previously bought in a leap of faith, kiss it good-bye, put it in a small box, bury it in your yard, and cry for the loss.[4]

Funeral for a Stillbirth Some couples decide that a funeral and memorial service for their stillborn baby is most appropriate. Naming the child and commemorating its death help to make the loss more tangible and legitimate in the eyes of society. Such a funeral may also help to mobilize friends, family, and other social support to comfort the grieving parents.[5]

Consider What is Most Important to You

Sometimes losses can serve as a "wake-up call" and give you a chance to re-evaluate your priorities. Certainly, having a baby is meaningful to you. However, we urge you to consider what specific parts of having a baby you regard as most important. How important is it that you be pregnant as opposed to being a parent? If parenting is more important to you than pregnancy, you may want to consider options like adoption. How important is it to you to pass along your genes? Again, if this is not as important to you as having a child, you may want to look into adoption. How important is it to you to be a parent as opposed to being a nurturer? Some people find that their need to nurture can be fulfilled by taking care of other people's children, pets, or even plants and flowers.

During our break from infertility treatments, we realized how much we had missed our life the way we had known it before infertility. We realized that there was a world out there without fertility drugs and needles, inseminations, waiting, and loss.

Sometimes the quest for a biologically related child can become so engrossing that a couple can forget about the other things in life that are meaningful to them. We urge you to talk with your partner about the kinds of things that bring meaning to your life and are important to you. If you have lost sight of these things, try remembering what mattered most to you before you knew about your fertility problems, or the goals and dreams you and your partner shared earlier on in your relationship.

Challenge Your Thoughtless Thinking[6]

Some aspects of grief can be based on irrational thoughts and perceptions. Examples include overgeneralizing that life is terrible, blaming past perceived transgressions for your fertility problems, and believing that you somehow could have prevented your fertility problems by doing something differently. Chapters 5 and 7 provide a full description of cognitive distortions and how they affect your mood.

Cognitive distortions can interfere with your grieving and retard your progress in moving through the stages of grief. It is very painful to have basic beliefs about the goodness of life challenged because of infertility. Infertility can make you feel that the world is a terrible place, that life is unfair, and that the self is unworthy. Although these new beliefs are very intense, it must be remembered that they are based on distorted thinking.

Overgeneralized Assumptions and World Views   Researchers[7] have found that grief threatens three assumptions or views that people have about the world. The first assumption, that the world is a good place, often gets turned into thinking that the world is a terrible place as a result of infertility. The second assumption, that the world is fair, changes into thinking that the world is unfair because of infertility. The last assumption that the self is worthy shifts into believing that the self is unworthy. Although it is very painful to have these most basic assumptions challenged, and although the new beliefs are very intense, it must be remembered that the new assumptions are based on distorted thinking—namely, on overgeneralization or overapplication of the original assumptions.

Examining the evidence in a logical manner and thinking in shades of gray can help point out these errors in thinking. For example, list all the good things about the world while not discounting the belief that your infertility is, indeed, terrible. Feeling that the world is unfair can be challenged by reminding yourself that many things in this world are fair even if your infertility is not. Feeling unworthiness as a person is certainly an overgeneralization. Just because parts of your reproductive system do not function as you would like is insufficient evidence to conclude that you are not a worthy wife/husband, man/woman, potential parent, or person.

Faulty Cause–Effect Relationships   Human beings seem to have a need to create cause–effect relationships for events that happen to them. When the cause cannot be readily found in the environment, humans tend to look inward for the cause. The result is self–blame, guilt, and often depression. Unfortunately, this is frequently based on illogical and inaccurate thinking. Scientists who specialize in studying how people think and how they interact socially have identified a number of cognitive errors that people tend to make in creating cause–effect relationships.[8] First, people very often fail to recognize countless potential causes that lie outside of themselves. In addition, people often confuse thinking that they "could have prevented" the loss with "causing" the loss. While it may be true that you *could have prevented* an STD by using a condom, it is not necessarily true that you *caused* your infertility by having unprotected sex. The difference is more than one of mere word choice. It is about accurate and logical thinking.

Monday Morning Quarterbacking   In football it is common for the coach to review the tape of the previous night's game and point out all the mistakes made by the players. Analyzing a situation with hindsight is much easier than trying to predict what could happen. Unfortunately, many people beat themselves up about what they wish they had done differently. For example, one woman with damaged tubes as a result of an infection told us how she wished she had taken antibiotics for her yeast infection instead of relying on homeopathic remedies. Hindsight made it easy for her to see how improper treatment of her infection led to the scarring of her tubes. However, she eventually stopped blaming herself for her fertility problems when she realized that she underwent the treatment that she thought was best at the time. Such "Monday morning quarterbacking" can be challenged by monitoring your use of

---

ASSIGNMENT 12.4

List the types of cognitive distortions you have had about infertility loss. Use Chapter 5 to help you come up with a rational response to challenge each distortion:

_____

_____

---

the words "should/should not have," "could/could not have," and "what if...?" Thinking about shoulds, coulds, and what-ifs will not change anything in the present except for impeding your grief, deflating your mood, and lowering your self-image.

Use General Coping Skills

Skills used to cope with stressors in general can help you cope with grief. Chapter 8 discussed many useful coping skills, including deep breathing, muscle relaxation, distraction, exercise, increasing social contacts, solving problems, and changing the way you think.

HELPING OTHERS GRIEVE INFERTILITY LOSSES: TEN TIPS FOR PARTNERS, FAMILY, AND FRIENDS

Very often people are clueless about what to say and how best to support the couple with fertility problems. While it is easy to direct anger towards acquaintances, friends, and family members for making insensitive comments, it must also be admitted that providing comfort to a person in grief is very difficult, especially when the grief is related to the loss of potential or to miscarriages. Many people, especially those who have never experienced infertility, do not understand how difficult the experience can be, and how painful it is when they ask about when you are going to have children. Friends and family can be insensitive to interpersonal cues and may not notice that you are hurt by their questions, joking, or probing about having children.

ASSIGNMENT 12.5

List the skills you can use this week to help you cope with grief:

_____

_____

Educating people around you about common reactions to infertility and how you would like to be treated during your grief process may be a true gift. It can lessen their anxiety about talking with you, provide an additional source of positive social support, and strengthen your relationship with them. Below are a number of tips created by grief experts[9] on how others can help you through your grief. You can hand them this section and ask them to read it. You can also use the suggestions to help your partner through his or her grieving process.

> *Tip 1: Give the person "permission" to grieve.* Infertility involves many losses. These losses can include the loss of a potential child that has been hoped for and dreamed about for many years, the loss of the pregnancy experience, and the loss of self-esteem. In addition, many couples face the loss of a fetus through miscarriages or stillbirth. Grieving these losses is not only normal, it is essential for the resolution of the loss. You can give the bereaved permission to grieve by listening to them, letting your caring and concern show, allowing them to express their feelings (even if it feels uncomfortable for you to witness them being sad or angry), and assuring them that their feelings are valid.
>
> *Tip 2: Be present with the griever.* There is tremendous therapeutic value in being in the presence of and sharing grief with a trusted person. Social support is critical throughout the grief process, so try not to allow the bereaved to remain isolated for too long. On the other hand, it is important to balance this by allowing the griever some space and discouraging inappropriate dependence. You may feel like you have to say or do just the right thing to help the bereaved, but really the best thing you can do is just be there and listen nonjudgmentally. Remember that you cannot take away the griever's pain. It will likely take great strength for you to listen without trying to assure them that everything will be okay. You may find yourself fighting your own sense of helplessness. Keep reminding yourself that the best help you can provide is your presence and your sympathetic ear.
>
> *Tip 3: Don't be surprised to see volatile emotional reactions in the bereaved.* Emotional reactions to infertility can involve surprise, denial, anxiety, anger, isolation, guilt, grief, and resolution. Displays of these emotions may be intense and volatile. In the early stages of grief, hostile emotions may be directed at others, such as yourself. Although reasonable limits should

be placed on the expression of anger by the bereaved, remind yourself that the griever is in pain. In addition, be prepared to have the griever find your help ineffective at first, since all he or she probably wants is the return of fertility.

Tip 4: Things to avoid saying to the bereaved. Do not try to explain the loss in religious or philosophical terms—e.g., "It is God's will" or "Everything happens for a reason." Although your intentions are good, saying such things will not help the bereaved. At worst, these types of statements can be interpreted as meaning that you don't think they would be worthy or fit parents, or that they don't deserve a child. Do not tell the bereaved couple they should feel better because they have other children (in the case of secondary infertility) or because there are so many other children in the world that they could adopt. Such comments rob the grievers of their legitimate losses and sadness. Do not try to unrealistically "pretty up" the situation. Instead, validate that the griever is in true pain and that the situation does not make sense to him or her.

Tip 5: Help the griever accept the loss. Accepting loss means coming to an emotional and intellectual acceptance that the loss has occurred, despite all wishes and hopes for the contrary. Acceptance of the loss will allow the griever to proceed with medical treatment (if it is warranted) and move through the remaining stages of grief. You can help the griever accept the losses of infertility by assisting in identifying and expressing the various feelings of grief. This means allowing the griever to talk (sometimes about the same things over and over again), cry, and review their story while you listen nonjudgmentally and with acceptance. Each retelling of the story and expression of emotion moves the bereaved that much closer to successful resolution of the grief.

Tip 6: Help the griever identify and mourn all the losses and potential losses involved in infertility. Infertility involves numerous losses. The bereaved must grieve for the potential child, as well as for all the hopes, dreams, fantasies, and expectations that went along with trying to conceive. Not only is the hope of having a genetically related child jeopardized by infertility, but so are any future plans that could involve a child or family. For example, if a career or school path has been shaped around being able to take maternity or paternity leave, these plans may have to be altered.

Tip 7: Help the griever recognize that the only way to get through grief is to yield to it. There is no escape from grief. The griever cannot go around it, over it, or under it. He or she must go directly through it, which means identifying losses and experiencing painful emotions. Avoiding or delaying grief will only make it worse, and the emotions will fester and boil over. However, taking time to grieve must be balanced with taking breaks from grief. Dwelling overly on grief is unhealthy. Encourage the griever to engage in occasional activities that will distract from his or her grief. Also, assure the griever that it is okay to enjoy other aspects of life or even to laugh while in grief.

Tip 8: Help the bereaved use skills to cope with the grief. Grief takes both an emotional and physical toll on the bereaved. It can be incredibly stressful to grieve losses. As such, encourage the griever to take good physical care of himself or herself to reduce vulnerability to physical illness and intense emotions. Grievers should be sure to eat and sleep properly, exercise, take medications as prescribed, avoid mood-altering drugs, and treat physical illnesses. In addition, they should engage in activities that increase their sense of self-esteem and sense of control over their lives. Participation in at least some social activities also is useful. The griever has been introduced to many coping skills throughout this book. These skills include strategies to deal with depression, stress, relationship problems, and grief. Encourage the griever to read and apply these skills to his or her life.

Tip 9: At the appropriate time, encourage the griever to invest in other aspects of life. Once the grievers have moved through the stages of grief and are nearing resolution, you can help them accept infertility as only one part of their identity and focus again on other facets of existence. If the couple has exhausted treatment options and has decided to stop pursuing conception, they may begin to consider alternatives such as adoption or remaining child-free (a more acceptable term than "childless"). You can support them in their adoption decision or help them make life plans that do not include children.

Tip 10: Help the griever plan rituals to mourn the loss and participate in these rituals. When a person dies, our society provides opportunities to mourn during rituals such as funerals or memorial services. These rituals help mourners move through the stages of grief. Unfortunately, there are no such rituals when it comes to infertility loss. Helping the bereaved create some type of ritual to commemorate the loss of the dream child or fetus can make the loss more tangible and "legitimate." Rituals symbolize healing and transition, and thus can be very therapeutic for the mourner.

SECTION V SUMMARY

- Infertility can include many losses: the loss of a dream child, the loss of experience, the loss of control, the loss of self-confidence, the loss of relationships, the loss of status or prestige, and the loss of security.
- Grief is likely to occur on many different occasions during the experience of infertility.
- The following stages of grief are common after receiving the diagnosis of infertility: surprise and denial, anger, bargaining, depression, and acceptance. These reactions are often re-experienced with each new loss involved in infertility.
- Because grief can take a lot out of you emotionally and physically, it is important for you to take especially good care of yourself during the grieving process.
- One of the best things you can do to move successfully through the stages of grief is to give yourself permission to grieve, which means allowing yourself to experience all the emotions that go along with the grief process.
- There are many skills you can use to cope with grief and all the emotions related to grief.
- Rituals can help you move through the stages of grief by providing a tangible and structured way to express your emotions and mourn your losses.
- Maximize your chances of receiving positive social support by educating those around you about how you would like to be treated and helped through your grieving process.

APPENDIX A: SUGGESTED READINGS

Barbach, Lonnie. *For Yourself: The Fulfillment of Female Sexuality*. Signet, New York, 2000.

Barlow, David H., & Michelle G. Craske. *Mastery of Your Anxiety and Panic*. Graywind Publications. Albany, N.Y., 1989.

Borg, Susan, & Judith Lasker. *When Pregnancy Fails: Families Coping with Miscarriage, Stillbirth, and Infant Death*. Beacon Press, Boston, 1990.

Burns, David. *Feeling Good: The New Mood Therapy*. Quill/HarperCollins Publishers, New York, 1999.

Burns, David. *The Feeling Good Handbook*. Plume Books, New York, 1989.

Carter, Jean W., & Michael Carter. *Sweet Grapes: How to Stop Being Infertile and Start Living Again*. Perspectives Press, Indianapolis, IN, 1989.

Cooper, Susan L., & Ellen S. Glazer. *Beyond Infertility: A Guide to the New Reproductive Options*. Macmillan Publishing/Lexington Books, New York, 1994.

Cooper, Susan L., & Ellen S. Glazer. *Choosing Assisted Reproduction: Social, Emotional and Ethical Considerations*. Perspectives Press, Indianapolis, IN, 1998.

DeCherney, Alan, & Mary Lake Polan. *Decision-Making in Infertility*. B. C. Decker, Philadelphia, 1988.

DeFrain, John. *Stillborn: The Invisible Death*. Lexington Books, Boston, 1986.

Deits, Bob. *Life After Loss*. Fisher Books, Tuscon, AZ, 1992.

Domar, Alice, & Henry Dreher. *Healthy Mind, Healthy Woman: Using the Mind-Body Connection to Manage Stress and Take Control of Your Life*. Henry Holt, New York, 1996.

Friedman, Rochelle, & Bonnie Gradstein. *Surviving Pregnancy Loss*. Little, Brown, Boston, 1992.

Gilman, Lois. *The Adoption Resource Book*. HarperCollins, New York, 1992.

Glazer, Ellen Sarasohn. *The Long-Awaited Stork: A Guide to Parenting After Infertility*. Main Street Books, 1995.

Gray, John. *Men Are from Mars, Women Are from Venus*. HarperCollins Publishers, New York, 1992.

Greil, Arthur L. *Not Yet Pregnant: Infertile Couples in Contemporary America*. Rutgers University Press, New Brunswick, NJ, 1991.

Harkness, Carla. *The Infertility Book: A Comprehensive Medical and Emotional Guide*. Celestial Arts, Berkeley, CA, 1992.

Hauri, Peter, & Shirley Linde. *No More Sleepless Nights*. J. Wiley, New York, 1990.

Heiman, Julia R., & Joseph LoPiccolo. *Becoming Orgasmic: A Sexual and Personal Growth Program for Women*. Simon and Schuster, New York, 1988.

Ilse, Sherokee. *Empty Arms: Coping After Miscarriage, Stillbirth, and Infant Death*. Wintergreen Press, Long Lake, MN, 1990.

Ilse, Sherokee, & Linda Hammer Burns. *Miscarriage: A Shattered Dream*. Wintergreen Press, Long Lake, MN, 1985.

Kabat-Zinn, Jon. *Full Catastrophe Living: Using the Wisdom of Your Body and Mind to Face Stress, Pain and Illness.* Delacorte Press, New York, 1991.

Kohn, Ingrid, & Perry-Lynn Moffitt. *A Silent Sorrow: Pregnancy Loss, Guidance and Support for You and Your Family.* Dell Publishing/A Delta Book, New York, 1992.

Kubler-Ross, Elisabeth. *On Death and Dying.* Macmillan, New York, 1969.

Linehan, Marsha M. *Skills Training Manual for Treating Borderline Personality Disorder.* Guilford Press, New York, 1993.

Marrs, Richard. *Dr. Marrs' Fertility Book.* Delacorte Press, New York, 1997.

Menning, Barbara Eck. *Infertility: A Guide for Childless Couples.* Prentice-Hall, Englewood Cliffs, NJ, 1988.

Morrow, Judith Gordon, & Nancy Gordon DeHammer. *Good Mourning: Help and Understanding in the Time of Pregnancy Loss.* Word Publishing, Dallas, 1989.

Notarius, Clifford, & Howard Markman. *We Can Work It Out.* G. P. Putman's Sons, New York, 1993.

Peck, Ellen. *The Baby Trap.* Bernard Geis Associates, New York, 1971.

Peck, Ellen, & Judy Senderowitz. *Pronatalism: The Myth of Mom and Apple Pie.* Thomas Crowell, New York, 1974.

Robin, Peggy. *How to Be a Successful Fertility Patient.* William Morrow and Company, Inc., 1993.

Rosenberg, Helane S., & Yakov M. Epstein. *Getting Pregnant When You Thought You Couldn't.* Warner Books, 1993.

Salzer, Linda P. *Surviving Infertility.* HarperCollins Publishers/Harper Perennial, New York, 1991.

Silber, Sherman J. *How to Get Pregnant with the New Technology.* Warner Books, 1998.

Staudacher, Carol. *Men and Grief: A Guide for Men Surviving the Death of a Loved One.* New Harbinger Publications, Oakland, CA, 1991.

Stephenson, Lynda R. *Give Us A Child: Coping With the Personal Crisis of Infertility.* Harper and Row, New York, 1987.

Zilbergeld, Bernie. *The New Male Sexuality: The Truth About Men, Sex, and Pleasure.* Bantam Books, New York, 1999.

Zoldbrod, Aline P. *Men, Women and Infertility.* Macmillan Publishing/ Lexington Books, New York, 1993.

APPENDIX B: RESOURCE DIRECTORY

MEDICAL RESOURCES

American College of Obstetricians and Gynecologists (ACOG)
409 12th Street SW
Washington, DC 20024-2188
202-638-5577
Web Site: www.acog.org

American Society for Reproductive Medicine (ASRM)
1209 Montgomery Highway
Birmingham, AL 35216-2809
205-978-5000
Web Site: www.asrm.org

American Urological Association
1120 N. Charles Street
Baltimore, MD 21201
301-727-1100

InterNational Council on Infertility Information Dissemination (INCIID)
P. O. Box 6836
Arlington, VA 22206
520-544-9548
Fax: 703-379-1593
E-mail: INCIIDinfo@inciid.org
Web Site: www.inciid.org

Society for Assisted Reproductive Technology (SART)
1209 Montgomery Highway
Birmingham, AL 35216
205-978-5000
Web Site: www.sart.org

Society for Reproductive Surgeons (SRS)
1209 Montgomery Highway
Birmingham, AL 35216
205-978-5000
Web Site: www.reprodsurgery.org

INTERNET RESOURCES AND INFORMATION

RESOLVE
1310 Broadway
Somerville, MA 02144-1731
Helpline: 617-623-0744
Business Line: 617-623-1156
Web Site: www.resolve.org

Internet Heath Resources
1133 Garden Lane
Lafayette, CA 94549
925-284-9362
Web Site: www.ihr.com

ADOPTION

***Adoptive Families* Magazine**
P.O. Box 5159
Brentwood, TN 37024
800-372-3300
Web Site: www.adoptivefamilies.com

American Adoption Congress
P.O. Box 42730
Washington, DC 20015
202-483-3399
Web Site: www.americanadoptioncongress.org

National Council for Single Adoptive Parents
P. O. Box 15084
Chevy Chase, MD 20825

International Alliance for Children, Inc.
Wellesley Office Park
55 William Street, Suite G-10
Wellesley, MA 02481-3902
781-431-7148
Web Site: www.allforchildren.org

National Adoption Center
1500 Walnut Street, Suite 701
Philadelphia, PA 19102
800-TO-ADOPT

Child Welfare Information Gateway
Children's Bureau/ACYF
1250 Maryland Avenue SW
Washington, DC 20024
800-394-3366
Web Site: www.childwelfare.gov

MISCARRIAGES

The Compassionate Friends
P. O. Box 3696
Oakbrook, IL 60522-3696
877-969-0010
Web Site: www.compassionatefriends.org

THIRD-PARTY REPRODUCTION

The American Surrogacy Center
638 Church Street NE
Marietta, GA 30063
770-426-1107
Web Site: www.surrogacy.com

Center for Surrogate Parenting & Egg Donation, Inc.
West Coast Office:
15821 Ventura Blvd., Suite 675
Encino, CA 91436
818-788-8288
East Coast Office:
9 State Circle, Suite 302
Annapolis, MD 21401
410-990-9862
Web Site: www.creatingfamilies.com and www.eggdonor.com

ENDNOTES

INTRODUCTION

1. Hull, M. G. R., Glazener, C. M. A., Kelly, N. J., Conway, D. I., Foster, P. A., Hinton, R. A., Coulson, C., Lambert, P. A., Watt, E. M., & Desai, K. M. (1985). Population study of causes, treatment, and outcome of infertility. *British Medical Journal, 291*, 1693–1697.
2. Mahlstedt, P. P., McDuff, S., & Bernstein, J. (1987). Emotional factors and the in vitro fertilization and embryo transfer process. *Journal of In Vitro Fertilization and Embryo Transfer, 4,* 232–236.
3. Freeman, E. W., Boxer, A. S., Rickels, K., Tureck, R., & Mastroianni, L. (1985). Psychological evaluation and support in a program of in vitro fertilization and embryo transfer. *Fertility and Sterility, 43,* 48–53.

CHAPTER 1

1. Harkness, C. (1992). *The infertility book: A comprehensive medical and emotional guide.* Berkeley, CA: Celestial Arts.
2. Menning, B. E. (1988). *Infertility: A guide for the childless couple*, 2nd edition. New York: Prentice Hall.
3. Tuschen-Caffier, B., Florin, I., Krause, W., & Pook, M. (1999). Cognitive-behavioral therapy for idiopathic infertile couples. *Psychotherapy and Psychosomatics, 68*(1), 15–21.
4. Liebmann-Smith, J., Nardi Egan, J., & Stangel, J. (1999). *The unofficial guide to overcoming infertility.* New York: Macmillan.
5. Ibid.
6. From Jessica Williams at www.preconception.com.
7. Menning, B. E. (1988). *Infertility: A guide for the childless couple* (2nd ed.). New York: Prentice Hall.
8. Harkness, C. (1992). *The infertility book: A comprehensive medical and emotional guide.* Berkeley, CA: Celestial Arts.
9. Keye, W. R. Jr. (1999). Medical aspects of infertility for the counselor. In L. H. Burns & S. N. Covington (Eds.), *Infertility counseling: A comprehensive text for clinicians.* New York: The Parthenon Publishing Group.

CHAPTER 2

1. Mosher, W. D., & Pratt, W. F. (1990). Fecundity and infertility in the United States, 1965–1988. *Advance Data, 192,* 1–9.
2. Liebmann-Smith, J., Nardi Egan, J., & Stangel, J. (1999). *The unofficial guide to overcoming infertility.* New York: Macmillan.
3. Ibid.
4. Zilbergeld, B. (1999). *The new male sexuality: The truth about men, sex, and pleasure.* New York: Bantam Books.
5. Liebmann-Smith, J., Nardi Egan, J., & Stangel, J. (1999). *The unofficial guide to overcoming infertility.* New York: Macmillan.
6. Menning, B. E. (1988). *Infertility: A guide for the childless couple* (2nd ed.). New York: Prentice Hall.

CHAPTER 3

1. Centers for Disease Control and Prevention (2005). 2003 Assisted reproductive technology success rates: National summary and fertility clinic reports. http://www.cdc.gov/ART/ART2003/index.htm.
2. Jones, H. W., Jr., & Toner, J. P. (1993). The infertile couple. *New England Journal of Medicine, 329,* 1710–1715.
3. Berger, G. S., Goldstein, M., & Fuerst, M. (1995). *The couple's guide to infertility: Updated with the newest scientific techniques to help you have a baby.* New York: Main Street Books/Doubleday.
4. Ibid.
5. Ibid.
6. Domar, A. D., & Seibel, M. (1990). Emotional aspects of infertility. In M. M. Seibel (Ed.), *Infertility: A comprehensive text.* Norwalk, CT: Appleton & Lange.
7. SART. (1998). Assisted reproductive technology in the United States and Canada: 1995 results generated from the American Society for Reproductive Medicine/Society for Assisted Reproductive Technology Registry. *Fertility and Sterility, 69,* 389–396.
8. Centers for Disease Control and Prevention (2005). 2003 Assisted reproductive technology success rates: National summary and fertility clinic reports. http://www.cdc.gov/ART/ART2003/index.htm.
9. Ibid.
10. Ibid.
11. Ibid.
12. Ibid.
13. SART. (1998). Assisted reproductive technology in the United States and Canada: 1995 results generated from the American Society for Reproductive Medicine/Society for Assisted Reproductive Technology Registry. *Fertility and Sterility, 69,* 389–396.
14. Diamond, R., Kequr, D., Meyers, M., Scharf, C. N., & Weinshel, M. (1999). *Couple therapy for infertility.* New York: Guilford Press.
15. Liebmann-Smith, J., Nardi Egan, J., & Stangel, J. (1999). *The unofficial guide to overcoming infertility.* New York: Macmillan.
16. Diamond, R., Kequr, D., Meyers, M., Scharf, C. N., & Weinshel, M. (1999). *Couple therapy for infertility.* New York: Guilford Press.

CHAPTER 5

1. Greil, A. L. (1997). Infertility and psychological distress: A critical review of the literature. *Social Science and Medicine,* 45(11), 1679–1704.
2. Cook, E. P. (1987). Characteristics of the biopsychosocial crisis of infertility. *Journal of Counseling & Development,* 65(9), 465–470.
3. Mahlstedt, P. P. (1985). The psychological component of infertility. *Fertility and Sterility,* 43, 335–346.
4. Menning, B. E. (1988). *Infertility: A guide for the childless couple,* 2nd ed. New York: Prentice Hall.
5. Stephenson, L. R. (1987). *Give us a child: Coping with the personal crisis of infertility.* New York: Harper & Row Publishers, Inc.
6. Williams, L., Bischoff, R., & Ludes, J. (1992). A biopsychosocial model for treating infertility. *Contemporary Family Therapy: An International Journal,* 14(4), 309–322.
7. Burns, D. D. (1999). *Feeling good: The new mood therapy.* New York: Quill.
8. Lewinshohn, P. M., Munoz, R. F., Youngren, M. A., & Zeiss, A. M. (1992). *Control your depression.* New York: Simon and Schuster.

CHAPTER 6

1. Burns, D. D. (1999). *Feeling good: The new mood therapy.* New York: Quill.
2. Beck, A. T., Rush, A. J., Shaw, B. F., & Emery, G. (1979). *Cognitive therapy of depression.* New York: Guilford Press.
3. Burns, D. D. (1999). *Feeling good: The new mood therapy.* New York: Quill.
4. Hunt, J., & Monach, J. H. (1997). Beyond the bereavement model: The significance of depression for infertility counseling. *Human Reproduction,* 12(11 Supplemental), 188-194.
5. Burns, D. D. (1999). *Feeling good: The new mood therapy.* New York: Quill..
6. Beck, A. T., Rush, A. J., Shaw, B. F., & Emery, G. (1979). *Cognitive therapy of depression.* New York: Guilford Press.
7. Burns, D. D. (1999). *Feeling good: The new mood therapy.* New York: Quill.
8. Ibid.
9. Lewinshohn, P. M., Munoz, R. F., Youngren, M. A., & Zeiss, A. M. (1992). *Control your depression.* New York: Simon and Schuster.
10. Linehan, M. M. (1993b). *Skills training manual for treating borderline personality disorder.* New York: Guilford Press.
11. Burns, D. D. (1999). *Feeling good: The new mood therapy.* New York: Quill.

CHAPTER 7

1. O'Moore, A. M., O'Moore, R. R., Harrison, R. F., Murphy, G., & Carruthers, M. E. (1983). Psychosomatic aspects in idiopathic infertility: Effects of treatment with autogenic training. *Journal of Psychosomatic Research,* 27(2), 145–151.
2. Stewart, D. E., Boydell, K. M., McCarthy, K., Swerdlyk, S., Redmond, C., & Cohrs, W. (1992). A prospective study of the effectiveness of brief professionally led support groups for infertility patients. *International Journal of Psychiatry and Medicine,* 22(2), 173–182.
3. Wasser, S. K., Sewall, G., & Soules, M. R. (1993). Psychosocial stress as a cause of infertility. *Fertility and Sterility,* 59(3), 685–689.
4. Wright, J., Allard, M., Lecours, A., & Sabourin, S. (1989). Psychosocial distress and infertility: A review of controlled research. *International Journal of Fertility,* 34(2), 126–142.

5. Bernstein, D. A., & Borkovec, T. D. (1973). *Progressive relaxation training: A manual for the helping professions.* Champaign, Illinois: Research Press. Burns, D. D. (1999). *Feeling good: The new mood therapy.* New York: Quill.

6. Burns, L. H., & Covington, S. N. (1999). Psychology of infertility. In L. H. Burns & S. N. Covington (Eds.), *Infertility counseling: A comprehensive text for clinicians.* New York: The Parthenon Publishing Group.

7. Greil, A. L. (1997). Infertility and psychological distress: A critical review of the literature. *Social Science and Medicine,* 45(11), 1679–1704.

8. Seibel, M. M., & Taymor, M. L. (1982). Emotional aspects of infertility. *Fertility and Sterility,* 37, 137–145.

9. Ulbrich, P. M., Coyle, A. T., & Llabre, M. M. (1990). Involuntary childlessness and marital adjustment: His and hers. *Journal of Sex and Marital Therapy,* 16(3), 147–158.

10. Domar, A. D., Seibel, M., & Benson, H. (1990). The mind/body program for infertility: A new behavioral treatment approach for women with infertility. *Fertility and Sterility,* 53(2), 246–249.

11. Domar, A. D., Zuttermeister, P. C., Seibel, M., & Benson, H. (1992). Psychological improvement in infertile women after behavioral treatment: A replication. *Fertility and Sterility,* 58(1), 144–147.

12. Domar, A. D., Friedman, R., & Zuttermeister, P. C. (1999). Distress and conception in infertile women: A complementary approach. *Journal of the American Women's Association,* 54(4), 196–198.

13. McNaughton-Cassill, M. E., Bostwick, M., Vanscoy, S. E., Arthur, N. J., Hichman, T. N., Robinson, R. D., & Neal, G. S. (2000). Development of brief stress management support groups for couples undergoing *in vitro* fertilization treatment. *Fertility and Sterility,* 74(1), 87–93.

14. Linehan, M. M. (1993b). *Skills training manual for treating borderline personality disorder.* New York: Guilford Press.

15. Burns, D. D. (1999). *Feeling good: The new mood therapy.* New York: Quill.

16. Meichenbaum, D. (1985). *Stress inoculation training. New York:* Pergamon Press.

17. Ibid.

18. Burns, D. D. (1999). *Feeling good: The new mood therapy.* New York: Quill.

CHAPTER 8

1. O'Moore, A. M., O'Moore, R. R., Harrison, R. F., Murphy, G., & Carruthers, M. E. (1983). Psychosomatic aspects in idiopathic infertility: Effects of treatment with autogenic training. *Journal of Psychosomatic Research,* 27(2), 145–151.

2. Domar, A. D., Seibel, M., & Benson, H. (1990). The mind/body program for infertility: A new behavioral treatment approach for women with infertility. *Fertility and Sterility,* 53(2), 246–249.

3. Domar, A. D., Zuttermeister, P. C., Seibel, M., & Benson, H. (1992). Psychological improvement in infertile women after behavioral treatment: A replication. *Fertility and Sterility,* 58(1), 144–147.

4. Domar, A. D., Friedman, R. & Zuttermeister, P. C. (1999). Distress and conception in infertile women: A complementary approach. *Journal of the American Women's Association,* 54(4), 196–198.

5. Bernstein, D. A., & Borkovec, T. D. (1973). *Progressive relaxation training: A manual for the helping professions.* Champaign, Illinois: Research Press.

6. Carlson, C. R., & Bernstein, D. A. (1995). Relaxation skills training: Abbreviated progressive relaxation. In W. T. O'Donohue & L. Krasner (Eds.), *Handbook of psychological skills training: Clinical techniques and applications*. Boston: Allyn and Bacon.

7. Linehan, M. M. (1993b). *Skills training manual for treating borderline personality disorder*. New York: Guilford Press.

8. Prattke, T. W., & Gass-Sternas, K. A. (1993). Appraisal, coping, and emotional health of infertile couples undergoing donor artificial insemination. *Journal of Obstetrics, Gynecology, and Neonatal Nursing*, 22(6), 516–527.

9. Stewart, D. E., Boydell, K. M., McCarthy, K., Swerdlyk, S., Redmond, C., & Cohrs, W. (1992). A prospective study of the effectiveness of brief professionally-led support groups for infertility patients. *International Journal of Psychiatry and Medicine*, 22(2), 173–182.

10. Meichenbaum, D. (1985). *Stress inoculation training*. New York: Pergamon Press.

11. From www.resolve.org.

CHAPTER 9

1. Epstein, Y. M., & Rosenberg, H. S. (1997). He does, she doesn't; she does, he doesn't: Couple conflicts about infertility. In S. R. Leiblum (Ed.), *Infertility: Psychological issues and counseling strategies*. New York: John Wiley and Sons, Inc.

2. Ibid.

3. Abbey, A., Andrews, F. M., & Halman, L. J. (1995). Provision and receipt of social support and disregard: What is their impact on the marital life quality of infertile and fertile couples? *Journal of Personality and Social Psychology*, 68(3), 455-469.

4. Berg, B. J., Wilson, J. F., & Weingartner, P. J. (1991). Psychological sequelae of infertility treatment: The role of gender and sex-role identification. *Social Science and Medicine*, 33(9), 1071-1080.

5. Cooper-Hilbert, B. (1998). *Infertility and involuntary childlessness: Helping couples cope*. New York: W. W. Norton & Co., Inc.

6. Daniluk, J. C. (1997). Gender and infertility. In S. R. Leiblum (Ed.), *Infertility: Psychological issues and counseling strategies*. New York: John Wiley & Sons.

7. Greil, A. L. (1991). *Not yet pregnant: Infertile couples in contemporary America*. New Brunswick: Rutgers University Press.

8. Salzer, L. P. (1986). *Infertility: How Couples Can Cope*. Boston, MA: G. K. Hall & Co.

9. Wright, J., Allard, M., Lecours, A., & Sabourin, S. (1989). Psychosocial distress and infertility: A review of controlled research. *International Journal of Fertility*, 34(2), 126-142.

10. Cooper-Hilbert, B. (1998). *Infertility and involuntary childlessness: Helping couples cope*. New York: W. W. Norton & Co., Inc.

CHAPTER 10

1. Jacobson, N. S., & Margolin, G. (1979). *Marital Therapy: Strategies Based on Social Learning and Behavior Exchange Principles*. New York: Brunner/Mazel Publishers.

2. Ibid.

3. Ibid.

4. Linehan, M. M. (1997). Validation and psychotherapy. In A. C. Bohart and L. S. Greenberg (Eds.). *Empathy reconsidered: New directions in psychotherapy*, pp. 353–392. Washington, DC: APA.

5. Jacobson, N. S., & Margolin, G. (1979). *Marital Therapy: Strategies Based on Social Learning and Behavior Exchange Principles*. New York: Brunner/Mazel Publishers.

6. Menning, B. E. (1988). *Infertility: A guide for the childless couple*, 2nd ed. New York: Prentice Hall.

7. Ibid.

8. Sadler, A. G., & Syrop, C. H. (1987).The stress of infertility: Recommendations for assessment and intervention. *Family Therapy Collections*, 22, 1–17.

9. Downey, J., Yingling, S., McKinney, M., Husami, N., Jewelewicz, R., & Maidman, J. (1989). Mood disorders, psychiatric symptoms, and distress in women presenting for infertility evaluation. *Fertility and Sterility*, 52(3), 425–432.

10. Leiblum, S. R. (1993). The impact of infertility on sexual and marital satisfaction. *Annual Review of Sex Research*, 4, 99–120.

11. Menning, B. E. (1988). *Infertility: A guide for the childless couple*, 2nd ed. New York: Prentice Hall.

12. Tuschen-Caffier, B., Florin, I., Krause, W., & Pook, M. (1999). Cognitive-behavioral therapy for idiopathic infertile couples. *Psychotherapy and Psychosomatics*, 68(1), 15–21.

CHAPTER 11

1. Menning, B. E. (1988). *Infertility: A guide for the childless couple*, 2nd ed. New York: Prentice Hall.

2. Cook, E. P. (1987). Characteristics of the biopsychosocial crisis of infertility. *Journal of Counseling & Development*, 65(9), 465-470.

3. Mahlstedt, P. P. (1985). The psychological component of infertility. *Fertility and Sterility*, 43, 335-346.

4. Menning, B. E. (1988). *Infertility: A guide for the childless couple*, 2nd edition. New York: Prentice Hall.

5. Stephenson, L. R. (1987). *Give us a child: Coping with the personal crisis of infertility*. New York: Harper & Row Publishers, Inc.

6. Williams, L., Bischoff, R., & Ludes, J. (1992). A biopsychosocial model for treating infertility. *Contemporary Family Therapy: An International Journal*, 14(4), 309-322.

7. Kubler-Ross, E. (1969). *On death and dying*. New York: Collier-Macmillan, Ltd.

8. Cook, E. P. (1987). Characteristics of the biopsychosocial crisis of infertility. *Journal of Counseling & Development*, 65(9), 465–470.

9. Menning, B. E. (1980). The emotional needs of infertile couples. *Fertility and Sterility*, 34(4), 313–319.

10. Patterson, J. E. (1986). But not alone: The grief of infertility. *Journal of the American Medical Association*, 255(17), 2293-2294.

11. Menning, B. E. (1980). The emotional needs of infertile couples. *Fertility and Sterility*, 34(4), 313–319.

12. Ibid.

13. Kubler-Ross, E. (1969). *On death and dying*. New York: Collier-Macmillan, Ltd.

14. Cook, E. P. (1987). Characteristics of the biopsychosocial crisis of infertility. *Journal of Counseling & Development*, 65(9), 465–470.

15. Kraft, A. D., Palombo, J., Mitchell, D., Dean, C., Meyers, S., & Schmidt, A. W. (1980). The psychological dimension of infertility. *American Journal of Orthopsychiatry*, 50(4), 618-628.

16. Mahlstedt, P. P. (1985). The psychological component of infertility. *Fertility and Sterility*, 43, 335-346.

17. Menning, B. E. (1980). The emotional needs of infertile couples. *Fertility and Sterility*, 34(4), 313–319.

18. Ibid.

19. Ibid.

20. Cook, E. P. (1987). Characteristics of the biopsychosocial crisis of infertility. *Journal of Counseling & Development,* 65(9), 465-470.

CHAPTER 12

1. From www.willowgreen.com.

2. Stroebe, M. S., Hansson, R. O., Stroebe, W., & Schut, H. (2001). *Handbook of bereavement research: Consequences, coping, and care.* Washington, DC: American Psychological Association.

3. Meyers, M., Diamond, R., Kezur, D., Scharf, C., Weinshel, M., & Rait, D. S. (1995). An infertility primer for family therapists: I. Medical, social, and psychological dimensions. *Family Process,* 34(2), 219–229.

4. Flinn, T. (1988). Taps in the cabbage patch. In E. Glazer and S. Cooper (Eds.) *Without child.* New York: Lexington Books.

5. Menning, B. E. (1988). *Infertility: A guide for the childless couple,* 2nd ed. New York: Prentice Hall.

6. Stroebe, M. S., Hansson, R. O., Stroebe, W., & Schut, H. (2001). *Handbook of bereavement research: Consequences, coping, and care.* Washington DC: American Psychological Association..

7. Ibid.

8. Ibid.

9. Rando, T. A. (1984). *Grief, dying, and death: Clinical interventions for caregivers.* Champaign, IL: Research Press Co.

AUTHORS

Negar Nicole Jacobs, Ph.D., is clinical psychologist at the VA Sierra Nevada Health Care System in Reno, Nevada, where she works as a clinician, researcher and educator. Aside from infertility, her main interests include behavioral medicine and the delivery of behavioral healthcare in medical settings, addictive disorders, and cross-cultural issues

William T. O'Donohue, Ph.D., is full professor of psychology at the University of Nevada, Reno. His major areas of research include mental health service delivery, human sexuality, forensic psychology, management, administration, behavior therapy, and philosophy of psychology.